LANGUAGE
IN
UNIFORM

A READER ON PROPAGANDA

LANGUAGE
IN
UNIFORM

A READER ON PROPAGANDA

Edited by
NICK AARON FORD
Morgan State College

THE ODYSSEY PRESS, INC. NEW YORK

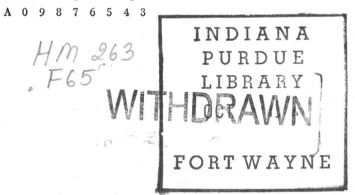

ACKNOWLEDGMENTS

"The Nature and Media of Propaganda." From *The Analysis of Propaganda;* by William Hummel and Keith Huntress; copyright 1949 by the authors. Reprinted by permission of Holt, Rinehart and Winston, Inc., publishers.

"How to Detect Propaganda." From *Propaganda Analysis* (November; 1937); by Clyde R. Miller. Reprinted by permission of the author.

"On Reading Propaganda." From *A Primer for Readers;* by Edward A. Tenney and Ralph M. Wardle; F. S. Crofts and Company; 1942. Reprinted by permission of the author.

"Stereotypes." From *Public Opinion;* by Walter Lippmann. Reprinted by permission of the Macmillan Company from *Public Opinion* by Walter Lippmann. Copyright 1922 by Walter Lippmann; copyright renewed 1950 by Walter Lippmann.

"Neither Blind Obedience Nor Uncivil Disobedience" by Sidney Hook; *New York Times Magazine,* June 5; 1966. ©1966 by The New York Times Company. Reprinted by permission.

"The All-White World of Children's Books" by Nancy Larrick; *Saturday Review,* September 11, 1965. Reprinted by permission.

"What the Historian Owes the Negro" by Benjamin Quarles; *Saturday Review; Review,* September 3, 1966. Reprinted by permission.

"Types of Anti-Catholicism" by Robert McAfee Brown; *Commonweal;* November 25; 1955. Reprinted by permission of the Commonweal Publishing Co.; Inc.

"The State." From *Mein Kampf*; Volume II; by Adolph Hitler; 1926; translated by Ralph Manheim. Reprinted by permission of Houghton Mifflin Company.

"Freedom to Read." Reprinted by permission of American Library Association; American Book Publishers Council; and other national organizations which have adopted the Statement.

"Nationalistic Bias in History Textbooks" by Stephen E. Ambrose; Baltimore *Sun*; May 15, 1966. Reprinted by permission.

"A Letter to Johnny's Mother" from *Why Johnny Can't Read* by Rudolph Flesch. Copyright ©1955 by Harper & Brothers. Reprinted by permission of Harper & Row, Publishers.

"The Tyranny of Multiple-Choice Tests" by Banesh Hoffmann. Copyright ©1961; by Harper's Magazine, Inc. Reprinted from the March 1961 issue of *Harper's Magazine* by permission of author and of *Harper's Magazine*.

"Education and Democracy" by Robert M. Hutchins; *School and Society*; June 18; 1949. Reprinted by permission.

"Whispers for Sale: Verbal Advertising" by Robert Littell and John J. McCarthy. Copyright © 1936, by Harper's Magazine, Inc. Reprinted from the February 1936 issue of *Harper's Magazine* by permission of Mrs. Robert Littell and John J. McCarthy. Copyright © renewed 1964.

"Forgotten Road to Success in Writing" by J. D. Ratcliff. Reprinted by permission of Famous Writing School, Inc.; Westport; Connecticut.

"The Good Life." Reprinted by permission of the Connecticut Development Commission.

"North Carolina's Baffling Mystery." Reprinted by permission of the North Carolina Department of Conservation and Development.

"Have You Ever Thought of Living and Working in Vermont." Reprinted by permission of Vermont Development Department.

Preface

We are living in an age of propaganda. It is impossible to live through a single day without being continually bombarded by a barrage of propaganda directed at men, women, and children of every age, class, and condition by the press, radio, television, billboards, and other media. We must choose carefully what part of this panorama of sights and sounds we will admit beyond the threshold of conscious attention. Unless we do, we shall be forever at the mercy of competing, contradicting, confusing, intimidating forces that can make life a frustrating experience.

But we cannot successfully meet this challenge without some knowledge of the nature and uses of the incessant propaganda with which we must deal. The purpose of LANGUAGE IN UNIFORM is to acquaint students with the most common varieties of propagandistic writings and to help them toward understanding how to analyze and evaluate such writings.

It is necessary first, however, to correct some false impressions about the meaning of propaganda, which many people mistakenly consider a synonym for *falsehood* or *lie*. It is only since the advent of Adolph Hitler that this word has acquired universally its sinister connotation. In 1622 Pope Gregory XV organized a College of Propaganda for the supervision of the foreign missions. At that time the word was highly respectable and signified the praiseworthy action of spreading an important doctrine or report.

Until the beginning of World War I, the word propaganda continued to represent the basic meaning it had in 1622. In fact, before 1915 the *Readers' Guide to Periodical Literature,* which records the titles of all articles published in reputable American magazines, did not have a single entry concerning propaganda. Today the entries are numerous.

There are many definitions of propaganda, but the key words, expressed or implied, in any satisfactory definition are "emotion" and "persuasion." Its aim is to persuade people by emotional means to do or not to do something that the propagandist desires. In some cases the desired action is for the common good of the community or the nation as a whole; in other cases it is opposed to the common good of the community or the nation. In some cases the appeal is based on truth supported by strong emotional overtones and is, therefore, *good* propaganda; in other cases the appeal is based on distortion, half-truths, and absolute falsehoods and is, therefore, *bad* propaganda.

Although propaganda can be harmful, it is often a powerful ally of education and an aid to beneficient social action. The major difference between it and education is education's complete commitment to truth. Education's chief concern is its search for truth; propaganda's chief concern is its determination to incite action or active belief. True education always seeks its goal by discarding all that it discovers to be false, biased, and misleading, while propaganda often seeks its goal by either hiding and ignoring the false and the misleading or deliberately distorting and using them to advantage in its efforts to support with emotional fervor biased attitudes and opinions.

The selections for study are organized in the following categories: Introduction (which consists of four essays intended to define the terms and give an overall view of the problems involved in the entire study); Political and Economic Discussion; Racial and Religious Considerations; In Pursuit of Educational Goals; and Effective Advertising: The Art of Hidden Persuasion. After each selection there are Questions for Study and Discussion, which include suggested writing assignments and vocabulary study. It is expected that the teacher will modify and add to these exercises in accordance with the needs of his particular students. For those who become interested enough to want to do further study on one or more aspects of the subject, a selective bibliography is provided at the end of the book.

N. A. F.

Contents

INTRODUCTION

The Nature and Media of Propaganda

William Hummel and Keith Huntress

WHAT IS PROPAGANDA?

"Propaganda" is a word of evil connotation. The average American, hearing it, is reminded of spies and secret police, of cynical reporters and biased magazines, of lobbies and special privilege and lies.

The reason for this is easy to understand. In wartime, when enemy nations report victories over our forces or publish news of terrifying new weapons, those reports are labeled in our newspapers and magazines as "propaganda." The implication is that such announcements are made in order to influence the people of this country to relax their efforts and that the claims are false. When we achieve victories or create atom bombs, our papers make much of such reports, and we call them "news." In general, we are inclined to call reports which favor our own interests true; reports from the opposition are called propaganda. And so the word has become a synonym for a lie. The creation of government bureaus of propaganda and of institutes for propaganda analysis, always with emphasis on slanted news and deceptive claims, has strengthened the prejudice against the word.

Let us take one example of "propaganda" and place it beside an example of "news." German newspapers reported the Battle of the Bulge as a German victory, cited tremendous Allied losses, and claimed that the front would be stabilized, that German arms would yet be victorious. American newspapers reported the Battle of the Bulge as a limited German success, headlined Allied heroism, and minimized the possibilities of further German exploitation of the break-through. In the event the American newspapers were right, but you must note that the news stories of the two countries were trying to do exactly the same thing— inform readers about some important events and give them confidence in the armies of their countries. The American stories were the more accurate, but the purpose was the same.

As another example, let us suppose you have made a new acquaintance whom you rather like. He invites you to a public meeting on a certain Tuesday; he has been to a number of such meetings, and they are always interesting. So you go. You sit and listen. The speaker criticizes your present way of life; he points out faults in the society around you and explains a system that will, he says, eliminate those faults, and that will make you a happier and better person. You are interested. But then you suddenly realize that his solution involves some difficulties, that you do not understand his new society. "But that's Communism!" you whisper. "Sure it is," answers your friend. Later you make another acquaintance, who invites you to another meeting. The speaker criticizes your present way of life; he points out faults in the society around you and explains a system that will, he says, eliminate those faults, and that will make you a happier and better person. You are interested. "I think I'll join this church," you whisper to your friend. "I'm a member now," he says.

Yet again, advertisements are propaganda for products. They are attempts to sell large quantities of shampoos and baby food and automobiles, sheets and roofing and zwieback. But the same methods are used to sell war bonds, to win support for the Red Cross, to obtain help for crippled children. The aims are different, but the methods are the same.

It is the contention of this book, therefore, that the idea that propaganda is always harmful, always false, is wrong. Propaganda can be used for a good cause as well as for a bad one. The motives and the ends are the important parts of any campaign; propaganda merely supplies the method of operation. In this book, propaganda means *any attempt to persuade anyone to a belief or to a form of action.* Any narrower definition will result in difficulties that must be avoided in the attempt to analyze this process.

Hence this book is not a warning against the "dangers of propaganda." The propaganda process is an essential feature of life in the modern world, no more evil because of its frequent misuse than drugs or dynamite, the characteristics of which it shares. We live our lives surrounded by propaganda; we create enormous amounts of it ourselves; and we form most or all of our cherished beliefs with its aid.

The sum of what we know through personal experience is small. In politics and economics, for example, where the facts are often not clear-cut and where rival authorities are common, all of us depend on sources outside ourselves for our opinions. Most Americans "know" their stands on Communism, big business, labor unions, and international relations. You have opinions on all these things. But do you know any Communists? Have you ever administered a big business? Are you a member of a labor union? A screen lies between each of us and the world of events, through which we allow certain kinds and amounts of information to filter, and our term "propaganda" describes the way in which that filtering occurs.

It follows that we cannot "guard against" propaganda; we should be lost without it. Most of us know that the earth moves round the sun because we have accepted the propaganda of mathematicians and astronomers, or that vaccination prevents smallpox because we believe the arguments of physicians and bacteriologists; but few laymen can produce adequate scientific evidence to support these propositions. So with most of our opinions and attitudes. We live in a reported universe, and our most essential information comes to us, at best, at second hand.

These remarks imply that anything may be labeled propaganda that attempts to make someone accept a fact or a point of view. On the basis of such a definition, a fish that imitates a rock in order to lure its luncheon a little closer is a propagandist, and so is a physicist who presents the results of his experiments to a group of his colleagues. And broadly speaking, both fish and physicists *are* propagandists.

But this book is to be concerned with propaganda as it reaches the citizens of the United States in the twentieth century, and for practical purposes we must limit our definition a little further. Most people sense an overtone in the word, an overtone that suggests *organized* attempts to persuade or systematic assaults on public beliefs. Thus we speak of the propaganda of the labor unions, or of the N.A.M., or of the Russians, Germans, or Chinese, and rarely of propaganda as something individual and personal. This qualification is useful, and dictionary definitions note the connotation of organized, group activity.

THE MEDIA OF PROPAGANDA

There are a number of channels of propaganda that are important to the average American. They are, in no special order, personal contacts, newspapers, magazines, radio programs, books, and visual media, such as motion pictures, the theater, and television. There is nothing final in this list. If you like, you may divide the propaganda that reaches you into the things you read, the things you hear, and the things you see. Every individual will have to make his own evaluation of the importance of these media. The man who gets most of his news through the radio and most of his entertainment from motion pictures lives in a different world from the man who reads carefully two or three newspapers a day and spends most of his evenings reading books and magazines of opinion. But everyone is affected by some of these channels of propaganda, and the more conscientiously one attempts to "keep up with things," the longer will grow the list of contenders for belief.

Most of the propaganda in our lives relates trivially to those lives—the small decisions, the tepid judgments that make up immensely the largest part of our days. Personal contacts are supreme in the field of such decisions. The attitudes of parents are often decisive in the lives of their children; teachers in their schools and ministers in their pulpits have moved all of us at one time or another. A few words from friends have changed most lives and much history, but it is impossible to assess such influences. They are with us always, like the poor and the air we breathe. The propaganda lines are as diverse as the speakers, and as numerous. Most strongly affective personal contacts are emotionally supercharged —one might be inclined to accept market tips from a dear friend even though the friend is on his way from filing petition in bankruptcy, for after all the old double room at college was a very pleasant place. Voting habits in America have a suspicious tendency to run in families. How many of your own most cherished beliefs are, by merest chance, those which you remember hearing around the family dinner table?

It might be worthwhile to analyze the influences that work upon us at such times, to scrutinize the gossip and the flung word, and tell exactly what they are and mean. But no one has time to question all his attitudes and decisions, and the purposes of this book restrict the analysis of propaganda to those things which affect other people, many other people. Chief among these media are newspapers, books and magazines, motion pictures, and radio and television.

THE MEDIA OF PROPAGANDA: NEWSPAPERS

The influence of newspapers is felt in almost every American home, and most of us form our first ideas of national and international problems from their pages, either directly or by hearing about them at second or twenty-second hand. During the last twenty years, we have had abundant proof that newspapers are less effective as propaganda agents that they once were or were thought to be. In five consecutive national elections the newspapers of the country have opposed the candidate who won and have been clearly defeated by such competing media as the radio or the personal-appearance tour or the record. Or, if you please, the newspapers of the country have so thoroughly lost touch with popular opinion on political issues that their views on these subjects are no longer of much importance. Whichever alternative you choose, it is an inescapable fact that for nearly twenty years the domestic political propaganda of most American newspapers has gone unheeded by most Americans.

But there are many other areas of opinion that the modern newspapers have claimed as their own. Your news of international affairs comes to you, if you are a reader of a daily of any pretensions at all, through one of the great wire services, such as A.P. or U.P. The odds are long that your local newspaper does not maintain a correspondent at any of the places mentioned in dispatches impressively headed Ankara, Moscow, or Aberystwyth, Wales; few dailies, and those only the largest, can afford the expense of a foreign staff. Americans dislike the word "censorship," but almost everything they read has been "censored" by correspondents and editors along a line that runs from the event to the newsstand and the breakfast table. There is an alternative. If you are a subscriber to a daily of no pretensions at all, you get no foreign news.

Generally speaking, this centralization of news-gathering machinery is probably an advantage, or at least a necessity. The reader of a big modern daily gets some foreign news, and he certainly gets more of it than he would get if his own newspaper had to save its pennies until it could afford to send a reporter to investigate the world outside. No one would trade the information he gets from a modern news service for the information his great-great-great-grandfather received in the occasional dispatches headed "Letter from Lisbon," which appeared in his weekly *Advertiser* or *Intelligencer*. Yet it is important to remember that "reading it in the paper" is not the same as "being there." You bear no scars from the wreck you read about this morning, and you did not fight in the revolution you so sternly opposed last week. One effect of the rise of the press associations is that we get better coverage of distant events; another is that a further conformity is forced on the American citizen. The subscriber in Boston and the subscriber in Medicine Hat read the same account of Rita Hayworth's latest marriage over their breakfast coffee.

There are dozens of good newspapers in the United States and scores of competent ones, but it is still difficult for many of us to hear the various sides of complicated issues. This situation has always existed to a certain extent, of course, but it is more true now than it used to be, and the difficulty is becoming greater every year. Time was when every sizeable town had its newspaper or, frequently, newspapers. Now there are only a half-dozen cities in the United States that offer any real competition for the reader's interest. The usual pattern, even for a large city, is one morning and one evening newspaper, and they are frequently owned by the same company.

The difficulty is one of expense. Seventy-five years ago one good journeyman, a set of type, and a press made a newspaper. Now the establishment of a big-city paper that can hope to compete with other such journals is a matter for millionaires alone. Our newspapers are better than they have ever been in coverage, in features, in the offering of trained intelligence, but the average newspaper reader can hear only one tune played year after year.

For years it was the fashion to hint darkly at the advertisers as the greatest threat to the freedom of the press in this country. The theory was that since a newspaper lives by its advertising, it must necessarily be at the beck and call of the owners of department stores and grocery chains. But this situation is not often the true one. If the newspaper depends on advertising, so does the grocery chain, and in many cases the owner of the newspaper is probably as rich as the store owner and much more powerful. Publishers seldom take dictation from anyone. And yet it is a fact that most American newspapers are conservative in political tone, more conservative by a good deal than the people who read them, if we can believe the evidence of election returns. The reason is probably a simple one. Publishers are necessarily wealthy and powerful individuals, and they naturally associate chiefly with people like themselves, whose interests are their interests. People who are wealthy and powerful in any society tend to resist changes—for obvious reasons. Hence newspapers, which are, to a certain extent, extensions of the personalities of their owners, tend also to be conservative. This generalization admits of individual exceptions, but it is broadly true.

Considered as vehicles for propaganda, newspapers make an almost ideal medium. There is something in every issue for everybody, and a reader naturally moves from the item of his first interest to other items which may also affect his opinions and decisions. It has been established that more people read the weather report than anything else in newspapers, but they read other sections as well.

Probably the news should be considered first—the headlines and the front-page stories that come to us hot from life and the A.P. wires. The news is not supposed to be colored by propaganda, by any effort to persuade or convince. Ideally each news story should tell us what happened and where and to whom and how and why; but reporters are human beings with human biases, as their stories show. And then each story must be edited and assigned its place in the makeup of the paper, and prejudice may decide whether a story deserves a front-page spread or a soberer inside column. Sometimes there is overt use of news articles for propaganda purposes. The Chicago *Tribune* has found political capital in the drama and in baseball, at different times.

The editorial page is, of course, where the newspaper is supposed to do its persuading. The one great difficulty is that so few readers ever turn to the editorials. If you do read them, though, you should know where the newspaper stands on controversial questions, and that is valuable in assessing the "slanting" of its news.

The last half-century has seen the rise of the columnists. Limited at first to wisecracks, humorous verse, and gossip, the columnists have lately assumed the role of prophets and seers. One can buy solutions to most of the world's evils for a mere nickel. Like the writers of editorials, the columnists are supposed to persuade and convince, and like them, too, the columnists are keys to the leanings of the paper. One seldom finds a Westbrook Pegler in a newspaper friendly to labor or a Samuel Grafton in a conservative Republican journal.

There is little propaganda in weather reports or daily recipes, but the rest of any newspaper is fair game. Comic strips extol the virtues of true love and the innocence of childhood—though one strip did have a villain who was the spitting image of John L. Lewis—and Al Capp has frequently bruised the sensibilities of the United States Senate.

THE MEDIA OF PROPAGANDA: MAGAZINES AND BOOKS

Magazine and book circulation in the United States is, of course, not so large as newspaper circulation, yet for several reasons these media must be considered among the most important vehicles of written propaganda.

Magazines vary much more widely than newspapers, their contents ranging from the primitive appeals of the pulps and comic books to the serious and often scholarly articles in such quality periodicals as *Harper's* and *The Atlantic Monthly*. The great mass-circulation weeklies and monthlies, which reach millions with every issue, are carefully tailored to editorial formulas that have gained and held large readerships. Thus the women's magazines combine sweetness and light with the value of true love and a sprinkling of household hints; the immensely successful *Reader's Digest* sells self-help and minimum reading time; the big news weeklies are departmentalized newspapers with a week's perspective and no comic strips.

The biases of magazines are usually milder than those of newspapers. Sharp competition for huge audiences makes it dangerous for a journal seriously or consistently to offend any group of its readers. What may seem like a bold discussion of a controversial issue may really be nothing of the kind; it may be only a fiery restatement of what the magazine's readership already believes and wants to hear reiterated. Analysis of the propaganda content and direction of a national magazine requires some familiarity with the publication over a period of several issues, and some notion of what audience is reached by it.

The propaganda effect of magazines on general attitudes is perhaps more noticeable than that on particular issues. The fiction in the big "slicks," for example, consistently reinforces a set of values which G. B. Shaw has unkindly dubbed "middle-class" morality—virtue triumphs, evil gets its deserts, and a white, middle-class hero is united with a white, middle-class heroine after a period of tribulation ranging from 2,500 to 30,000 words. Even the advertisements in these periodicals have an effect upon our general ideas about what is desirable for and typical of the American people. They have been as effective as the motion pictures and Sears-Roebuck in bringing about the end of hayseed rural America, and what many people think of as the typical American standard of living is probably the standard of the "typical" family which smiles at them from the beer and refrigerator ads.

Books are read by two groups—less than one per cent of the population, and students. The average American reads less than one book a year. *Gone with the Wind* has been the best-selling novel of our time, with six million copies sold. But *The Reader's Digest* sells more copies than that every month, and the New York *Daily News* sells the same number in a little over two days. Books are a luxury item with a limited market. Yet they are among the best media for propaganda, and to underestimate their importance is to ignore the very special groups that read books in large numbers. The people who control our government, our industries, our art, and our education are the readers of books, and their influence is out of all proportion to their numbers. *Mein Kampf* and *Das Kapital* and *The Origin of Species* have made our world, though *Life's* circulation for a year would cover all those who have read these books, with enough readers to spare for several digests.

THE MEDIA OF PROPAGANDA: MOTION PICTURES AND THEATER

In general, motion pictures are made for profit. Since that is so, and since any "message" beyond the vaguest affirmatives is certain to offend some potential customer, motion pictures have tended to steer clear of controversial material. They have tried, successfully, to sell entertainment, with an occasional bow in favor of love and democracy. They are propaganda, but they are propaganda for the great myths of our time, because they must please Everyman.

The great box-office hits are likely to be literally out of this world: costume dramas like *Gone with the Wind* and the comic sagas of Crosby and Hope have nothing to do with our lives. Occasionally, though, a motion picture may have a real propaganda point—you will remember *The Grapes of Wrath, Mission to Moscow,* and *Gentleman's Agreement* —and these are likely to be more effective than any number of factual reports. A few documentary films like *The Plow That Broke the Plains* and *The River* have been successful, and they show what motion pictures can do when they turn their attention to overt propaganda. There are thousands of training and educational films that are persuasive in their purpose, but they are not easily available to the public. The same comment that we have already made about magazines may be made about motion pictures: They help to determine our values and social beliefs, and, in part, our behavior. But their influence is long-range and pervasive rather than immediate and particular.

The professional theater, except in the largest cities, is a dying art; yet it deserves to be mentioned because like books it has a wider influence than could be expected from the number of its patrons. There is direct influence through the fact that successful plays are often bought and produced as movies in Hollywood, and there is indirect influence through reviews and word of mouth. Nevertheless, few lives are changed by plays; they are an excellent propaganda medium, but they reach far too few people directly to be comparable to newspapers and magazines.

THE MEDIA OF PROPAGANDA: RADIO AND TELEVISION

Radio is dominated by networks like the National Broadcasting Company, the Columbia Broadcasting System, and the Mutual and American Broadcasting companies. These associations present the most popular shows and the best-known commentators. There are also hundreds of local radio stations which serve the news and advertising and home-talent needs of the smaller cities. As propaganda media, radio stations are most important because of two features—the news and advertising. In general, the news is a straight recital of events with only indirect editorial comment, and the advertising is straight selling, even by way of the soap opera. The only really complicated propaganda coming to us through radio is the work of commentators, who have a role similar to that of columnists in newspapers. Indeed, they are often the same people. With them, of course, every opinion or statement is only as valuable as the source. How much does the commentator know? Why should he be believed? ...

FREEDOM FOR PROPAGANDA

As we have seen, outlets for propaganda are necessary in any society, and they are particularly necessary in a democracy. Our freedom of the press is really only a freedom to be propagandized, but it deserves to be defended on that ground. One of the great dangers of our time is the threat against freedom of speech and freedom of the press, two liberties that are unknown through a large part of our world.

And there is another freedom that is equally important—the freedom to hear all sides of a question, to be able to choose among alternative versions of the truth. The editors of *Pravda* and *Izvestia* are doubtless free to print the news as they see it. But they would not be editors of those newspapers if they did not see news in the proper light, Kremlinically speaking. The people of Russia have no freedom of choice, no alternative versions. They read the gospel according to *Pravda* and *Izvestia* or they do not read at all. Freedom of the press without freedom for more than one kind of press means nothing.

The average American has alternative sources of information now. His newspaper is likely to be the only one easily available in his town, and it is likely to have a definite bias, but he can subscribe to an outstanding paper like the New York *Times,* and he can dial a dozen radio stations with a turn of his hand. Some of them may present views that differ from those of his newspaper. He can go to motion pictures that may express views on economics or international affairs, though there are not many, and he can read magazines or books that advocate everything from aeronautics to yoga. And that is as it should be. If we can hear all sides of a question, then there is hope for an honest and intelligent choice among the alternatives that continually face us. But the tendency of the last three decades has been toward greater and greater control of the media of mass propaganda by fewer and fewer great owners and publishers. This tendency is dangerous beyond any doubt, as dangerous, perhaps, as a corresponding growth of government control would have been. It is a tendency on which the propaganda-conscious citizen should keep a very wary eye.

Questions for Study and Discussion

1. What definition of propaganda do Hummel and Huntress give? Why do they qualify their definition?

2. Describe propaganda, giving examples from the three categories all propaganda can be divided into.

3. What proof is offered that newspapers have lost considerable propagandistic influence in recent years?

4. Can you suggest an incident to prove that newspapers are influential propagandists?

5. Even though news may be presented in an unbiased manner, by what means does a newspaper legitimately express its biased attitudes?

6. Although less than one percent of the population reads books, why do the authors maintain that books are among the best media for propaganda?

7. What type of propaganda is usually presented in motion pictures and plays?

8. Can you name several motion pictures or stage plays other than those listed here which differ from the average in their use of propaganda?

9. What dangerous tendency in the control of mass media do the authors suggest has been developing in recent years?

Vocabulary Study

Define or identify the following words as used in this essay: connotation, cynical, tepid, affective, scrutinize, hayseed, *Pravda, Izvestia.*

Writing Assignment

The foregoing selection was written in 1949. Write a composition updating the facts and trends of one of the authors' discussions of media, and expressing your own reaction to the authors' points of view.

How to Detect Propaganda

Clyde R. Miller

If American citizens are to have a clear understanding of present-day conditions and what to do about them, they must be able to recognize propaganda, to analyze it, and to appraise it.

But what is propaganda?

As generally understood, propaganda is expression of opinion or action by individuals or groups deliberately designed to influence opinions or actions of other individuals or groups with reference to predetermined ends. Thus propaganda differs from scientific analysis. The propagandist is trying to "put something across," good or bad, whereas the scientist is trying to discover truth and fact. Often the propagandist does not want careful scrutiny and criticism; he wants to bring about a specific action. Because the action may be socially beneficial or socially harmful to millions of people, it is necessary to focus upon the propagandist and his activities the searchlight of scientific scrutiny. Socially desirable propaganda will not suffer from such examination, but the opposite type will be detected and revealed for what it is.

We are fooled by propaganda chiefly because we don't recognize it when we see it. It may be fun to be fooled but, as the cigarette ads used to say, is is more fun to know. We can more easily recognize propaganda when we see it if we are familiar with the seven common propaganda devices. These are:

1. The Name Calling Device
2. The Glittering Generalities Device
3. The Transfer Device
4. The Testimonial Device
5. The Plain Folks Device
6. The Card Stacking Device
7. The Band Wagon Device

Why are wo fooled by these devices? Because they appeal to our emotions rather than to our reason. They make us believe and do something we would not believe or do if we thought about it calmly, dispassionately. In examining these devices, note that they work most effectively at those times when we are too lazy to think for ourselves; also, they tie into emotions which sway us to be "for" or "against" nations, races, religions, ideals, economic and political policies and practices, and so on through automobiles, cigarettes, radios, toothpastes, presidents, and wars. With our emotions stirred, it may be fun to be fooled by these propaganda devices, but it is more fun and infinitely more to our own interests to know how they work.

Lincoln must have had in mind citizens who could balance their emotions with intelligence when he made his remark: "...but you can't fool all of the people all of the time."

NAME CALLING

"Name Calling" is a device to make us form a judgment without examining the evidence on which it should be based. Here the propagandist appeals to our hate and fear. He does this by giving "bad names" to those individuals, groups, nations, races, policies, practices, beliefs, and ideals which he would have us condemn and reject. For centuries the name "heretic" was bad. Thousands were oppressed, tortured, or put to death as heretics. Anybody who dissented from popular or group belief or practice was in danger of being called a heretic. In the light of today's knowledge, some heresies were bad and some were good. Many of the pioneers of modern science were called heretics; witness the cases of Copernicus, Galileo, Bruno. Today's bad names include: Fascist, demagogue, dictator, Red, financial oligarchy, Communist, muckraker, alien, outside agitator, economic royalist, Utopian, rabble-rouser, troublemaker, Tory, Constitution wrecker.

"Al" Smith called Roosevelt a Communist by implication when he said in his Liberty League speech, "There can be only one capital, Washington or Moscow." When "Al" Smith was running for the presidency, many called him a tool of the Pope, saying in effect, "We must choose between Washington and Rome." That implied that Mr. Smith, if elected President, would take his orders from the Pope. Likewise Mr. Justice Hugo Black has been associated with a bad name, Ku Klux Klan. In these cases some propagandists have tried to make us form judgments without examining essential evidence and implications. "Al Smith is a Catholic. He must never be President." "Roosevelt is a Red. Defeat his program." "Hugo Black is or was a Klansman. Take him out of the Supreme Court."

Use of "bad names" without presentation of their essential meaning, without all their pertinent implications, comprises perhaps the most common of all propaganda devices. Those who want to maintain the status quo apply bad names to those who would change it. For example, the Hearst press applies bad names to Communists and Socialists. Those who want to change the status quo apply bad names to those who would maintain it. For example, the Daily Worker and the American Guardian apply bad names to conservative Republicans and Democrats.

GLITTERING GENERALITIES

"Glittering Generalities" is a device by which the propagandist identifies his program with virtue by use of "virtue words." Here he appeals to our emotions of love, generosity, and brotherhood. He uses words like truth, freedom, honor, liberty, social justice, public service, the right to work, loyalty, progress, democracy, the American way, Constitution defender. These words suggest shining ideals. All persons of good will believe in these ideals. Hence the propagandist, by identifying his individual group, nation, race, policy, practice, or belief with such ideals, seeks to win us to his cause. As Name Calling is a device to make us form a judgment to reject and condemn, without examining the evidence, Glittering Generalities is a device to make us accept and approve, without examining the evidence.

For example, use of the phrases, "the right to work" and "social justice," may be a device to make us accept programs for meeting the labor-capital problem which, if we examined them critically, we would not accept at all.

In the Name Calling and Glittering Generalities devices, words are used to stir up our emotions and to befog our thinking. In one device "bad words" are used to make us mad; in the other "good words" are used to make us glad.

The propagandist is most effective in use of these devices when his words make us create devils to fight or gods to adore. By his use of the "bad words," we personify as a "devil" some nation, race, group, individual, policy, practice, or ideal; we are made fighting mad to destroy it. By use of "good words," we personify as a godlike idol some nation, race, group, etc. Words which are "bad" to some are "good" to others, or may be made so. Thus, to some the New Deal is "a prophecy of social salvation" while to others it is "an omen of social disaster."

From consideration of names, "bad" and "good," we pass to institutions and symbols, also "bad" and "good." We see these in the next device.

TRANSFER

"Transfer" is a device by which the propagandist carries over the authority, sanction, and prestige of something we respect and revere to something he would have us accept. For example, most of us respect and revere our church and our nation. If the propagandist succeeds in getting church or nation to approve a campaign in behalf of some program, he thereby transfers its authority, sanction, and prestige to that program. Thus we may accept something which otherwise we might reject.

In the Transfer device, symbols are constantly used. The cross represents the Christian Church. The flag represents the nation. Cartoons like Uncle Sam represent a consensus of public opinion. Those symbols stir emotions. At their very sight, with the speed of light, is aroused the whole complex of feelings we have with respect to church or nation. A cartoonist by having Uncle Sam disapprove a budget for unemployment relief would have us feel that the whole United States disapproves relief costs. By drawing an Uncle Sam who approves the same budget, the cartoonist would have us feel that the American people approve it. Thus, the Transfer device is used both for and against causes and ideas.

TESTIMONIAL

The "Testimonial" is a device to make us accept anything from a patent medicine or a cigarette to a program of national policy. In this device the propagandist makes use of testimonials. "When I feel tired, I smoke a Camel and get the grandest lift." "We believe the John L. Lewis plan of labor organization is splendid; C.I.O. should be supported." This device works in reverse also; counter-testimonials may be employed. Seldom are these used against commercial products like patent medicines and cigarettes, but they are constantly employed in social, economic, and political issues. "We believe the John L. Lewis plan of labor organization is bad; C.I.O. should not be supported."

PLAIN FOLKS

"Plain Folks" is a device used by politicians, labor leaders, business men, and even by ministers and educators to win our confidence by appearing to be people like ourselves—"just plain folks among the neighbors." In election years especially do candidates show their devotion to little children and the common, homey things of life. They have front porch campaigns. For the newspaper men they raid the kitchen cupboard finding there some of the good wife's apple pie. They go to country picnics; they attend service at the old frame church; they pitch hay and go fishing; they show their belief in home and mother. In short, they would win our votes by showing that they're just as common as the rest of us—"just plain folks," and therefore, wise and good. Business men often are "plain folks" with the factory hands. Even distillers use the device. "It's our family's whiskey, neighbor; and neighbor, it's your price."

CARD STACKING

"Card Stacking" is a device in which the propagandist employs all the arts of deception to win our support for himself, his group, nation, race, policy, practice, belief, or ideal. He stacks the cards against the truth. He uses under-emphasis and over-emphasis to dodge issues and evade facts. He resorts to lies, censorship, and distortion. He omits facts. He offers false testimony. He creates a smokescreen of clamor by raising a new issue when he wants an embarrassing matter forgotten.

He draws a red herring across the trail to confuse and divert those in quest of facts he does not want revealed. He makes the unreal appear real and the real appear unreal. He lets half-truth masquerade as truth. By the Card Stacking device, a mediocre candidate, through the "build-up," is made to appear an intellectual titan; an ordinary prize fighter a probable world champion; a worthless patent medicine a beneficent cure. By means of this device propagandists would convince us that a ruthless war of aggression is a crusade for righteousness.... Card Stacking employs sham, hypocrisy, effrontery.

THE BAND WAGON

The "Band Wagon" is a device to make us follow the crowd, to accept the propagandist's program en masse. Here his theme is: "Everybody's doing it." His techniques range from those of medicine show to dramatic spectacle. He hires a hall, fills a great stadium, marches a million men in parade. He employs symbols, colors, music, movement, all the dramatic arts. He appeals to the desire, common to most of us, to "follow the crowd." Because he wants us to "follow the crowd" in masses, he directs his appeal to groups held together by common ties of nationality, religion, race, environment, sex, vocation. Thus propagandists campaigning for or against a program will appeal to us as Catholics, Protestants, or Jews; as members of the Nordic race or as Negroes; as farmers or as school teachers; as housewives or as miners. All the artifices of flattery are used to harness the fears and hatreds, prejudices and biases, convictions and ideals common to the group; thus emotion is made to push and pull the group on to the Band Wagon. In newspaper articles and in the spoken word this device is also found. "Don't throw your vote away. Vote for our candidate. He's sure to win." Nearly everybody wins in every election—before the votes are in.

PROPAGANDA AND EMOTION

Observe that in all these devices our emotion is the stuff with which propagandists work. Without it they are helpless; with it, harnessing it to their purposes, they can make us glow with pride or burn with hatred, they can make us zealots in behalf of the program they espouse. As we said at the beginning, propaganda as generally understood is expression of opinion or action by individuals or groups with reference to predetermined ends. Without the appeal to our emotion—to our fears and to our courage, to our selfishness and unselfishness, to our loves and to our hates—propagandists would influence few opinions and few actions.

To say this is not to condemn emotion, an essential part of life, or to assert that all predetermined ends of propagandists are "bad." What we mean is that the intelligent citizen does not want propagandists to utilize his emotions, even to the attainment of "good" ends, without knowing that is going on. He does not want to be "used" in the attainment of ends he may later consider "bad." He does not want to be gullible. He does not want to be fooled. He does not want to be duped, even in a "good" cause. He wants to know the facts and among these is included the fact of the utilization of his emotions.

Keeping in mind the seven common propaganda devices, turn to today's newspapers and almost immediately you can spot examples of them all. At election time or during any campaign, Plain Folks and Band Wagon are common. Card Stacking is hardest to detect because it is adroitly executed or because we lack the information necessary to nail the lie. A little practice with the daily newspapers in detecting these propaganda devices soon enables us to detect them elsewhere—in radio, news-reel, books, magazines, and in expressions of labor unions, business groups, churches, schools, political parties.

Questions for Study and Discussion

1. Define propaganda.

2. Why is it necessary to be able to recognize, analyze, and appraise propaganda?

3. Why are we so easily fooled by propaganda devices?

4. Should honest, intelligent writers and readers reject as unfair all emotional appeals? Explain.

5. Is all propaganda bad? Explain.

6. Which one of the seven propaganda devices is most difficult to detect?.

Writing Assignment

Write a summary paragraph of seven sentences, expressing in each sentence the essence of one of the common propaganda devices.

Vocabulary Study

Define the following words as used in this selection: scrutiny, dispassionately, heresies, demagogue, Utopian, consensus, effrontery, gullible.

On Reading Propaganda

E. A. Tenney

The greatest menace to our democracy, to our existence as a free, independent, and peace-loving people, is that insidious thing called *Propaganda.* Like the thief and the outcast it lurks in dark corners and in broken-down alleys, and like the pickpocket it stealthily insinuates its slimy, snakelike fingers into the pockets of the mind and filches from us our intellectual integrity. One touch of its corroding influence debases the purest passion, and one whiff of its breath contaminates the purest air. The stench of those thousands upon thousands of God-fearing Americans infected and diseased by it is greater than the stench that arose from the putrefying bodies of the unburied victims of the bubonic plague. The more one considers the ghastly effect of propaganda upon modern life the more one hates it for the evil thing it is and the evil it has wrought. Speak propaganda and please the devil, your master, all of you who traffic in unclean words and in foul perverted thoughts!

In the foregoing paragraph, I practiced my hand at writing some propaganda against *propaganda* just to see whether I could do it and also to give you, my reader, a chance to test yourself to see whether you are susceptible and are readily taken in. I observed the rules not for writing honest propaganda but for writing inferior or unscrupulous propaganda, insincere stuff. The difference between good and bad propaganda is the difference between good and bad persuasion—a topic treated in the next paragraph. Before turning to it, I wish to point out the principles upon which I wrote in composing the preceding paragraph. In the first place I posed the questions to myself, "How shall I prejudice my readers against this word? How shall I give to the word an evil connotation so that in the future they will feel an emotion of hate or loathing or anger when next I use it?" The paragraph itself is an answer to the question. I was insincere in that I wrote only half of what I believe to be true; I was unscrupulous in that I employed glittering generalities, appealed to the conventional stock prejudices, resorted to name-calling, personified the word into an evil thing and associated it with bad smells, unsavory places, the slimy snake, and the devil. Now it so happens that I dislike propaganda of the type I wrote—it does not play the game fairly; but I admire much propaganda, i.e., persuasion which makes no attempt to conceal its aim and which argues its case with intelligence and sincere emotion. Of late a great cry has gone up against propaganda as though it were some new evil thing which must be exterminated. In New York City a number of men have organized an "Institute for Propaganda Analysis," and each month they publish a leaflet to warn their readers against various propagandas. The paradox is that they are propagandists propagandizing against propaganda. What these men are doing is analyzing bad propaganda and striving to raise the quality.

Whenever there is an organized movement to persuade people to believe or do something, whenever an effort is made to "propagate" a creed or set of opinions or convictions or to make people act as we want them to act, the means employed are called propaganda. When the means are base, then the propaganda is base; when the means are honorable, it is honorable. The means which I employed in the opening paragraph were unworthy of a good citizen or honorable and just man, for they were intended to create an emotional prejudice against propaganda without giving the word a fair trial. On the contrary, in this paragraph I am writing good propaganda because I am honestly using what means I have to persuade you, the reader, that the word has a good connotation as well as a sinister one. The word has many synonyms—persuasion, publicity, proselytism, conversion, advertisement. Missionaries, salesmen, advertisers, publicity or public relations men—for colleges, political parties, business firms, etc., "ambassadors of good will" are all propagandists to be admired or despised in proportion to the quality of the means they use in converting others to their opinions. When Edmund Burke said that there are ways and means by which a good man will not save even his country, he meant that there are some devices of propaganda to which a sincere and honorable man will not stoop. Bad propaganda is a species of fraud; good propaganda is a process of enlightenment. The subtle, hidden, indirect lie, the lie which is intended to arouse the base passions of hate and by so doing enable the liar to achieve some unjust end—this is propaganda in its lowest, most fraudulent form. Its opposite is propaganda at its best. Between these two extremes lie all imaginable degrees of worth and worthlessness.

Questions for Study and Discussion

1. What is this author's definition of propaganda?
2. How does the author differentiate good propaganda from bad propaganda?
3. Point out the similarities and differences between this selection and "How to Detect Propaganda."

Vocabulary Study

Define the following words as used in this selection: paradox, proselytism, fraudulent.

Stereotypes

Walter Lippmann

Each of us lives and works on a small part of the earth's surface, moves in a small circle, and of these acquaintances knows only a few intimately. Of any public event that has wide effects we see at best only a phase and an aspect. This is as true of the eminent insiders who draft treaties, make laws, and issue orders, as it is of those who have treaties framed for them, laws promulgated to them, order given at them. Inevitably our opinions cover a bigger space, a longer reach of time, a greater number of things, than we can directly observe. They have, therefore, to be pieced together out of what others have reported and what we can imagine.

Yet even the eyewitness does not bring back a naive picture of the scene. For experience seems to show that he himself brings something to the scene which later he takes away from it, that oftener than not what he imagines to be the account of an event is really a transfiguration of it. Few facts in consciousness seem to be merely given. Most facts in consciousness seem to be partly made. A report is the joint product of the knower and known, in which the role of the observer is always selective and usually creative. The facts we see depend on where we are placed, and the habit of our eyes. . . .

For the most part we do not first see, and then define, we define first and then see. In the great blooming, buzzing confusion of the outer world we pick out what our culture has already defined for us, and we tend to perceive that which we have picked out in the form stereotyped for us by our culture. Of the great men who assembled at Paris to settle the affairs of mankind, how many were there who were able to see much of the Europe about them, rather than their commitments about Europe? Could anyone have penetrated the mind of M. Clemanceau, would he have found there images of the Europe of 1919, or a great sediment of stereotyped ideas accumulated and hardened in a long and pugnacious existence? Did he see the Germans of 1919, or the German type as he had learned to see it since 1871? He saw the type, and among the reports that came to him from Germany, he took to heart those reports, and, it seems, those only, which fitted the type that was in his mind. If a junker blustered, that was an authentic German; if a labor leader confessed the guilt of the empire, he was not an authentic German.

At a Congress of Psychology in Gottingen an interesting experiment was made with a crowd of presumably trained observers.

Not far from the hall in which the Congress was sitting there was a public fete with a masked ball. Suddenly the door of the hall was thrown open and a clown rushed in madly pursued by a Negro, revolver in hand. They stopped in the middle of the room fighting; the clown fell, the Negro leapt upon him, fired, and then both rushed out of the hall. The whole incident hardly lasted twenty seconds.

The President asked those present to write immediately a report since there was sure to be a judicial inquiry. Forty reports were sent in. Only one had less than 20% of mistakes in regard to the principal facts; fourteen had 20% to 40% of mistakes; twelve from 40% to 50%; thirteen more than 50%. Moreover in twenty-four accounts 10% of the details were pure inventions and this proportion was exceeded in ten accounts and diminished in six. Briefly a quarter of the accounts were false.

It goes without saying that the whole scene had been arranged and even photographed in advance. The ten false reports may then be relegated to the category of tales and legends; twenty-four accounts are half legendary, and six have a value approximating to exact evidence.

Thus out of forty trained observers writing a responsible account of a scene that had just happened before their eyes, more than a majority saw a scene that had not taken place. What then did they see? One would suppose it was easier to tell what had occurred, than to invent something which had not occurred. They saw their stereotype of such a brawl. All of them had in the course of their lives acquired a series of images of brawls, and these images flickered before their eyes. In one man these images displaced less than 20% of the actual scene, in thirteen men more than half. In thirty-four out of the forty observers the stereotypes preempted at least one-tenth of the scene.

A distinguished art critic has said that "what with the almost number-less shapes assumed by an object ... what with our insensitiveness and inattention, things scarcely would have for us features and outlines so determined and clear that we could recall them at will, but for the stereotyped shapes art has lent them." The truth is even broader than that, for the stereotyped shapes lent to the world come not merely from art, in the sense of painting and sculpture and literature, but from our moral codes and our social philosophies and our political agitations as well. Substitute in the following passage of Mr. Berenson's the words 'politics,' 'business,' and 'society,' for the word 'art' and the sentences will be no less true: "... unless years devoted to the study of all schools of art have taught us also to see with our own eyes, we soon fall into the habit of moulding whatever we look at into the forms borrowed from the one art with which we are acquainted. There is our standard of artistic reality. Let anyone give us shapes and colors which we cannot instantly match in our paltry stock of hackneyed forms and tints, and we shake our heads at his failure to reproduce things as we know they certainly are, or we accuse him of insincerity."

Mr. Berenson speaks of our displeasure when a painter "does not visualize objects exactly as we do," and of the difficulty of appreciating the art of the Middle Ages because since then "our manner of visualizing forms has changed in a thousand ways." He goes on to show how in regard to the human figure we have been taught to see what we do see. "Created by Donatello and Masaccio, and sanctioned by the Humanists, the new canon of the human figure, the new cast of features . . . presented to the ruling classes of that time the type of human being most likely to win the day in the combat of human forces. . . . Who had the power to break through this new standard of vision and, out of the chaos of things, to select shapes more definitely expressive of reality than those fixed by men of genius? No one had such power. People had perforce to see things in that way and in no other, and to see only the shapes depicted, to love only the ideals presented. . . ."

2

If we cannot fully understand the acts of other people, until we know what they think they know, then in order to do justice we have to appraise not only the information which has been at their disposal, but the minds through which they have filtered it. For the accepted types, the current patterns, the standard versions, intercept information on its way to consciousness. Americanization, for example, is superficially at least the substitution of American for European stereotypes. Thus the peasant who might see his landlord as if he were the lord of the manor, his employer as he saw the local magnate, is taught by Americanization to see the landlord and employer according to American standards. This constitutes a change of mind, which is, in effect, when the inoculation succeeds, a change of vision. His eye sees differently. One kindly gentlewoman has confessed that the stereotypes are of such overweening importance, that when hers are not indulged, she at least is unable to accept the brotherhood of man and the fatherhood of God: "We are strangely affected by the clothes we wear. Garments create a mental and social atmosphere. What can be hoped for the Americanism of a man who insists on employing a London tailor? One's very food affects his Americanism. What kind of American consciousness can grow in the atmosphere of sauerkraut and Limburger cheese? Or what can you expect of the Americanism of the man whose breath always reeks of garlic?"

This lady might well have been the patron of a pageant which a friend of mine once attended. It was called the Melting Pot, and it was given on the Fourth of July in an automobile town where many foreign-born workers are employed. In the center of the baseball park at second base stood a huge wooden and canvas pot. There were flights of steps up to the rim on two sides. After the audience had settled itself, and the band had played, a procession came through an opening at one side of the field. It was made up of men of all the foreign nationalities employed in the factories. They wore their native costumes, they were singing their national songs; they danced their folk dances, and carried the banners of all Europe. The master of ceremonies was the principal of the grade school dressed as Uncle Sam. He led them to the pot. He directed them up the steps to the rim, and inside. He called them out again on the other side. They came, dressed in derby hats, coats, pants, vest, stiff collar and polka-dot tie, undoubtedly, said my friend, each with an Eversharp pencil in his pocket, and all singing "The Star-Spangled Banner."

To the promoters of this pageant, and probably to most of the actors, it seemed as if they had managed to express the most intimate difficulty to friendly association between the older peoples of America and the newer. The contradiction of their stereotypes interfered with the full recognition of their common humanity. The people who change their names know this. They mean to change themselves, and the attitude of strangers toward them.

There is, of course, some connection between the scene outside and the mind through which we watch it, just as there are some long-haired men and short-haired women in radical gatherings. But to the hurried observer a slight connection is enough. If there are two bobbed heads and four beards in the audience, it will be a bobbed and bearded audience to the reporter who knows beforehand that such gatherings are composed of people with these tastes in the management of their hair. There is a connection between our vision and the facts, but it is often a strange connection. A man has rarely looked at a landscape, let us say, except to examine its possibilities for division into building lots, but he has seen a number of landscapes hanging in the parlor. And from them he has learned to think of a landscape as a rosy sunset, or as a country road with a church steeple and a silver moon. One day he goes to the country, and for hours he does not see a single landscape. Then the sun goes down looking rosy. At once he recognizes a landscape and exclaims that it is beautiful. But two days later, when he tries to recall what he saw, the odds are that he will remember chiefly some landscape in a parlor.

Unless he has been drunk or dreaming or insane he did see a sunset, but he saw in it, and above all remembers from it, more of what the oil painting taught him to observe, than what an impressionist painter, for example, or a cultivated Japanese would have seen and taken away with him. And the Japanese and the painter in turn will have seen and remembered more of the form they had learned, unless they happen to be the very rare people who find fresh sight for mankind. In untrained observation we pick recognizable signs out of the environment. The signs stand for ideas, and these ideas we fill out with our stock of images. We do not so much see this man and that sunset; rather we notice that the thing is man or sunset, and then see chiefly what our mind is already full of on those subjects.

3

There is economy in this. For the attempt to see all things freshly and in detail, rather than as types and generalities, is exhausting, and among busy affairs practically out of the question. In a circle of friends, and in relation to close associates or competitors, there is no shortcut through, and no substitute for, an individualized understanding. Those whom we love and admire most are the men and women whose consciousness is peopled thickly with persons rather than with types, who know us rather than the classification into which we might fit. For even without phrasing it to ourselves, we feel intuitively that all classification is in relation to some purpose not necessarily our own; that between two human beings no association has final dignity in which each does not affirm as an axiom the personal inviolability of both.

But modern life is hurried and multifarious; above all physical distance separates men who are often in vital contact with each other, such as employer and employee, official and voter. There is neither time nor opportunity for intimate acquaintance. Instead we notice a trait which marks a well-known type, and fill in the rest of the picture by means of the stereotypes we carry about in our heads. He is an agitator. That much we notice, or are told. Well, an agitator is this sort of person, and so he is this sort of person. He is an intellectual. He is a plutocrat. He is a foreigner. He is a "South European." He is from Back Bay. He is a Harvard Man. How different from the statement: he is a Yale Man. He is a regular fellow. He is a West Pointer. He is an old army sergeant.

He is a Greenwich Villager: what don't we know about him then, and about her? He is an international banker. He is from Main Street.

The subtlest and most pervasive of all influences are those which create and maintain the repertory of stereotypes. We are told about the world before we see it. We imagine most things before we experience them. And those pre-conceptions, unless education has made us acutely aware, govern deeply the whole process of perception. They mark out certain objects as familiar or strange, emphasizing the difference, so that the slightly familiar is seen as very familiar, and the somewhat strange as sharply alien. They are aroused by small signs, which may vary from a true index to a vague analogy. Aroused, they flood fresh vision with older images, and project into the world what has been resurrected in memory. Were there no practical uniformities in the environment, there would be no economy and only error in the human habit of accepting foresight for sight. But there are uniformities sufficiently accurate, and the need of economizing attention is so inevitable, that the abandonment of all stereotypes for a wholly innocent approach to experience would impoverish human life.

What matters is the character of the stereotypes, and the gullibility with which we employ them. And these in the end depend upon those inclusive patterns which constitute our philosophy of life. If in that philosophy we assume that the world is codified according to a code which we possess, we are likely to make our reports of what is going on describe a world run by our code. But if our philosophy tells us that each man is only a small part of the world, that his intelligence catches at best only phases and aspects in a coarse net of ideas, then, when we use our stereotypes, we tend to know that they are only stereotypes, to hold them lightly, to modify them gladly. We tend, also, to realize more and more clearly when our ideas started, where they started, how they came to us, why we accepted them. All useful history is antiseptic in this fashion. It enables us to know what fairy tale, what school book, what tradition, what novel, play, picture, phrase, planted one preconception in this mind, another in that mind.

4

Those who wish to censor art do not at least underestimate this influence. They generally misunderstand it, and almost always they are absurdly bent on preventing other people from discovering anything not sanctioned by them. But at any rate, like Plato in his argument about the poets, they feel vaguely that the types acquired through fiction tend to be imposed on reality. Thus there can be little doubt that the moving picture is steadily building up imagery which is then evoked by the words people read in their newspapers. In the whole experience of the race there has been no aid to visualization comparable to the cinema. If a Florentine wished to visualize the saints, he could go to the frescoes in his church, where he might see a vision of saints standardized for his time by Giotto. If an Athenian wished to visualize the gods he went to the temples. But the number of objects which were pictured was not great. And in the East, where the spirit of the second commandment was widely accepted, the portraiture of concrete practical decision was by so much reduced. In the western world, however, during the last few centuries there has been an enormous increase in the volume and scope of secular description, the word picture, the narrative, the illustrated narrative, and finally the moving picture and . . . the talking picture.

Photographs have the kind of authority over imagination today, which the printed word had yesterday, and the spoken word before that. They seem utterly real. They come, we imagine, directly to us without human meddling, and they are the most effortless food for the mind conceivable. Any description in words, or even any inert picture, requires an effort of memory before a picture exists in the mind. But on the screen the whole process of observing, describing, reporting, and then imagining, has been accomplished for you. Without more trouble than is needed to stay awake the result which your imagination is always aiming at is reeled off on the screen. The shadowy idea becomes vivid; your hazy notion, let us say, of the Ku Klux Klan, thanks to Mr. Griffith, takes vivid shape when you see *The Birth of a Nation*. Historically it may be the wrong shape, morally it may be a pernicious shape, but it is a shape, and I doubt whether anyone who has seen the film and does not know more about the Ku Klux Klan than Mr. Griffith, will ever hear the name again without seeing those white horsemen.

5

And so when we speak of the mind of a group of people, of the French mind, the militarist mind, the bolshevik mind, we are liable to serious confusion unless we agree to separate the instinctive equipment from the stereotypes, the patterns, and the formulae which play so decisive a part in building up the mental world to which the native character is adapted and responds. Failure to make this distinction accounts for oceans of loose talk about collective minds, national souls, and race psychology. To be sure a stereotype may be so consistently and authoritatively transmitted in each generation from parent to child that it seems almost like a biological fact. In some respects, we may indeed have become, as Mr. Wallas says, biologically parasitic upon our social heritage. But certainly there is not the least scientific evidence which would enable anyone to argue that men are born with the political habits of the country in which they are born. In so far as political habits are alike in a nation, the first places to look for an explanation are the nursery, the school, the church, not in that limbo inhabited by Group Minds and National Souls. Until you have thoroughly failed to see tradition being handed on from parents, teachers, priests, and uncles, it is a solecism of the worst order to ascribe political differences to the germ plasm.

It is possible to generalize tentatively and with a decent humility about comparative differences within the same category of education and experience. Yet even this is a tricky enterprise. For almost no two experiences are exactly alike, not even of two children in the same household. The older son never does have the experience of being the younger. And therefore, until we are able to discount the difference in nurture, we must withhold judgment about differences of nature. As well judge the productivity of two soils by comparing their yield before you know which is in Labrador and which in Iowa, whether they have been cultivated and enriched, exhausted, or allowed to run wild.

Questions for Study and Discussion

1. According to the experiment cited by the author, how many of the forty trained observers gave a written report approximating the truth of what had happened in their presence?

2. What does Mr. Lippmann attempt to prove by the foregoing example?

3. What four sources listed by the author furnish most of our stereotyped shapes or ideas of things?

4. What does the author wish to demonstrate by the pageant of the Melting Pot?

5. According to the author, what does the average observer see in a beautiful sunset or a live Indian?

6. What is he attempting to prove by this conclusion?

7. What are the subtlest and most pervasive of all influences?

8. What is the author's justification of stereotypes?

9. What is the author's chief advice about the proper use of stereotypes?

10. In what terms does the author state the great power of motion pictures?

11. Point out the major similarities and differences between ideas in this selection and in "The Nature and Media of Propaganda."

Vocabulary Study

Define the following words as used in this selection: transfiguration, culture, pugnacious, junker, preempted, paltry, hackneyed, Humanist, canon, multifarious, pervasive, repertory, pernicious, solecism.

Writing Assignment

Write one paragraph describing the stereotyped impression of a member of a minority group; write a second paragraph describing an individual impression of a member of the same minority group.

CHAPTER 1

POLITICAL AND ECONOMIC DISCUSSION

On Liberty

John Stuart Mill

The subject of this essay is not the so-called liberty of the will, so unfortunately opposed to the misnamed doctrine of philosophical necessity; but civil, or social liberty: the nature and limits of the power which can be legitimately exercised by society over the individual. A question seldom stated, and hardly ever discussed, in general terms, but which profoundly influences the practical controversies of the age by its latent presence, and is likely soon to make itself recognized as the vital question of the future. It is so far from being new, that, in a certain sense, it has divided mankind, almost from the remotest ages; but in the stage of progress into which the more civilized portions of the species have now entered, it presents itself under new conditions, and requires a different and more fundamental treatment.

The struggle between liberty and authority is the most conspicuous feature in the portions of history with which we are earliest familiar, particularly in that of Greece, Rome, and England. But in old times this contest was between subjects, or some classes of subjects, and the government. By liberty, was meant protection against the tyranny of the political rulers. The rulers were conceived (except in some of the popular governments of Greece) as in a necessarily antagonistic position to the people whom they ruled. They consisted of a governing One, or a governing tribe or caste, who derived their authority from inheritance or conquest, who, at all events, did not hold it at the pleasure of the governed, and whose supremacy men did not venture, perhaps did not desire, to contest, whatever precautions might be taken against its oppressive exercise. Their power was regarded as necessary, but also as highly dangerous; as a weapon which they would attempt to use against their subjects, no less than against external enemies. To prevent the weaker members of the community from being preyed upon by innummerable vultures, it was needful that there should be an animal of prey stronger than the rest, commissioned to keep them down. But as the king of the vultures would be no less bent upon preying on the flock than any of the minor harpies, it was indispensable to be in a perpetual attitude of defence against his beak and claws. The aim, therefore, of patriots, was to set limits to the power which the ruler should be suffered to exercise over the community; and this limitation was what they meant by liberty. It was attempted in two ways. First, by obtaining a recognition of certain immunities, called political liberties or rights, which it was to be regarded as a breach of duty in the ruler to infringe, and which, if he did infringe, specific resistance, or general rebellion, was held to be justifiable. A second, and generally a later expedient, was the establishment of constitutional checks; by which the consent of the community, or of a body of some sort supposed to represent its interests, was made a necessary condition to some of the more important acts of the governing power. To the first of these modes of limitations, the ruling power in most European countries, was compelled, more or less, to submit. It was not so with the second; and to attain this, or when already in some degree possessed, to attain it more completely, became everywhere the principal object of the lovers of liberty. And so long as mankind were content to combat one enemy by another, and to be ruled by a master, on condition of being guaranteed more or less efficaciously against his tyranny, they did not carry their aspirations beyond this point.

A time, however, came, in the progress of human affairs, when men ceased to think it a necessity of nature that their governors should be an independent power, opposed in interest to themselves. It appeared to them much better that the various magistrates of the State should be their tenants or delegates, revocable at their pleasure. In that way alone, it seemed, could they have complete security that the powers of government would never be abused to their disadvantage. By degrees, this new demand for elective and temporary rulers became the prominent object of the exertions of the popular party, wherever any such party existed; and superseded, to a considerable extent, the previous efforts to limit the power of rulers. As the struggle proceeded for making the ruling power emanate from the periodical choice of the ruled, some persons began to think that too much importance had been attached to the limitation of the power itself. *That* (it might seem) was a resource against rulers whose interests were habitually opposed to those of the people. What was now wanted was, that the rulers should be identified with the people; that their interest and will should be the interest and will of the nation. The nation did not need to be protected against its own will. There was no fear of its tyrannizing over itself. Let the rulers be effectually responsible to it, promptly removable by it, and it could afford to trust them with power of which it could itself dictate the use to be made. Their power was but the nation's own power, concentrated, and in a form convenient for exercise. This mode of thought, or rather perhaps of feeling, was common among the last generation of European liberalism, in the Continental section of which, it still apparently predominates. Those who admit any limit to what government may do, except in the case of such governments as they think ought not to exist, stand out as brilliant exceptions among the political thinkers of the Continent. A similar tone of sentiment might by this time have been prevalent in our own country, if the circumstances which for a time encouraged it had continued unaltered.

But, in political and philosophical theories, as well as in persons, success discloses faults and infirmities which failure might have con cealed from observation. The notion, that the people have no need to limit their power over themselves, might seem axiomatic, when popular government was a thing only dreamed about, or read of as having existed at some distant period of the past. Neither was that notion necessarily disturbed by such temporary aberrations as those of the French Revolution, the worst of which were the work of an usurping few, and which, in any case, belonged, not to the permanent working of popular institutions, but to a sudden and convulsive outbreak against monarchical and aristocratic despotism. In time, however, a democratic republic came to occupy a large portion of the earth's surface, and made itself felt as one of the most powerful members of the community of nations; and elective and responsible government became subject to the observations and criticisms which wait upon a great existing fact. It was now perceived that such phrases as "self-government," and "the power of the people over themselves," do not express the true state of the case. The "people" who exercise the power, are not always the same people with those over whom it is exercised; and the self-government spoken of is not the government of each by himself, but of each by all the rest. The will of the people, moreover, practically means the will of the most numerous or the most active part of the people; the majority, or those who succeed in making themselves accepted as the majority: the people, consequently, *may* desire to oppress a part of their number; and precautions are as much needed against this, as against any other abuse of power. The limitation, therefore, of the power of government over individuals, loses none of its importance when the holders of power are regularly accountable to the community, that is, to the strongest party therein. This view of things, recommending itself equally to the intelligence of thinkers and to the inclination of those important classes in European society to whose real or supposed interests democracy is adverse, has had no difficulty in establishing itself; and in political speculations "the tyranny of the majority" is now generally included among the evils against which society requires to be on its guard.

Like other tyrannies, the tyranny of the majority was at first, and is still vulgarly, held in dread, chiefly as operating through the acts of the public authorities. But reflecting persons perceived that when society is itself the tyrant—society collectively, over the separate individuals who compose it—its means of tyrannizing are not restricted to the acts which it may do by the hands of its political functionaries. Society can and does execute its own mandates: and if it issues wrong mandates instead of right, or any mandates at all in things with which it ought not to meddle, it practices a social tyranny more formidable than many kinds of political oppression, since, though not usually upheld by such extreme penalties, it leaves fewer means of escape, penetrating much more deeply into the details of life, and enslaving the soul itself. Protection, therefore, against the tyranny of the magistrate is not enough; there needs protection also against the tyranny of the prevailing opinion and feeling; against the tendency of society to impose, by other means than civil penalties, its own ideas and practices as rules of conduct on those who dissent from them; to fetter the development, and if possible, prevent the formation, of any individuality not in harmony with its ways, and compel all characters to fashion themselves upon the model of its own.

There is a limit to the legitimate interference of collective opinion with individual independence; and to find that limit, and maintain it against encroachment, is as indispensable to a good condition of human affairs, as protection against political despotism.

But though this proposition is not likely to be contested in general terms, the practical question, where to place the limit—how to make the fitting adjustment between individual independence and social control—is a subject on which nearly everything remains to be done. All that makes existence valuable to any one, depends on the enforcement of restraints upon the actions of other people. Some rules of conduct, therefore, must be imposed, by law in the first place, and by opinion on many things which are not fit subjects for the operation of law. What these rules should be is the principal question in human affairs; but if we except a few of the most obvious cases, it is one of those which least progress has been made in resolving. No two ages, and scarcely any two countries, have decided it alike; and the decision of one age or country is a wonder to another. Yet the people of any given age and country no more suspect any difficulty in it, than if it were a subject on which mankind had always been agreed. The rules which obtain among themselves appear to them self-evident and self-justifying. This all but universal illusion is one of the examples of the magical influence of custom, which is not only, as the proverb says, a second nature, but is continually mistaken for the first. The effect of custom, in preventing any misgiving respecting the rules of conduct which mankind impose on one another, is all the more complete because the subject is one which it is not generally considered necessary that reasons should be given, either by one person to others, or by each to himself. People are accustomed to believe, and have been encouraged in the belief by some who aspire to the character of philosophers, that their feelings, on subjects of this nature, are better than reasons, and render reasons unnecessary. The practical principle which guides them to their opinions on the regulation of human conduct, is the feeling in each person's mind that everybody should be required to act as he, and those with whom he sympathizes, would like them to act. No one, indeed, acknowledges to himself that his standard of judgment is his own liking; but an opinion on a point of conduct, not supported by reasons, can only count as one person's preference; and if the reasons, when given, are a mere appeal to a similar preference felt by other people, it is still only many people's liking instead of one. To an ordinary man, however, his own preference, thus supported, is not only a perfectly satisfactory reason, but the only one he generally has for any of his notions of morality, taste, or propriety, which are not expressly written in his religious creed; and his chief guide in the interpretation even of that. Men's opinions, accordingly, on what is laudable or blameable, are affected by all the multifarious causes which influence their wishes in regard to the conduct of others, and which are as numerous as those which determine their wishes on any other subject. Sometimes their reason—at other times their prejudices or superstitions: often their social affections, not seldom their antisocial ones, their envy or jealousy, their arrogance or contemptuousness: but most commonly, their desires or fears for themselves—their legitimate or illegitimate self-interest. Wherever there is an ascendant class, a large portion of the morality of the country emanates from its class interests, and its feelings of class superiority. The morality between Spartans and Helots, between planters and Negroes, between princes and subjects, between nobles and roturiers, between men and women, has been for the most part the creation of these class interests and feelings of the members of the ascendant class, in their relations among themselves. Where, on the other hand, a class, formerly ascendant, has lost its ascendancy, or where its ascendancy is unpopular, the prevailing moral sentiments frequently bear the impress of an impatient dislike of superiority. Another grand determining principle of the rules of conduct, both in act and forbearance, which have been enforced by law or opinion, has been the servility of mankind towards the supposed preferences or aversions of their temporal masters, or of their gods. This servility, though essentially selfish, is not hypocrisy; it gives rise to perfectly genuine sentiments of abhorrence; it made men burn magicians and heretics. Among so many baser influences, the general and obvious interests of society have of course had a share, and a large one, in the direction of the moral sentiments: less, however, as a matter of reason, and on their own account, than as a consequence of the sympathies and antipathies which grew out of them: and sympathies and antipathies which had little or nothing to do with the interests of society, have made themselves felt in the establishment of moralities with quite as great force.

The likings and dislikings of society, or of some powerful portion of it, are thus the main thing which has practically determined the rules laid down for general observance, under the penalties of law or opinion. And in general, those who have been in advance of society in thought and feeling, have left this condition of things unassailed in principle, however they may have come into conflict with it in some of its details. They have occupied themselves rather in inquiring what things society ought to like or dislike, than in questioning whether its likings or dislikings should be a law to individuals. They preferred endeavoring to alter the feelings of mankind on the particular points on which they were themselves heretical, rather than make common cause in defence of freedom, with heretics generally. The only case in which the higher ground has been taken on principle and maintained with consistency, by any but an individual here and there, is that of religious belief: a case instructive in many ways, and not least so as forming a most striking instance of the fallibility of what is called the moral sense: for the *odium theologicum*, in a sincere bigot, is one of the most unequivocal cases of moral feeling. Those who first broke the yoke of what called itself the Universal Church, were in general as little willing to permit difference of religious opinion as that church itself. But when the heat of the conflict was over, without giving a complete victory to any party, and each church or sect was reduced to limit its hopes to retaining possession of the ground it already occupied; minorities, seeing that they had no chance of becoming majorities, were under the necessity of pleading to those whom they could not convert, for permission to differ. It is accordingly on this battle-field, almost solely, that the rights of the individual against society have been asserted on broad grounds of principle, and the claim of society to exercise authority over dissentients openly controverted. The great writers to whom the world owes what religious liberty it possesses, have mostly asserted freedom of conscience as an indefeasible right, and denied absolutely that a human being is accountable to others for his religious belief. Yet so natural to mankind is intolerance in whatever they really care about, that religious freedom has hardly anywhere been practically realized, except where religious indifference, which dislikes to have its peace disturbed by theological quarrels, has added its weight to the scale. In the minds of almost all religious persons, even in the most tolerant countries, the duty of toleration is admitted with tacit reserves. One person will bear with dissent in matters of church government, but not of dogma; another can tolerate everybody, short of a Papist or an Unitarian; another, every one who believes in revealed religion; a few extend their charity a little further, but stop at the belief in a God and in a future state. Wherever the sentiment of the majority is still genuine and intense, it is found to have abated little of its claim to be obeyed.

In England, from the peculiar circumstances of our political history, though the yoke of opinion is perhaps heavier, that of law is lighter, than in most other countries of Europe; and there is considerable jealousy of direct interference, by the legislative or the executive power, with private conduct; not so much from any just regard for the independence of the individual, as from the still subsisting habit of looking on the government as representing an opposite interest to the public. The majority have not yet learnt to feel the power of the government their power, or its opinions their opinions. When they do so, individual liberty will probably be as much exposed to invasion from the government, as it already is from public opinion. But, as yet, there is a considerable amount of feeling ready to be called forth against any attempt of the law to control individuals in things in which they have not hitherto been accustomed to be controlled by it; and this with very little discrimination as to whether the matter is, or is not, within the legitimate sphere of legal control; insomuch that the feeling, highly salutary on the whole, is perhaps quite as often misplaced as well grounded in the particular instances of its application. There is, in fact, no recognized principle by which the propriety or impropriety of government interference is customarily tested. People decide according to their personal preferences. Some, whenever they see any good to be done, or evil to be remedied, would willingly instigate the government to undertake the business; while others prefer to bear almost any amount of social evil, rather than add one to the departments of human interests amenable to governmental control. And men range themselves on one or the other side in any particular case, according to this general direction of their sentiments; or according to the degree of interest which they feel in the particular thing which it is proposed that the government should do; or according to the belief they entertain that the government would, or would not, do it in the manner they prefer; but very rarely on account of any opinion to which they consistently adhere, as to what things are fit to be done by a government. And it seems to me that, in consequence of this absence of rule or principle, one side is at present as often wrong as the other; the interference of government is, with about equal frequency, improperly invoked and improperly condemned.

The object of this essay is to assert one very simple principle, as entitled to govern absolutely the dealings of society with the individual in the way of compulsion and control, whether the means used by physical force in the form of legal penalties, or the moral coercion of public opinion. That principle is, that the sole end for which mankind are warranted, individually or collectively, in interfering with the liberty of action of any of their number, is self-protection. That the only purpose for which power can be rightfully exercised over any member of a civilized community, against his will, is to prevent harm to others. His own good, either physical or moral, is not a sufficient warrant. He cannot rightfully be compelled to do or forbear because it will be better for him to do so, because it will make him happier, because, in the opinions of others, to do so would be wise, or even right. These are good reasons for remonstrating with him, or reasoning with him, or persuading him, or entreating him, but not for compelling him, or visiting him with any evil, in case he do otherwise. To justify that, the conduct from which it is desired to deter him must be calculated to produce evil to some one else. The only part of the conduct of any one, for which he is amenable to society, is that which concerns others. In the part which merely concerns himself, his independence is, of right, absolute. Over himself, over his own body and mind, the individual is sovereign.

It is, perhaps, hardly necessary to say that this doctrine is meant to apply only to human beings in the maturity of their faculties. We are not speaking of children, or of young persons below the age which the law may fix as that of manhood or womanhood. Those who are still in a state to require being taken care of by others, must be protected against their own actions as well as against external injury. For the same reason, we may leave out of consideration those backward states of society in which the race itself may be considered as in its nonage. The early difficulties in the way of spontaneous progress are so great, that there is seldom any choice of means for overcoming them; and a ruler full of the spirit of improvement is warranted in the use of any expedients that will attain an end, perhaps otherwise unattainable. Despotism is a legitimate mode of government in dealing with barbarians, provided the end be their improvement, and the means justified by actually effecting that end. Liberty, as a principle, has no application to any state of things anterior to the time when mankind have become capable of being improved by free and equal discussion. Until then, there is nothing for them but implicit obedience to an Akbar or a Charlemagne, if they are so fortunate as to find one. But as soon as mankind have attained the capacity of being guided to their own improvement by conviction or persuasion (a period long since reached in all nations with whom we need here concern ourselves), compulsion, either in the direct form or in that of pains and penalties for non-compliance, is no longer admissable as a means to their own good, and justifiable only for the security of others.

It is proper to state that I forego any advantage which could be derived to my argument from the idea of abstract right, as a thing independent of utility. I regard utility as the ultimate appeal on all ethical questions; but it must be utility in the largest sense, grounded on the permanent interests of man as a progressive being. Those interests, I contend, authorize the subjection of individual spontaneity to external control, only in respect to those actions of each, which concern the interest of other people. If any one does an act hurtful to others there is a *prima facie* case for punishing him, by law, or, where legal penalties are not safely applicable, by general disapprobation. There are also many positive acts for the benefit of others, which he may rightfully be compelled to perform, such as, to give evidence in a court of justice; to bear his fair share in the common defence, or in any other joint work necessary to the interest of the society of which he enjoys the protection; and to perform certain acts of individual beneficence, such as saving a fellow creature's life, or interposing to protect the defenceless against ill-usage, things which whenever it is obviously a man's duty to do, he may rightfully be made responsible to society for not doing. A person may cause evil to others not only by his actions but by his inaction, and in either case he is justly accountable to them for the injury. The latter case, it is true, requires a much more cautious exercise of compulsion than the former. To make any one answerable for doing evil to others, is the rule; to make him answerable for not preventing evil, is, comparatively speaking, the exception. Yet there are many cases clear enough and grave enough to justify that exception. In all things which regard the external relations of the individual, he is *de jure* amenable to those whose interests are concerned, and if need be, to society as their protector. There are often good reasons for not holding him to the responsibility; but these reasons must arise from the special expediences of the case: either because it is a kind of case in which he is on the whole likely to act better, when left to his own discretion, than when controlled in any way in which society have it in their power to control him; or because the attempt to exercise control would produce other evils, greater than those which it would prevent. When such reasons as these preclude the enforcement of responsibility, the conscience of the agent himself should step into the vacant judgment-seat, and protect those interests of others which have not external protection; judging himself all the more rigidly, because the case does not admit of his being made account-able to the judgment of his fellow-creatures.

But there is a sphere of action in which society, as distinguished from the individual, has, if any, only an indirect interest; comprehending all that portion of a person's life and conduct which affects only himself, or, if it also affects others, only with their free, voluntary, and undeceived consent and participation. When I say only himself, I mean directly, and in the first instance: for whatever affects himself, may affect others through himself; and the objection which may be grounded on this contingency, will receive consideration in the sequel. This, then, is the appropriate region of human liberty. It comprises, first, the inward do-main of consciousness; demanding liberty of conscience, in the most comprehensive sense; liberty of thought and feeling; absolute freedom of opinion and sentiment on all subjects, practical or speculative, scien-tific, moral, or theological. The liberty of expressing and publishing opinions may seem to fall under a different principle, since it belongs to that part of the conduct of an individual which concerns other people; but, being almost of as much importance as the liberty of thought itself, and resting in great part on the same reasons, is practically inseparable from it. Secondly, the principle requires liberty of tastes and pursuits; of framing the plan of our life to suit our own character; of doing as we like, subject to such consequences as may follow; without impediment from our fellow-creatures, so long as what we do does not harm them, even though they should think our conduct foolish, perverse, or wrong. Thirdly, from this liberty of each individual, follows the liberty, within the same limits, of combination among individuals; freedom to unite, for any purpose not involving harm to others: the persons combining being supposed to be of full age, and not forced or deceived.

No society in which these liberties are not, on the whole, respected, is free, whatever may be its form of government; and none is completely free in which they do not exist absolute and unqualified. The only free-dom which deserves the name, is that of pursuing our own good in our own way, so long as we do not attempt to deprive others of theirs, or impede their efforts to obtain it. Each is the proper guardian of his own health, whether bodily, or mental and spiritual. Mankind are greater gainers by suffering each other to live as seems good to themselves, than by compelling each to live as seems good to the rest.

Though this doctrine is anything but new, and, to some persons, may have the air of a truism, there is no doctrine which stands more directly opposed to the general tendency of existing opinion and practice. Society has expended fully as much effort in the attempt (according to its lights) to compel people to conform to its notions of personal, as of social excellence. The ancient commonwealths thought themselves entitled to practise, and the ancient philosophers countenanced, the regulation of every part of private conduct by public authority, on the ground that the State had a deep interest in the whole bodily and mental discipline of every one of its citizens; a mode of thinking which may have been admissible in small republics surrounded by powerful enemies, in constant peril of being subverted by foreign attack or internal commotion, and to which even a short interval of relaxed energy and self-command might so easily be fatal, that they could not afford to wait for the salutary permanent effects of freedom. In the modern world, the greater size of political communities, and above all, the separation between the spiritual and temporal authority (which placed the direction of men's consciences in other hands than those which controlled their worldly affairs), prevented so great an interference by law in the details of private life; but the engines of moral repression have been wielded more strenuously against divergence from the reigning opinion in self-regarding, than even in social matters; religion, the most powerful of the elements which have entered into the formation of moral feeling, having almost always been governed either by the ambition of a hierarchy, seeking control over every department of human conduct, or by the spirit of Puritanism. And some of those modern reformers who have placed themselves in strongest opposition to the religions of the past, have been noway behind either churches or sects in their assertion of the right of spiritual domination: M. Comte, in particular, whose social system, as unfolded in his *Traite de Politique Positive*, aims at establishing (though by moral more than by legal appliances) a despotism of society over the individual, surpassing anything contemplated in the political ideal of the most rigid disciplinarian among the ancient philosophers.

Apart from the peculiar tenets of individual thinkers, there is also in the world at large an increasing inclination to stretch unduly the powers of society over the individual, both by the force of opinion and even by that of legislation: and as the tendency of all the changes taking place in the world is to strengthen society, and diminish the power of the individual, this encroachment is not one of the evils which tend spontaneously to disappear, but, on the contrary, to grow more and more formidable. The disposition of mankind, whether as rulers or as fellow-citizens, to impose their own opinions and inclinations as a rule of conduct on others, is so energetically supported by some of the best and by some of the worst feelings incident to human nature, that it is hardly ever under restraint by anything but want of power; and as the power is not declining, but growing, unless a strong barrier of moral conviction can be raised against the mischief, we must expect, in the present circumstances of the world, to see it increase. . . .

Questions for Study and Discussion

1. How does Mill define liberty?

2. In what two ways did early patriots seek to guarantee liberty for themselves and their countrymen?

3. Explain Mill's concept of "the tyranny of the majority."

4. What does Mill mean by "social tyranny"?

5. What is the practical principle which guides a person's opinions on the regulation of human conduct?

6. What are the two most powerful influences which generally determine the moralities of a society?

7. What is the one principle which Mill insists should alone determine society's right to interfere with the liberty of action of an individual?

8. Why, according to Mill, is a person responsible to society for not doing things like going to the aid of defenseless animals being ill used?

9. According to this principle does society have the right to legally restrain an individual from acts of self-destruction?

10. Under what conditions does Mill admit that the principle referred to in question 7 should not apply?

11. What does Mill regard as the ultimate appeal on all ethical questions? Explain.

12. Give the substance of Mill's summary of the three regions of human liberty.

13. What is Mill's overall appraisal of the success of the individual's struggle against the tyranny of society?

14. Explain the propaganda elements in the following expressions:
    a. preyed upon by . . . vultures (page 32)
    b. beak and claws (page 32)
    c. tyranny of the majority (page 34)
    d. class superiority (page 36)
    e. yoke of opinion (page 38)

Vocabulary Study

Define the following words or phrases as used in this essay: tyranny, immunities, efficaciously, revocable, axiomatic, aberrations, despotism, vulgarly, mandates, illusion, dogma, salutary, nonage, *prima facie, de jure.*

Writing Assignment

Write a composition of not less than 300 words on one of the following topics:
1. The Individual Versus Society
2. The Individual's Right to Dissent
3. The Protection of Minority Rights in a Democracy

A Modest Proposal

Jonathan Swift

It is a melancholy object to those who walk through this great town or travel in the country, when they see the streets, the roads, and cabin-doors crowded with beggars of the female sex, followed by three, four, or six children, all in rags, and importuning every passenger for an alms. These mothers instead of being able to work for their honest livelihood, are forced to employ all their time in strolling to beg sustenance for their helpless infants, who, as they grow up, either turn thieves for want of work, or leave their dear native country, to fight for the Pretender in Spain, or sell themselves to the Barbadoes.

I think it is agreed by all parties, that this prodigious number of children in the arms, or on the backs, or at the heels of their mothers, and frequently of their fathers, is in the present deplorable state of the kingdom a very great additional grievance; and therefore whoever could find out a fair, cheap, and easy method of making these children sound and useful members of the common-wealth, would deserve so well of the public as to have his statue set up for a preserver of the nation.

But my intention is very far from being confined to provide only for the children of professed beggars; it is of a much greater extent, and shall take in the whole number of infants at a certain age, who are born of parents in effect as little able to support them, as those who demand our charity in the streets.

As to my own part, having turned my thoughts, for many years, upon this important subject, and maturely weighed the several schemes of other projectors, I have always found them grossly mistaken in their computation. It is true, a child just dropt from its dam, may be supported by her milk for a solar year with little other nourishment, at most not above the value of two shillings, which the mother may certainly get, or the value in scraps, by her lawful occupation of begging; and it is exactly at one year old that I propose to provide for them in such a manner, as, instead of being a charge upon their parents, or the parish, or wanting food and raiment for the rest of their lives, they shall, on the contrary, contribute to the feeding and partly to the clothing of many thousands.

There is likewise another great advantage in my scheme, that it will prevent those voluntary abortions, and that horrid practice of women murdering their bastard children, alas! too frequent among us—sacrificing the poor innocent babes, I doubt, more to avoid the expense than the shame—which would move tears and pity in the most savage and inhuman breast.

The number of souls in this kingdom being usually reckoned one million and a half, of these I calculate there may be about two hundred thousand couples whose wives are breeders; from which number I subtract thirty thousand couples, who are able to maintain their own children, although I apprehend there cannot be so many, under the present distresses of the kingdom; but this being granted, there will remain an hundred and seventy thousand breeders. I again subtract fifty thousand, for those women who miscarry, or whose children die by accident or disease within the year. There only remain an hundred and twenty thousand children of poor parents annually born: The question therefore is, How this number shall be reared, and provided for? which, as I have already said, under the present situation of affairs, is utterly impossible by all the methods hitherto proposed; for we can neither employ them in handicraft or agriculture; we neither build houses (I mean in the country) nor cultivate land: They can very seldom pick up a livelihood by stealing till they arrive at six years old, except where they are of towardly parts, although, I confess, they learn the rudiments much earlier; during which time they can however be properly looked upon only as probationers; as I have been informed by a principal gentleman in the county of Cavan, who protested to me, that he never knew above one or two instances under the age of six, even in a part of the kingdom so renowned for the quickest proficiency in the art.

I am assured by our merchants, that a boy or a girl before twelve years old, is no saleable commodity, and even when they come to this age, they will not yield above three pounds, or three pounds and half a crown at most, on the exchange; which cannot turn to account either to the parents or kingdom, the charge of nutriment and rags having been at least four times that value.

I shall now therefore humbly propose my own thoughts, which I hope will not be liable to the least objection.

I have been assured by a very knowing American of my acquaintance in London, that a young healthy child well nursed is at a year old a most delicious, nourishing, and wholesome food, whether stewed, roasted, baked, or broiled; and I make no doubt that it will equally serve in a fricassee, or a ragout.

I do therefore humbly offer it to publick consideration, that of the hundred and twenty thousand children, already computed, twenty thousand may be reserved for breed, whereof only one fourth part to be males; which is more than we allow to sheep, black cattle, or swine; and my reason is that these children are seldom the fruits of marriage, a circumstance not much regarded by our savages; therefore one male will be sufficient to serve four females. That the remaining hundred thousand may, at a year old, be offered in the sale to the persons of quality and fortune through the kingdom; always advising the mother to let them suck plentifully in the last month, so as to render them plump and fat for a good table. A child will make two dishes at an entertainment for friends; and when the family dines alone, the fore or hind quarter will make a reasonable dish, and seasoned with a little pepper or salt will be very good boiled on the fourth day, especially in winter.

I have reckoned upon a medium that a child just born will weigh 12 pounds, and in a solar year, if tolerably nursed, increaseth to 28 pounds.

I grant this food will be somewhat dear, and therefore very proper for landlords, who, as they have already devoured most of the parents, seem to have the best title to the children.

Infants' flesh will be in season throughout the year, but more plentiful in March, and a little before and after; for we are told by a grave author, an eminent French physician, that fish being a prolific diet, there are more children born in Roman Catholic countries about nine months after Lent than at any other season; therefore, reckoning a year after Lent, the markets will be more glutted than usual, because the number of popish infants is at least three to one in this kingdom: and therefore it will have one other collateral advantage, by lessening the number of papists among us.

I have already computed the charge of nursing a beggar's child (in which list I reckon all cottagers, laborers, and four-fifths of the farmers) to be about two shillings per annum, rags included; and I believe no gentleman would repine to give ten shillings for the carcass of a good fat child, which, as I have said, will make four dishes of excellent nutritive meat, when he hath only some particular friend of his own family to dine with him. Thus the squire will learn to be a good landlord, and grow popular among his tenants; the mother will have eight shillings net profit, and be fit for work till she produces another child.

Those who are more thrifty (as I must confess the times require) may flay the carcass, the skin of which artificially dressed will make admirable gloves for ladies, and summer boots for fine gentlemen.

As to our city of Dublin, shambles may be appointed for this purpose in the most convenient parts of it, and butchers we may be assured will not be wanting; although I rather recommend buying the children alive and dressing them hot from the knife, as we do roasting pigs.

A very worthy person, a true lover of his country, and whose virtues I highly esteem, was lately pleased in discoursing on this matter to offer a refinement upon my scheme. He said that many gentlemen of this kingdom, having of late destroyed their deer, he conceived that the want of venison might be well supplied by the bodies of young lads and maidens, not exceeding fourteen years of age nor under twelve; so great a number of both sexes in every country being now ready to starve for want of work and service; and these to be disposed of by their parents if alive, or otherwise by their nearest relations. But with due deference to so excellent a friend, and so deserving a patriot, I cannot be altogether in his sentiments; for as to the males, my American acquaintance assured me from frequent experience, that their flesh was generally tough and lean, like that of our schoolboys, by continual exercise, and their taste disagreeable, and to fatten them would not answer the charge. Then as to the females, it would, I think with humble submission, be a loss to the publick, because they soon would become breeders themselves: And besides it is not improbable that some scrupulous people might be apt to censure such a practice (although indeed very unjustly) as a little bordering upon cruelty, which, I confess, hath always been with me the strongest objection against any project, how well soever intended.

But in order to justify my friend, he confessed that this expedient was put into his head by the famous Psalmanazar, a native of the island Formosa, who came from thence to London, above twenty years ago, and in conversation told my friend, that in his country when any young person happened to be put to death, the executioner sold the carcass to persons of quality, as a prime dainty, and that, in his time, the body of a plump girl of fifteen, who was crucified for an attempt to poison the Emperor, was sold to his Imperial Majesty's prime minister of state, and other great mandarins of the court, in joints from the gibbet, at four hundred crowns. Neither indeed can I deny, that if the same use were made of several plump young girls in this town, who, without one single groat to their fortunes, cannot stir abroad without a chair, and appear at a play-house and assemblies in foreign fineries which they never will pay for, the kingdom would not be the worse.

Some persons of a desponding spirit are in great concern about that vast number of poor people, who are aged, diseased, or maimed, and I have been desired to employ my thoughts what course may be taken, to ease the nation of so grievous an encumbrance. But I am not in the least pain upon that matter, because it is very well known, that they are every day dying, and rotting, by cold, and famine, and filth, and vermin, as fast as can be reasonably expected. And as to the younger labourers, they are now in almost as hopeful a condition. They cannot get work, and consequently pine away for want of nourishment, to a degree, that if at any time they are accidentally hired to common labour, they have not strength to perform it, and thus the country and themselves are happily delivered from the evils to come.

I have too long digressed, and therefore shall return to my subject. I think the advantages by the proposal which I have made are obvious and many, as well as of the highest importance.

For first, as I have already observed, it would greatly lessen the number of papists, with whom we are yearly over-run, being the principal breeders of the nation, as well as our most dangerous enemies, and who stay at home on purpose with a design to deliver the kingdom to the Pretender, hoping to take their advantage by the absence of so many good Protestants, who have chosen rather to leave their country, than stay at home, and pay tithes against their conscience to an Episcopal curate.

Secondly, the poorer tenants will have something valuable of their own, which by law may be made liable to distress and help to pay their landlord's rent, their corn and cattle being already seized, and money a thing unknown.

Thirdly, whereas the maintenance of an hundred thousand children, from two years old and upward, cannot be computed at less than ten shillings apiece per annum, the nation's stock will be thereby increased fifty thousand pounds per annum, besides the profit of a new dish introduced to the tables of all gentlemen of fortune in the kingdom who have any refinement in taste. And the money will circulate among ourselves, the goods being entirely of our own growth and manufacture.

Fourthly, the constant breeders, beside the gain of eight shillings sterling per annum by the sale of their children, will be rid of the charge of maintaining them after the first year.

Fifthly, this food would likewise bring great custom to taverns, where the vintners will certainly be so prudent as to procure the best receipts for dressing it to perfection, and consequently have their houses frequented by all the fine gentlemen who justly value themselves upon their knowledge in good eating; and a skillful cook, who understands how to oblige his guests, will contrive to make it as expensive as they please.

Sixthly, this would be a great inducement to marriage, which all wise nations have either encouraged by rewards or enforced by laws and penalties. It would increase the care and the tenderness of mothers toward their children, when they were sure of a settlement for life to the poor babes, provided in some sort by the public, to their annual profit instead of expense. We should soon see an honest emulation among the married women, which of them could bring the fattest child to the market. Men would become as fond of their wives during the time of their pregnancy as they are now of their mares in foal, their cows in calf, their sows when they are ready to farrow; nor offer to beat or kick them (as is too frequent a practice) for fear of a miscarriage.

Many other advantages might be enumerated. For instance, the addition of some thousand carcasses in our exportation of barreled beef, the propagation of swine's flesh, and improvement in the art of making good bacon, so much wanted among us by the great destruction of pigs, too frequent at our tables; which are no way comparable in taste or magnificence to a well-grown, fat, yearling child, which roasted whole will make a considerable figure at a lord mayor's feast or any other public entertainment. But this and many others I omit, being studious of brevity.

Supposing that one thousand families in this city would be constant customers for infants' flesh, besides others who might have it at merry meetings, particularly at weddings and christenings, I compute that Dublin would take off annually about twenty thousand carcasses; and the rest of the kingdom (where probably they will be sold somewhat cheaper) the remaining eighty thousand.

I can think of no one objection that will possibly be raised against this proposal, unless it should be urged that the number of people will be thereby much lessened in the kingdom. This I freely own, and 'twas indeed one principal design in offering it to the world. I desire the reader will observe that I calculate my remedy for this one individual kingdom of Ireland, and for no other that ever was, is, or, I think, ever can be upon earth. Therefore let no man talk to me of other expedients: of taxing our absentees at five shillings a pound: of using neither clothes, nor household furniture, except what is of our own growth and manufacture: of utterly rejecting the materials and instruments that promote foreign luxury: of curing the expensiveness of pride, vanity, idleness, and gaming in our women: of introducing a vein of parsimony, prudence and temperance: of learning to love our country, where in we differ even from Laplanders, and the inhabitants of Topinamboo: of quitting our animosities, and factions, nor act any longer like the Jews, who were murdering one another at the very moment their city was taken: of being a little cautious not to sell our country and consciences for nothing: of teaching landlords to have at least one degree of mercy towards their tenants. Lastly, of putting a spirit of honesty, industry, and skill into our shopkeepers, who, if a resolution could now be taken to buy only our native goods, would immediately unite to cheat and exact upon us in the price, the measure, and the goodness, nor could ever yet be brought to make one fair proposal of just dealing, though often and earnestly invited to it.

Therefore I repeat, let no man talk to me of these and the like expedients, till he hath at least some glimpse of hope, that there will ever be some hearty and sincere attempt to put them in practice.

But as to my self, having been wearied out for many years with offering vain, idle, visionary thoughts, and at length utterly despairing of success, I fortunately fell upon this proposal, which as it is wholly new, so it hath something solid and real, of no expense and little trouble, full in our own power, and whereby we can incur no danger in disobliging England. For this kind of commodity will not bear exportation, the flesh being of too tender a consistence, to admit a long continuance in salt, although perhaps I could name a country, which would be glad to eat up our whole nation without it.

After all, I am not so violently bent upon my own opinion, as to reject any offer, proposed by wise men, which shall be found equally innocent, cheap, easy, and effectual. But before something of that kind shall be advanced in contradiction to my scheme, and offering a better, I desire the author or authors, will be pleased maturely to consider two points. First, as things now stand, how they will be able to find food and raiment for a hundred thousand useless mouths and backs. And secondly, there being a round million of creatures in human figure throughout this kingdom, whose whole subsistence put into a common stock would leave them in debt two millions of pounds sterling, adding those who are beggars by profession, to the bulk of farmers, cottagers and labourers, with their wives and children, who are beggars in effect; I desire those politicians, who dislike my overture, and may perhaps be so bold to attempt an answer, that they will first ask the parents of these mortals, whether they would not at this day think it a great happiness to have been sold for food at a year old, in the manner I prescribe, and thereby have avoided such a perpetual scene of misfortunes as they have since gone through, by the oppression of landlords, the impossibility of paying rent without money or trade, the want of common sustenance, with neither house nor clothes to cover them from the inclemencies of the weather, and the most inevitable prospect of entailing the like or greater miseries upon their breed for ever.

I profess, in the sincerity of my heart, that I have not the least personal interest in endeavoring to promote this necessary work, having no other motive than the public good of my country, by advancing our trade, providing for infants, relieving the poor, and giving some pleasure to the rich. I have no children by which I can propose to get a single penny; the youngest being nine years old, and my wife past child-bearing.

Questions for Study and Discussion

1. What is the substance of Swift's proposal?

2. What reasons does he give to support his proposal?

3. At what point in the essay do you begin to suspect that the writer is not serious? Cite the paragraph.

4. What caused you to doubt the author's seriousness?

5. What is the real purpose of this essay?

6. What is the name of the method used by the author to achieve his purpose?

7. What is the advantage of such a method?

8. Which paragraph is the most effective in summarizing the evils Swift seeks to expose?

9. Explain the propaganda elements in the following expressions:

    a. a child just dropt from its dam (page 45)

    b. women murdering their bastard children (page 45)

    c. child . . . a most delicious, nourishing, and wholesome food, whether stewed, roasted, baked, or broiled (page 46)

    d. popish infants (page 47)

    e. dressing them hot from the knife, as we do roasting pigs (page 47)

    f. dying and rotting by cold, and famine, and filth, and vermin, as fast as can reasonably be expected (page 48)

Vocabulary Study

Define the following words as used in this essay: prodigious, probationers, collateral, gibbet, tithes, parsimony.

Writing Assignment

Write a paragraph of not less than 100 words summarizing in strong emotional language Swift's major criticisms against the ruling classes of England.

Civil Disobedience

Henry David Thoreau

I heartily accept the motto,—"That government is best which governs least"; and I should like to see it acted up to more rapidly and systematically. Carried out, it finally amounts to this, which also I believe,— "That government is best which governs not at all": and when men are prepared for it, that will be the kind of government which they will have. Government is at best but an expedient; but most governments are usually, and all governments are sometimes, inexpedient. The objections which have been brought against a standing army, and they are many and weighty, and deserve to prevail, may also at last be brought against a standing government. The standing army is only an arm of the standing government. The government itself, which is only the mode which the people have chosen to execute their will, is equally liable to be abused and perverted before the people can act through it. Witness the present Mexican war, the work of comparatively a few individuals using the standing government as their tool; for, in the outset, the people would not have consented to this measure.

This American government,—what is it but a tradition, though a recent one, endeavoring to transmit itself unimpaired to posterity, but each instant losing some of its integrity? It has not the vitality and force of a single living man; for a single man can bend it to his will. It is a sort of wooden gun to the people themselves. But it is not the less necessary for this; for the people must have some complicated machinery or other, and hear its din, to satisfy that idea of government which they have. Governments show thus how successfully men can be imposed on, even impose on themselves, for their own advantage. It is excellent, we must all allow. Yet this government never of itself furthered any enterprise, but by the alacrity with which it got out of its way. *It* does not keep the country free. *It* does not settle the West. *It* does not educate. The character inherent in the American people has done all that has been accomplished; and it would have done somewhat more, if the government had not sometimes got in its way. For government is an expedient by which men would fain succeed in letting one another alone; and, as has been said, when it is most expedient, the governed are most let alone by it. Trade and commerce, if they were not made of India-rubber, would never manage to bounce over the obstacles which legislators are continually putting in their way; and, if one were to judge these men wholly by the effects of their actions and not partly by their intentions, they would deserve to be classed and punished with those mischievous persons who put obstructions on the railroads.

But, to speak practically and as a citizen, unlike those who call themselves no-government men, I ask for, not at once no government, but *at once* a better government. Let every man make known what kind of government would command his respect, and that will be one step toward obtaining it.

After all, the practical reason why, when the power is once in the hands of the people, a majority are permitted, and for a long period continue, to rule is not because they are most likely to be in the right, nor because this seems fairest to the minority, but because they are physically the strongest. But a government in which the majority rule in all cases cannot be based on justice, even as far as men understand it. Can there not be a government in which majorities do not virtually decide right and wrong, but conscience?—in which majorities decide only those questions to which the rule of expediency is applicable? Must the citizen ever for a moment, or in the least degree, resign his conscience to the legislator? Why has every man a conscience, then? I think that we should be men first, and subjects afterward. It is not desirable to cultivate a respect for the law, so much as for the right. The only obligation which I have a right to assume is to do at any time what I think right. It is truly enough said that a corporation has no conscience; but a corporation of conscientious men is a corporation *with* a conscience. Law never made men a whit more just; and, by means of their respect for it, even the well-disposed are daily made the agents of injustice. A common and natural result of an undue respect for law is, that you may see a file of soldiers, colonel, captain, corporal, privates, powder-monkeys, and all, marching in admirable order over hill and dale to the wars, against their wills, ay, against their common sense and consciences, which makes it very steep marching indeed, and produces a palpitation of the heart. They have no doubt that it is a damnable business in which they are concerned; they are all peaceably inclined. Now, what are they? Men at all? or small movable forts and magazines, at the service of some unscrupulous man in power? Visit the Navy-Yard, and behold a marine, such a man as an American government can make, or such as it can make a man with its black arts,—a mere shadow and reminiscence of humanity, a man laid out alive and standing, and already, as one may say, buried under arms with funeral accompaniments, though it may be

> Not a drum was heard, not a funeral note,
> As his corse to the rampart we hurried;
> Not a soldier discharged his farewell shot
> O'er the grave where our hero we buried.

The mass of men serve the state thus, not as men mainly, but as machines, with their bodies. They are the standing army, and the militia, jailers, constables, *posse comitatus*, etc. In most cases there is no free exercise whatever of the judgment or of the moral sense; but they put themselves on a level with wood and earth and stones; and wooden men can perhaps be manufactured that will serve the purpose as well. Such command no more respect than men of straw or a lump of dirt. They have the same sort of worth only as horses and dogs. Yet such as these even are commonly esteemed good citizens. Others—as most legislators, politicians, lawyers, ministers, and office-holders—serve the state chiefly with their heads; and, as they rarely make any moral distinctions, they are as likely to serve the Devil without *intending* it, as God. A very few, as heroes, patriots, martyrs, reformers in the great sense, and *men*, serve the state with their consciences also, and so neces-

sarily resist it for the most part; and they are commonly treated as
enemies by it. A wise man will only be useful as a man, and will not
submit to be "clay," and "stop a hole to keep the wind away," but leave
that office to his dust at least:

> I am too high-born to be propertied,
> To be a secondary at control,
> Or useful serving-man and instrument
> To any sovereign state throughout the world.

He who gives himself entirely to his fellowmen appears to them useless and selfish; but he who gives himself partially to them is pronounced
a benefactor and philanthropist.

How does it become a man to behave toward this American government today? I answer, that he cannot without disgrace be associated
with it. I cannot for an instant recognize that political organization as
my government which is the *slave's* government also.

All men recognize the right of revolution; that is, the right to refuse
allegiance to, and to resist, the government, when its tyranny or its in-
efficiency are great and unendurable. But almost all say that such is not
the case now. But such was the case, they think, in the Revolution of '75.
If one were to tell me that his was a bad government because it taxed
certain foreign commodities brought to its ports, it is most probable
that I should not make an ado about it, for I can do without them. All
machines have their friction; and possibly this does enough good to
counterbalance the evil. At any rate, it is a great evil to make a stir
about it. But when the friction comes to have its machine, and oppression
and robbery are organized, I say, let us not have such a machine any
longer. In other words, when a sixth of the population of a nation which
has undertaken to be the refuge of liberty are slaves, and a whole
country is unjustly overrun and conquered by a foreign army, and subjected to military law, I think that it is not too soon for honest men to
rebel and revolutionize. What makes this duty the more urgent is the
fact that the country so overrun is not our own, but ours is the invading
army.

Paley, a common authority with many on moral questions, in his
chapter on the "Duty of Submission to Civil Government," resolves all
civil obligation into expediency; and he proceeds to say, "that so long as
the interest of the whole society requires it, that is, so long as the
established government cannot be resisted or changed without public
inconveniency, it is the will of God that the established government be

obeyed, and no longer.... This principle being admitted, the justice of every particular case of resistance is reduced to a computation of the quantity of the danger and grievance on the one side, and of the probability and expense of redressing it on the other." Of this, he says, every man shall judge for himself. But Paley appears never to have contemplated those cases to which the rule of expediency does not apply, in which a people, as well as an individual, must do justice, cost what it may. If I have unjustly wrested a plank from a drowning man, I must restore it to him though I drown myself. This, according to Paley, would be inconvenient. But he that would save his life, in such a case, shall lose it. This people must cease to hold slaves, and to make war on Mexico, though it cost them their existence as a people.

In their practice, nations agree with Paley; but does any one think that Massachusetts does exactly what is right at the present crisis?

> A drab of state, a cloth-o'-silver slut,
> To have her train borne up, and her soul trail in the dirt.

Practically speaking, the opponents to a reform in Massachusetts are not a hundred thousand politicians at the South, but a hundred thousand merchants and farmers here, who are more interested in commerce and agriculture than they are in humanity, and are not prepared to do justice to the slave and to Mexico, *cost what it may.* I quarrel not with far-off foes, but with those who, near at home, co-operate with, and do the bidding of, those far away, and without whom the latter would be harmless. We are accustomed to say, that the mass of men are unprepared; but improvement is slow, because the few are not materially wiser or better than the many. It is not so important that many should be as good as you, as that there be some absolute goodness somewhere; for that will leaven the whole lump. There are thousands who are *in opinion* opposed to slavery and to the war, who yet in effect do nothing to put an end to them; who, esteeming themselves children of Washington and Franklin, sit down with their hands in their pockets, and say that they know not what to do, and do nothing; who even postpone the question of freedom to the question of free-trade, and quietly read the prices-current along with the latest advices from Mexico, after dinner, and, it may be, fall asleep over them both. What is the price-current of an honest man and patriot to-day? They hesitate, and they regret, and sometimes they petition; but they do nothing in earnest and with effect. They will wait, well disposed, for others to remedy the evil, that they may no longer have it to regret. At most, they give only a cheap vote, and a feeble countenance and God-speed, to the right, as it goes by them. There are nine hundred and ninety-nine patrons of virtue to one virtuous man. But it is easier to deal with the real possessor of a thing than with the temporary guardian of it.

All voting is a sort of gaming, like checkers or backgammon, with a slight moral tinge to it, a playing with right and wrong, with moral questions; and betting naturally accompanies it. The character of the voters is not staked. I cast my vote, perchance, as I think right; but I am not vitally concerned that that right should prevail. I am willing to leave it to the majority. Its obligation, therefore, never exceeds that of expediency. Even voting *for the right* is *doing* nothing for it. It is only expressing to men feebly your desire that it should prevail. A wise man will not leave the right to the mercy of chance nor wish it to prevail through the power of the majority. There is but little virtue in the action of masses of men. When the majority shall at length vote for the abolition of slavery, it will be because they are indifferent to slavery, or because there is but little slavery left to be abolished by their vote. *They* will then be the only slaves. Only *his* vote can hasten the abolition of slavery who asserts his own freedom by his vote.

I hear of a convention to be held at Baltimore, or elsewhere, for the selection of a candidate for the Presidency, made up chiefly of editors, and men who are politicians by profession; but I think, what is it to any independent, intelligent, and respectable man what decision they may come to? Shall we not have the advantage of his wisdom and honesty, nevertheless? Can we not count upon some independent votes? Are there not many individuals in the country who do not attend conventions? But no: I find that the respectable man, so called, has immediately drifted from his position, and despairs of his country, when his country has more reason to despair of him. He forthwith adopts one of the candidates thus selected as the only *available* one, thus proving that he is himself *available* for any purposes of the demagogue. His vote is of no more worth than that of any unprincipled foreigner or hireling native, who may have been bought. O for a man who is a *man*, and, as my neighbor says, has a bone in his back which you cannot pass your hand through! Our statistics are at fault: the population has been returned too large. How many *men* are there to a square thousand miles in this country? Hardly one. Does not America offer any inducement for men to settle here? The American has dwindled into an Odd Fellow,—one who may be known by the development of his organ of gregariousness, and a manifest lack of intellect and cheerful self-reliance; whose first and chief concern, on coming into the world, is to see that the Almshouses are in good repair; and, before yet he has lawfully donned the virile garb, to collect a fund for the support of the widows and orphans that may be; who, in short, ventures to live only by the aid of the Mutual Insurance company, which has promised to bury him decently.

It is not a man's duty, as a matter of course, to devote himself to the eradication of any, even the most enormous wrong; he may still properly have other concerns to engage him; but it is his duty, at least, to wash his hands of it, and, if he gives it no thought longer, not to give it practically his support. If I devote myself to other pursuits and contemplations, I must first see, at least, that I do not pursue them sitting upon another man's shoulders. I must get off him first, that he may pursue his contemplations too. See what gross inconsistency is tolerated. I have heard some of my townsmen say, "I should like to have them order me out to help put down an insurrection of the slaves, or to march to Mexico;—see if I would go"; and yet these very men have each, directly by their allegiance, and so indirectly, at least, by their money, furnished a substitute. The soldier is applauded who refuses to serve in an unjust war by those who do not refuse to sustain the unjust government which makes the war; is applauded by those whose own act and authority he disregards and sets at naught; as if the state were penitent to that degree that it hired one to scourge it while it sinned, but not to that degree that it left off sinning for a moment. Thus, under the name of Order and Civil Government, we are all made at last to pay homage to and support our own meanness. After the first blush of sin comes its indifference; and from immoral it becomes, as it were, *un*moral, and not quite unnecessary to that life which we have made.

The broadest and most prevalent error requires the most disinterested virtue to sustain it. The slight reproach to which the virtue of patriotism is commonly liable, the noble are most likely to incur. Those who, while they disapprove of the character and measures of a government, yield to it their allegiance and support are undoubtedly its most conscientious supporters, and so frequently the most serious obstacles to reform. Some are petitioning the state to dissolve the Union, to disregard the requisitions of the President. Why do they not dissolve it themselves,—the union between themselves and the state,—and refuse to pay their quota into its treasury? Do not they stand in the same relation to the state that the state does to the Union? And have not the same reasons prevented the state from resisting the Union which have prevented them from resisting the state?

How can a man be satisfied to entertain an opinion merely, and enjoy *it?* Is there any enjoyment in it, if his opinion is that he is aggrieved? If you are cheated out of a single dollar by your neighbor, you do not rest satisfied with knowing that you are cheated, or with saying that you are cheated, or even with petitioning him to pay you your due; but you take effectual steps at once to obtain the full amount, and see that you are never cheated again. Action from principle, the perception and the performance of right, changes things and relations; it is essentially revolutionary, and does not consist wholly with anything which was. It not only divides states and churches, it divides families; ay, it divides the *individual,* separating the diabolical in him from the divine.

Unjust laws exist: shall we be content to obey them, or shall we endeavor to amend them, and obey them until we have succeeded, or shall we transgress them at once? Men generally, under such a government as this, think that they ought to wait until they have persuaded the majority to alter them. They think that, if they should resist, the remedy would be worse than the evil. But it is the fault of the government itself that the remedy *is* worse than the evil. *It* makes it worse. Why is it not more apt to anticipate and provide for reform? Why does it not cherish its wise minority? Why does it cry and resist before it is hurt? Why does it not encourage its citizens to be on the alert to point out its faults, and *do* better than it would have them? Why does it always crucify Christ, and excommunicate Copernicus and Luther, and pronounce Washington and Franklin rebels?

One would think that a deliberate and practical denial of its authority was the only offense never contemplated by government; else, why has it not assigned its definite, its suitable and proportionate penalty? If a man who has no property refuses but once to earn nine shillings for the state, he is put in prison for a period unlimited by any law that I know, and determined only by the discretion of those who placed him there; but if he should steal ninety times nine shillings from the state, he is soon permitted to go at large again.

If the injustice is part of the necessary friction of the machine of government, let it go, let it go: perchance it will wear smooth,—certainly the machine will wear out. If the injustice has a spring, or a pulley, or a rope, or a crank, exclusively for itself, then perhaps you may consider whether the remedy will not be worse than the evil; but if it is of such a nature that it requires you to be the agent of injustice to another, then, I say, break the law. Let your life be a counter friction to stop the machine. What I have to do is to see, at any rate, that I do not lend myself to the wrong which I condemn.

As for adopting the ways which the state has provided for remedying the evil, I know not of such ways. They take too much time, and a man's life will be gone. I have other affairs to attend to. I came into this world, not chiefly to make this a good place to live in, but to live in it, be it good or bad. A man has not everything to do, but something; and because he cannot do *everything*, it is not necessary that he should do *something* wrong. It is not my business to be petitioning the Governor or the Legislature any more than it is theirs to petition me; and if they should not hear my petition, what should I do then? But in this case the state has provided no way: its very Constitution is the evil. This may seem to be harsh and stubborn and unconciliatory; but it is to treat with the utmost kindness and consideration the only spirit that can appreciate or deserves it. So is all change for the better, like birth and death, which convulse the body.

I do not hesitate to say, that those who call themselves Abolitionists should at once effectually withdraw their support, both in person and property, from the government of Massachusetts, and not wait till they constitute a majority of one, before they suffer the right to prevail through them. I think that it is enough if they have God on their side, without waiting for that other one. Moreover, any man more right than his neighbors constitutes a majority of one already.

I meet this American government, or its representative, the state government, directly, and face to face, once a year—no more—in the person of its tax-gatherer; this is the only mode in which a man situated as I am necessarily meets it; and it then says distinctly, Recognize me; and the simplest, the most effectual, and, in the present posture of affairs, the indispensablest mode of treating with it on this head, of expressing your little satisfaction with and love for it is to deny it then. My civil neighbor, the tax-gatherer, is the very man I have to deal with,— for it is, after all, with men and not with parchment that I quarrel,—and he has voluntarily chosen to be an agent of the government. How shall he ever know well what he is and does as an officer of the government, or as a man, until he is obliged to consider whether he shall treat me, his neighbor, for whom he has respect, as a neighbor and well-disposed man, or as a maniac and disturber of the peace, and see if he can get over this obstruction to his neighborliness without a ruder and more impetuous thought or speech corresponding with his action. I know this well, that if one thousand, if one hundred, if ten men whom I could name,—if ten *honest* men only,—ay, if one HONEST man, in this State of Massachusetts, *ceasing to hold slaves,* were actually to withdraw from this copartnership, and be locked up in the county jail therefor, it would be the abolition of slavery in America. For it matters not how small the beginning may seem to be: what is once well done is done forever. But we love better to talk about it: that we say is our mission. Reform keeps many scores of newspapers in its service, but not one man. If my esteemed neighbor, the State's ambassador, who will devote his days to the settlement of the question of human rights in the Council Chamber, instead of being threatened with the prisons of Carolina, were to sit down the prisoner of Massachusetts, that State which is so anxious to foist the sin of slavery upon her sister,—though at present she can discover only an act of inhospitality to be the ground of a quarrel with her,— the Legislature would not wholly waive the subject the following winter.

Under a government which imprisons any unjustly, the true place for a just man is also a prison. The proper place today, the only place which Massachusetts has provided for her freer and less desponding spirits, is in her prisons, to be put out and locked out of the State by her own act, as they have already put themselves out by their principles. It is there that the fugitive slave, and the Mexican prisoner on parole, and the Indian come to plead the wrongs of his race should find them; on that separate, but more free and honorable ground, where the State places those who are not *with* her, but *against* her,—the only house in a slave State in which a free man can abide with honor. If any think that their influence would be lost there, and their voices no longer afflict the ear of the State, that they would not be as an enemy within its walls, they do not know by how much truth is stronger than error, nor how much more eloquently and effectively he can combat injustice who has experienced a little in his own person. Cast your whole vote, not a strip of paper merely, but your whole influence. A minority is powerless while it conforms to the majority; it is not even a minority then; but it is irresistible when it clogs by its whole weight. If the alternative is to keep all just men in prison, or give up war and slavery, the State will not hesitate which to choose. If a thousand men were not to pay their tax-bills this year, that would not be a violent and bloody measure, as it would be to pay them, and enable the State to commit violence and shed innocent blood. This is, in fact, the definition of a peaceable revolution, if any such is possible. If the tax-gatherer, or any other public officer, asks me, as one has done, "But what shall I do?" my answer is, "If you really wish to do anything, resign your office." When the subject has refused allegiance, and the officer has resigned his office, then the revolution is accomplished. But even suppose blood should flow. Is there not a sort of blood shed when the conscience is wounded? Through this wound a man's real manhood and immortality flow out, and he bleeds to an everlasting death. I see this blood flowing now.

· · ·

The authority of government, even such as I am willing to submit to, —for I will cheerfully obey those who know and can do better than I, and in many things even those who neither know nor can do so well,— is still an impure one: to be strictly just, it must have the sanction and consent of the governed. It can have no pure right over my person and property but what I conceded to it. The progress from an absolute to a limited monarchy, from a limited monarchy to a democracy, is a progress toward a true respect for the individual. Even the Chinese philosopher was wise enough to regard the individual as the basis of the empire. Is a democracy, such as we know it, the last improvement possible in government? Is it not possible to take a step further towards recognizing and organizing the rights of man? There will never be a really free and enlightened State until the State comes to recognize the individual as a higher and independent power, from which all its own power and authority are derived, and treats him accordingly. I please myself with imagining a State at last which can afford to be just to all men, and to treat the individual with respect as a neighbor; which even would not think it inconsistent with its own repose if a few were to live aloof from it, not meddling with it, nor embraced by it, who fulfilled all the duties of neighbors and fellow-men. A State which bore this kind of fruit, and suffered it to drop off as fast as it ripened, would prepare the way for a still more perfect and glorious State, which also I have imagined, but not yet anywhere seen.

Questions for Study and Discussion

1. What is Thoreau's purpose in this essay?

2. According to Thoreau, why is the majority always permitted to rule?

3. Why does the author disagree with majority rule?

4. What is the substance of Paley's doctrine quoted by Thoreau? Does he agree or disagree?

5. What two major "evils" tolerated by the American government were mainly responsible for Thoreau's strongest criticism of it?

6. According to Thoreau, what is one's minimum duty in respect to enormous wrongs being practiced by or with the approval of the government?

7. According to Thoreau, what should citizens do about unjust laws?

8. According to Thoreau, what is the only house in a slave state where a free man can abide with honor? Why?

9. How can a minority best make its influence felt?

10. What is Thoreau's conception of the ideal State?

11. What propagandistic devices does Thoreau use in this discussion?

12. Point out five passages that contain strong emotional appeals in favor of the author's point of view.

Vocabulary Study

Define the following words as used in this essay: expedient, alacrity, fain, gregariousness, unconciliatory.

Writing Assignment

Choose a statement from the essay with which you strongly disagree, and write an effective refutation in a propagandistic manner.

Neither Blind Obedience
Nor Uncivil Disobedience

Sidney Hook

During the past decade of tension and turmoil in American life, there has developed a mass phenomenon of civil disobedience even among those who profess devotion to democratic ideals and institutions. This phenomenon has taken on something of the character of a tidal wave that has not yet reached its crest. It has swept from the field of race relations to the campuses of some universities, subtly altering the connotation of the term "academic." It is being systematically developed as an instrument for influencing foreign policy. It is leaving its mark on popular culture. I am told that it is not only a theme of comic books but that children in our more sophisticated families no longer resort to tantrums in defying parental discipline—they go limp!

In the wake of civil disobedience there has occasionally developed *uncivil* disobedience, sometimes as a natural psychological development, and often because of the failure of law-enforcement agencies, particularly in the South, to respect and defend legitimate expression of social protest. The line between civil and uncivil disobedience is not only an uncertain and wavering one in practice; in some quarters it has become so in theory. A recent prophet of the philosophy of the absurd, in recommending civil disobedience as a form of creative disorder in a democracy, cited as an illustration of it Shays's Rebellion, the 18th-century revolt in Massachusetts. And indeed some of the techniques of protesting American involvement in Vietnam have departed so far from traditional ways of civil disobedience as to make it likely that they are inspired by the same confusion between civil and uncivil disobedience.

All this has made focal the perennial problems of the nature and limits of the citizen's obligation to obey the law, of the relation between the authority of conscience and the authority of the state, of the rights and duties of a democratic moral man in an immoral democratic society. The classical writings on these questions have acquired a burning relevance to the political condition of man today. I propose briefly to clarify some of these problems.

To begin with, I wish to stress the point that there is no problem concerning "social protest" as such in a democracy. Our Bill of Rights was adopted not only to make protest possible but to facilitate it. The political logic, the very ethos of any democracy that professes to rest, no matter how indirectly, upon freely given consent *requires* that peaceful social protest be permitted—and not only permitted but protected from interference by those opposed to the protest, which means protected by the agencies of law enforcement.

Not social protest but *illegal* social protest constitutes our problem. It raises the question of when, if ever, illegal protest is justified in a democratic society. It is of the first importance to bear in mind that we are raising the question as principled democrats in a democratic society. To urge that illegal social protests, motivated by exalted ideals, are sanctified in a democratic society by precedents like the Boston Tea Party, is to lapse into political illiteracy. For such actions occurred in societies in which those affected by unjust laws had no power peacefully to change them.

Further, many actions dubbed civilly disobedient by local authorities are strictly speaking not such at all. An action launched in violation of a local law or ordinance, and undertaken to test it, on the ground that the law itself violates state or Federal law, or launched in violation of a state law in the sincerely held belief that the state law outrages the Constitution, the supreme law of the land, is not civilly disobedient.

In large measure the sympathy with which the original sit-ins were received—especially the Freedom Rides, marches and demonstrations that flouted local Southern laws—was due to the conviction that they were constitutionally justified, in accordance with the heritage of freedom enshrined in the amendments, and enjoyed in other regions of the country. Practically everything the marchers did was sanctioned by the phrase of the First Amendment which upholds "the right of the people peaceably to assemble and to petition the Government for a redress of grievances." Actions of this kind may be wise or unwise, timely or untimely, but they are not civilly disobedient.

They become civilly disobedient when they are in deliberate violation of laws that have been enacted and sustained by the highest legislative and judicial bodies of the nation; e.g., tax laws, conscription laws, laws forbidding segregation in education, and discrimination in public accommodations and employment. Another class of examples consists of illegal social protest against local and state laws that clearly do not conflict with Federal law.

•   •   •

The mark of an enlightened democracy is, as far as its security allows, to respect the religious commitment of a citizen who believes, on grounds of conscience or any other ground, that his relation to God involves duties superior to those arising from any human relation. It, therefore, exempts him from his duty as a citizen to protect his country.

But the mark of the genuine conscientious objector in a democracy is to respect the democratic process. He does not use his exemption as a political weapon to coerce where he has failed to convince or persuade. Having failed to influence national policy by rational means *within* the law, in the political processes open to him in a free society, he cannot justifiably try to defeat that policy by resorting to obstructive techniques *outside* the law—and still remain a democrat.

It is one thing on grounds of conscience or religion to plead exemption from the duty of serving one's country when drafted. It is quite another to adopt harassing techniques to prevent others from volunteering or responding to the call of duty. It is one thing to oppose American involvement in Vietnam by teach-ins, petitions, electoral activity. It is quite another to attempt to stop troop trains; to take possession of the premises of draft boards where policies are not made; to urge recruits to sabotage their assignments and to feign illness in order to win discharge.

The first class of actions falls within the sphere of legitimate social protest; the second class is implicitly insurrectionary since it is directed against the authority of a democratic government which it seeks to overthrow not by argument and discussion but by resistance—albeit passive resistance.

Nonetheless, since we have rejected legal absolutism we must face the possibility that individuals on ethical grounds may in protest refuse to obey some law they regard as uncommonly immoral or uncommonly foolish. If they profess to be democrats, their behavior must scrupulously respect the following conditions:

It must be nonviolent—peaceful not only in form but in actuality. After all, the protestors are seeking to dramatize a great evil that the community allegedly has been unable to overcome because of compla-

cency or moral weakness. They must therefore avoid the guilt of imposing hardship or harm on others who in the nature of the case can hardly
be responsible for the situation under protest.

Second, resort to civil disobedience is never morally legitimate where
other methods of remedying the evil complained of are available. Existing grievance procedures were not available to the Southern Negroes.
The courts often shared the prejudices of the community and offered
little relief, often not even minimal protection. But such procedures
are available in the areas of industry and education. For example, where
charges against students are being heard, such procedures may result
in the dismissal of the charges, not the students. Or the faculty on appeal may decide to suspend the rules rather than the students. To jump
the gun to civil disobedience in by-passing these procedures is tell-tale
evidence that those who are calling the shots are after other game than
preserving the rights of students.

Third, those who resort to civil disobedience are duty bound to accept
the legal sanctions and punishments imposed by the laws. Attempts to
evade and escape them really involve not only a betrayal of the community—Socrates' argument in the Crito is especially valid where democratic political premises obtain—they erode the moral foundations of
civil disobedience itself. The rationale of the protesters is the hope that
the pain and hurt and indignity they voluntarily accept will stir their
fellow citizens to compassion, open their minds to second thoughts, and
move them to undertake the necessary healing action. But when we observe the heroics of defiance being followed by the dialectics of legal
evasion, we question the sincerity of the action.

Fourth, civil disobedience is unjustified if a major moral issue is not
clearly at stake. Differences about negotiable details that can easily be
settled with a little patience should not be fanned into a blaze of legal
opposition.

Fifth, where intelligent men of goodwill and character differ on large
and complex moral issues, discussion and agitation are more appropriate
than civilly disobedient action. E.g., those who feel strongly about animal rights and regard the consumption of animal flesh as morally evil
would have a just cause for civil disobedience if their freedom to obtain
other food was threatened. But they would have no moral right to resort
to similar action to prevent their fellow-citizens from consuming meat.
(Similarly, with fluoridation.)

Sixth, where civil disobedience is undertaken, there must be some
rhyme and reason in the time, place and targets selected. If one is con-

vinced, as I am not, that the Board of Education in New York City is remiss in its policy of desegregation, what is the point of dumping garbage on bridges to produce traffic jams that seriously discomfort commuters who have not the remotest connection with educational policies in New York? Such action can only obstruct the progress of desegregation in the communities of Long Island. Gandhi, who inspired the civil-disobedience movement in the 20th century, was a better technician than many who invoke his name but ignore his teachings. When he organized his campaign against the salt tax, he marched with his followers to the sea to make salt. He did not hold up food trains or tie up traffic.

Finally, there is such a thing as historical timing. Democrats who resort to civil disobedience must ask themselves whether the cumulative consequences of their action may in the existing climate of opinion undermine the peace and order on which the effective exercise of other human rights depend. This is a cost which one may be willing to pay but which must be taken into the reckoning.

All of these considerations are cautionary, not categorical. We have ruled out only two positions—blind obedience to any and all laws in a democracy, and unreflective violation of laws at the behest of individual consciences. Between these two obviously unacceptable extremes, there is a spectrum of views which shade into one another. Intelligent persons can differ on their application to specific situations. These differences will reflect different assessments of the historical mood of a culture, of the proper timing of protest and acquiescence, and of what the most desirable emphasis and direction of our teaching should be in order to extend "the blessings of liberty" as we preserve "domestic tranquillity."

Without essaying the role of a prophet, here is my reading of the needs of the present. It seems to me that the Civil Rights Act of 1964 and the Voting Acts of 1965 mark a watershed in the history of social and civil protest in the U.S. Upon their enforcement a great many things we hold dear depend, especially those causes in behalf of which in the last decade so many movements of social protest were launched.

The enforcement of the new civil-rights legislation depends on many factors—most notably the behavior of the hitherto recalcitrant elements in the Southern communities. Their *uncivil*, violent disobedience has proved unavailing; we need not fear that it will succeed better in the future. What we need to fear more is that in their opposition to the new legislation they will adopt the strategies and techniques of the civil-disobedience movement itself.

On the other hand, I think that in regions of the country where Negroes have made substantial advances, the civil-disobedience movement is not likely to make new gains commensurate with the risks. Those risks are that what is begun as civil disobedience will be perverted by extremists into uncivil disobedience, which will alienate large numbers who have firmly supported the cause of freedom.

One of the unintended consequences of the two world wars is that in many ways they strengthened the position of the Negroes and all other minorities in American political life. We do not need a third world war—or a civil war—to continue the process of liberation. We can do it in peace. The Civil Rights and the Voting Acts of 1964 and 1965 are in advance, far in advance, of the actual situation in some of the regions of the country where discrimination is still rife. Our present task is to bring home to, and reinforce, popular consciousness that those who violate the provisions of these acts are violating the highest law of the land, that their actions are outside the law.

Therefore, our goal must *now* be to build up and strengthen a mood of respect for the law, for civil obedience to laws even by those who deem them unwise or who opposed them in the past. Our hope is that those who abide by the law may learn not only to tolerate these acts but, in time, to accept them.

Judge Learned Hand once observed that if the spirit of liberty dies in the hearts of men, "no constitution, no law, no court can save it." But it is also true that where it is struggling to be born or beset by danger, the spirit of liberty may be strengthened by the timely legislation of just laws. To have the positive law on the side of right and justice is to have a powerful weapon that makes for voluntary compliance—but only if the *reasonableness* of the *prima facie* obligation to obey the law is recognized.

To one observer, at least, that reasonableness is being more and more disregarded in the country. The current mood is one of growing indifference to and disregard of even the reasonable legalities. The year's headlines from New York to California tell the story. I am not referring to the crime rate, which has made frightening advances, or to the fact that some of our metropolitan centers have become dangerous jungles. I am referring to a growing mood toward law generally, something comparable to the attitude toward the Volstead Act during the Prohibition era. The mood is more diffuse today. To be law-abiding in some circles is to be a "square."

In part, the community itself has been responsible for the emergence of this mood. This is especially true in those states which have failed to abolish the *unreasonable* legalities, particularly in the field of marriage, divorce, birth control, sex behavior, therapeutic abortion, voluntary euthanasia. The failure to repeal foolish laws, which make morally upright individuals legal offenders, tends to generate skepticism and indifference toward the reasonable legalities.

This mood must change if the promise of new civil-rights legislation is to be realized. Respect for law today can give momentum to the liberal upswing of the political and social pendulum in American life. In a democracy we cannot make an absolute of obedience to law or to anything else except, in John Erskine's memorable phrase, "the moral obligation to be intelligent." More than ever must we stress the wisdom of expressing dissent and opposition—the oxygen of free society—within the forms of civic obedience. Legal dissent and legal opposition still remain the most effective means within a democracy of making ordered progress toward a better society.

Questions for Study and Discussion

1. What is the author's purpose as stated in paragraph 3, page 65?
2. What does the author say about peaceful social protest?
3. What reasons does the author give for not regarding the original civil rights demonstrations and sit-ins as civilly disobedient?
4. When do demonstrations become civilly disobedient?
5. Under what seven conditions should an individual be permitted to disobey a law he considers immoral or unjust on ethical grounds?
6. What does the author mean by stating that the seven foregoing conditions are cautionary, not categorical?
7. What two positions has the author ruled out?
8. According to the author, what are the most effective means within a democracy of making ordered progress toward a better society?
9. What propagandistic devices are used in this selection?
10. What are the major agreements and disagreements between Hook and Thoreau?
11. Which of these two authors is less biased in his discussion? Explain.

Vocabulary Study

Define the following words and phrases as used in this essay: Shays's Rebellion, focal, perennial, ethos, categorical, watershed, recalcitrant, commensurate, Volstead Act, euthanasia.

Writing Assignment

Write a composition on one of the following topics or one of your own choosing based on the selections by Thoreau and Hook:

1. Hook Versus Thoreau on the Nature and Justification of Civil Disobedience

2. Civil Rights Demonstrations as a Legitimate Exercise of Civil Disobedience

3. Abuses of the Legitimate Exercise of Civil Disobedience by Certain Types of Civil Rights Demonstrations

---

America's Retreat From Victory

Senator Joseph McCarthy

Mr. President, in closely following the CONGRESSIONAL RECORD testimony before the Joint Committee on Foreign Relations and Armed Services, sitting jointly, which is conducting an investigation of the dismissal of Douglas MacArthur, I have become more and more impressed by two inescapable facts:

First. That it is impossible to develop the facts in the MacArthur inquiry without at the same time bringing to light some of the facts which bear on the question of why we fell from our position as the most powerful Nation on earth at the end of World War II to a position of declared weakness by our leadership.

Second. That it will be equally impossible to obtain the answers to the above without uncovering a conspiracy so immense and an infamy so black as to dwarf any previous such venture in the history of man. During the Marshall testimony, one of the Senators obviously troubled by the odor of the conspiracy which was commencing to rise as a result of the constant probing by the members of the committee—troubled by the fringes of the conspiracy which were commencing to show—came to my office and asked me for information on a subject which was troubling and puzzling him greatly. While I cannot quote him verbatim, the questions he asked were substantially as follows:

First. Who was close to Marshall and succeeded in deceiving this great American at Yalta when his military advice was that we turn Manchuria over to Russia, thereby signing at least the first section in the death warrant of the Republic of China?

Second. Who twisted and perverted the thinking of this great American and misguided him into the folly of his disastrous mission to China?

Third. Who, of tortured disloyalty to America, succeeded in deceiving this great general during the course of World War II to the end that he always sided with Stalin and against Churchill when history's great decisions were being made—decisions which turned out so bad for the free world and so good for international communism?

Upon searching for the answers for the Senator, I found to my surprise that Marshall, who, by the alchemy of propaganda, became the "greatest living American," and the recently proclaimed "master of global strategy" for the party in power, has never had his record subjected to the searching light of any historian. In view of the fact that the committee, the Congress, and the American people are being called upon either to endorse or reject Marshall's global strategy, I felt that it was urgent that such a study be made and submitted to the Russell committee.

MARSHALL'S RECORD FROM FRIENDLY SOURCES

I decided that the record of Marshall's unbroken series of decisions and acts, contributing so greatly to the strategy of defeat, should be given not from the pens and lips of his critics, but from sources friendly to him. In view of the fact that the archives of this Nation and other nations are not available to me, I have been unable to document all of the important details of his record. However, sufficient evidence is available to give a picture which is complete in its general outline. I have drawn on the written record; on the memoirs of the principal actors in the great events of the last 10 years; I have drawn heavily from the books out of which the history of these times will be written for the next 500 years; I have drawn from the pens of Admiral Leahy, Winston Churchill, Mark Clark, Robert Sherwood speaking for Harry Hopkins, Henry L. Stimson, James F. Byrnes, Edward B. Stettinius, Jr., Sumner Wells, Cordell Hull, General Arnold, General Deane, General Chennault, and Jonathan Daniels. No one of them alone was trying to or did give anything remotely approaching a complete record of Marshall. The picture emerges, however, as we piece together their recollection of the events in which he figures—oftentimes fragmentary, never directly uncomplimentary, but often, when fitted together, pointing unerringly to one conclusion. . . .

It is needless to tell you that this was a monumental task, but one which I felt had to be done, for unless we understand the record of Marshall it will be impossible to even remotely grasp the planned steady retreat from victory which commenced long before World War II ended. Unless we carefully study the records of Marshall and Acheson,* who have worked together so closely, it will be impossible to foretell the next move on the timetable of the great conspiracy.

I realize full well how unpopular it is to lay hands on the laurels of a man who had been built into a great hero. I very much dislike this unpleasant task, but I feel that it must be done if we are to intelligently make the proper decisions in the issues of life and death before us.

ELEMENTS OF AMERICA'S STRENGTH

Before embarking upon the documentation of the history of Marshall, let us first briefly review the elements of our strength. Primarily, of course, we have the great industrial potential of this the mightiest of industrial lands—a potential which during the late hostilities poured forth the weapons of war to such an extent that in the closing months the enemy was hopelessly overmastered. That is one element we may take for granted unless the Russians by, among other things, gaining command of the western Pacific could successfully threaten it from air bases in Alaska and northern Canada. We may assume our industrial potential for the time being.

*Dean Acheson, Secretary of State.

The other great constant factor is the will of the American people to resist. I think that will is not weakened, and I am proud, as other Senators are, of the magnificent evidence of that will which we have seen in Korea. And yet will and arms are not in themselves entirely sufficient. The mountains of materials which we may produce and the valor of American arms, as it has been demonstrated on a thousand battlefields in every corner of the globe from King Phillip's War to the current engagements in Korea, are not enough.

The variable factor in all this is politics and military strategy. What is strategy? Webster tells us that it is "the science or art of projecting and directing great military movements." In our case those military movements must be projected on a world-wide scale.

It is here that we come to the enigmatic, powerful figure of General Marshall. Why should we seek, as we shall, to understand General Marshall's strategic decisions in World War II? Because we are asked today to accept General Marshall as the paramount strategist of the present and the oncoming wars. The issue of these times has been partly framed in terms of the widely contrasted personalities and judgments of General MacArthur and General Marshall. We are asked to make the choice between MacArthur and Marshall. The issue in the great controversy that ensued upon the dismissal of General MacArthur by President Truman "in the dead, vast, and middle of the night" is at bottom a strategical issue.

THE STRANGE WAR OF 1951

As a backdrop to the investigation being conducted by the joint committee there is being waged a strange war, an undeclared and unacknowledged war; a war such as never before has been seen on sea or land. It is a war into which we were launched on the impulse of a President in the name of the United Nations, which has been striving ever since to disavow its paternity. If we are to believe the administration's spokesmen, it is a war without point or objective, a war without meaning except in the high personal and tragic sense in which it appears to the men who are consecrating the hills and valleys of Korea with their blood and to the wives and families of those men.

There is a nightmare quality about this war. In the eyes of the distinguished General Bradley it is a war fought against the "wrong enemy." The chairman of the Joint Chiefs of Staff, it is clear, has succumbed to the general confusion, and while it is not given to General

Bradley to know that in Korea we are fighting the Russian Empire, we in this Chamber may be supposed to know better. This being an unacknowledged war, we endure all the disadvantages of war without any of the advantages. We are powerless to exercise the political or military initiatives customary to a belligerent.

In everything that concerns the deadly and ruinous aspects of war—the casualty rolls, the immense cost in treasure, the domestic strains, the fears—we are at war. In everything that has to do with the constructive, hopeful aspects of war—for war has such aspects too—we are not at war. Because of the maddening ambiguity of the administration's policy, we cannot pursue intelligent policies that would bring victory, nor can we make use of sound military principles which might minimize bloodshed and prevent the appalling destruction of Korea. We are in a war of alliance, yet our allies are at best of nominal assistance and are at worst a conflicting hindrance. When they could really support us, then we and we alone are at war. Nor are we willing to make use of true friends, such as the Chinese Nationalists, who never have swerved in purpose.

WHO IS RUNNING THE WAR?

As the hearings progress, the question of what power is making decisions is becoming more and more confused. In one breath we hear that we, as the agent of the United Nations, can do all that is necessary to bring the war to a speedy and victorious conclusion. In the next breath we hear that actions which our military leaders consider necessary cannot be taken because the United Nations is running the war. The best example is found in the testimony of the Joint Chiefs and Acheson in regard to the hot pursuit of enemy planes. It was the unanimous opinion of General MacArthur, General Stratemeyer, the Secretary of Defense and the Joint Chiefs that our Air Force be allowed to engage in hot pursuit. The testimony was that Acheson was instructed to take the necessary steps to get the consent of our 13 "allies." He testified, however, that he only contacted six of them.

When asked why he did not present this question to the United Nations in view of the fact that the United Nations is allegedly the final authority in the operation of this war, he stated—and listen to this—that could not be done because Russia as a member of the United Nations would veto this military action. From this it would appear that we are in the fantastically incredible position of supplying a vast majority of the manpower (outside of Korean manpower) and the weapons of war, while at the same time we are in the position of having the war run by an organization in which our principal enemy, in the words of our Secretary of State, can veto any action which would promise us victory.

There will be found among us, Mr. President, many views regarding the United Nations. Some may see it with the infatuated and cloudy vision of President Truman and Secretary Acheson, as the only hope of mankind. Others, taking a moderate view, may see in it a still hopeful instrument for future peace and world order. Still others look upon the United Nations, so hastily improvised by the late President Roosevelt, the late Secretary Stettinius, and the presently incarcerated Alger Hiss, as a misbegotten fraud. All must admit that it is sown with our enemies and with false friends. It is, nevertheless, in the name of the United Nations that our sons and brothers are committed to the carnage of Korea.

DANGER OF A SUDDEN SELL-OUT

Worst of all, we cannot be sure as we sit here that suddenly behind the screen of chicanery and evil purpose we may not be committed to an ignominious peace. In January the Messrs. Truman, Acheson, and Marshall were ready to negotiate a truce that would have rewarded the Chinese hirelings of the Kremlin with a seat in the United Nations and the island bastion of Formosa. As recently as last March, these same gentlemen, in collaboration with the British, with the impudent National Socialist Nehru, and their tools and minions throughout Europe and the Middle East, were on the verge again of surrendering to the Asiatic power drive of Moscow. It is not a pleasant sight to see Uncle Sam, with purse in one hand and hat in the other, begging on bended knee for the things which are ours. But it was to be done cleverly, so that we would appear to be opposing what by our actions would have been inescapable results. Let me explain that the future of our allies on Formosa and the question of unseating the Republic of China in the United Nations and replacing her with Red China was to be settled by a jury composed of Red China, Red Russia, Socialist Britain, and the United States—a packed jury, if I ever heard of one.

There was no question about how three of the four would vote. There was no possible question how the Attlee government's representative would vote, because they have long stood 100 percent with Red China in her claims to Formosa and her claims to a seat in the United Nations. Our State Department had instructed our delegate to the United Nations to vote to settle the fate of our friends by a fixed jury—a jury stacked with the enemies of the Republic of China; a jury which had the whole-hearted and publicly expressed approval of the great Marshall, of course.

We are told that only the prompt action of General MacArthur in issuing a field ultimatum to the bloody pawns of Peiping forestalled that disaster. The President of the United States has explained that it was this act of General MacArthur that precipitated his dismissal. If that is indeed true, this single deed of MacArthur's, preserving for yet a little while our vital position in the Western Pacific, may well be regarded by history as the foremost among his many services to his country.

We cannot be secure today in the confidence that this administration will not again put our security in the Pacific to the hazard of its muddy and perverted purposes. Certainly Dean Acheson will not foresake the high-minded executioners of the Kremlin who are turning the public squares of Chinese city after Chinese city into charnel houses. The administration, which procured the surrender of China to Russia, is obviously well pleased with the results of its endeavors and has no desire to disturb the Russian Empire in its possession of the mainland of China.

And among the journalistic voices that invariably echo the administration's will, we have had fresh evidence within recent days of their eagerness that Russia be not molested in Asia. Many of those journalistic satraps have been demanding the punishment of Dean Rusk for his belated and partial acknowledgement that American policy has been betrayed in China.

I hope the press will understand that I am only referring to the left-wing, bleeding-heart elements of the press, because, thank God, we do have essentially a good press in this Nation.

POLICY OF WAR

This administration, which has given us this caricature of a war, is now bent on an even worse horror—a phony and fraudulent peace. It is planned by Secretary Marshall and the elegant and alien Acheson—Russian as to heart, British as to manner. We even hear cries for a fraudulent peace within this Chamber. In support of their campaign for a fraudulent peace, its advocates wage a campaign of fear.

The President threatens us with the destruction of our cities by Russian bombs unless we continue to pursue his empty, defeatist strategy in the Far East. The President's only answer to the splendid counsel of General MacArthur is that we must on no account offend the Soviet Union. One of the administration's two principal spokesmen on this matter seeks to frighten us with the admonition that unless we mind our P's and Q's in Korea, "This very Capitol Building, this very Senate Chamber may be blown to smithereens next week or the week after." Mr. President, that is not the great heart of America speaking.

I do not think we need fear too much about the Communists dropping atomic bombs on Washington. They would kill too many of their friends that way.

I never thought that I would live to see the day that Senators representing sovereign States would rise on the floor of the Senate and actually debate and argue to the effect that we should not protect the lives of our young men, whom we ourselves have sent into battle, merely because, if we were to fight back, we might make someone angry.

In my boyhood in Wisconsin, we had a deep pride in our country, in its strength as well as its wealth, in its high destiny as a great free society as well as in its opportunities for individual riches or position. We were simple, uncomplicated Americans, not above dying, if need be, for the land we love. We had self-assurance, too, and we assumed that whenever our security, our way of life, and our ideals were threatened by a hostile force, we would have the physical strength, and also the strength of character, to defend those values by force of arms, and to the utmost, regardless of consequences. We were not misled and enfeebled by abstractions such as collective security and by the tortured, twisted reasoning of men of little minds and less morals who for the first time in the history of this Nation argue that we should not vigorously fight back when attacked and in every possible way protect the lives of our men for fear of making an enemy or potential enemy mad, and that we dare not win a war. We hear the President in a Nation-wide broadcast saying, "Even if we win," Mr. President, listen to those words— "even"—"even if we win the war." When before in the history of this Nation has a President been so craven? Imagine George Washington, when he was leading his small, physically weak Nation against mighty and powerful England, saying to his troops, "Even if we win." Imagine

Lincoln, in even the darkest days of the Civil War, saying, "Even if we win." Imagine Churchill in England's darkest days during World War II when invasion was imminent, saying, "Even if we win." Imagine what might well have happened to England if those had been his words instead of his immortal words, "We shall fight on the beaches, we shall fight on the landing grounds, we shall fight in the fields and in the hills; we shall never surrender." Imagine Roosevelt, when he addressed the Congress on that fateful December 8, saying, "Even if we win."

As I listen to the debates in this Chamber and hear the testimony of the President's spokesmen, it makes me sick down deep inside. But when I get out of Washington into the United States, it is a healthy feeling— for then is answered the question: Where stand the people? Not with the Gospel of fear which is being preached to us. Not with the craven fears of the President and his spokesmen but rather with the wholesome American view regarding the integrity and self-reliance of America.

WHY ARE WE WEAK?

The administration explicity announces to the world that we are too weak to resist the Soviet Empire.

When World War II ended, the United States had the most powerful military machine the world had ever witnessed. It could have rolled across Asia, over the Ural Mountains, and on to the Pacific Ocean, and Korea would not have even been considered a minor mopping up operation by one of Patton's armored divisions. Since then the administration has been given every cent that it has asked, and more, to maintain a powerful military machine. Yet during the hearings, Chief of the Air Force General Vandenberg testified—page 3630 of the MacArthur hearings—that the United States is operating a shoestring air force, and Secretary Marshall testified—page 880 of the MacArthur hearings—that we had almost nothing in the summer of 1950 in the way of available troops in this country other than one airborne division and a part of a Marine division.

This is the same administration which, as we shall again demonstrate today, deliberately—and I use the word "deliberately" advisedly—assisted the Russian conquest of China—a conquest that General Marshall conceded in his recent testimony had taken place—and in so doing reversed the American policy toward the East that had been maintained by every President, Republican or Democrat, for the last half a century.

This is the administration which has sheltered the friends and puppets of the Russian Empire high in its own councils and when challenged, has turned the batteries of its anger and its camp-following propaganda agents, not upon the enemies of our country in its ranks but turned them upon the enemies of those enemies.

This is the administration that has allowed priceless atomic secrets to slip through its dubiously loyal fingers—stolen by spies who, according to the President, never existed, and to make the very bombs with which it now threatens us. Moreover—and this is a fact of equal significance which I propose to reveal if you will forgive the lengthy exposition required by the evidence—the administration preceding this one, by its pursuit of a fateful high strategy in World War II itself produced the might of the Russian Empire which General Marshall now so greatly fears.

MARSHALL'S ROLE IN THE STRUGGLE
BETWEEN CHURCHILL AND STALIN

In order to draw clearly the picture of Marshall, it is necessary to sketch in some detail the vast, history-making struggle between Churchill and Stalin and the decisive role which Marshall played in the struggle. During those wartime days, Marshall sometimes overbore Churchill; he was sometimes overborne by Churchill. Each was striving to guide the decisions of Roosevelt, who, because of the great weight of American military and industrial power, had the last word. The President moderated between these two men, as we shall see, but I think it entirely fair to say that in those procedures General Marshall more often than not swayed the historic decisions.

That estimate may strike some of us as novel. It does not accord with the accepted and popular view of those times, which places Roosevelt as the all-powerful voice, only modified, often to America's hurt, by the strong desires of Churchill. We have not been properly instructed. The truth is that among the three great powers of that day, Stalin had a policy, Churchill had a policy, and we operated between the two, almost invariably in support of the Russian line rather than the British.

If Senators will bear with me I shall document the fact in detail. We had no discernible policy except the superficial one of defeating the enemy in battle as fast as possible. This will become more manifest as we proceed to review the high strategy of World War II.

THE NATION'S PERIL

The history of those events would not deserve extended treatment in this Chamber at this time unless its lessons afforded us insight into our present perils. I think we are in the greatest danger ever faced by this Republic. I think that for the first time in our history we are in danger from which we may not be able to escape as a distinguishable, a free, and a hopeful society. The continued existence of this country has never before been called into question. Even had the Confederate States succeeded in establishing their independence we would be today two countries instead of one, but they would be countries of a common civilization and way of life.

The danger we face today is different not only in its magnitude but in its intrinsic nature. If the Communist empire, which alone threatens us and which alone is the only power able so to do, were to accomplish the objective it seeks—and which so many Americans in high places either consciously or unconsciously assist—we will not only cease to be the country we have known and loved, but those of us who are allowed to stay alive will no longer be allowed to exist as civilized men.

While the peril is great, the great and shining hope of ultimate victory for free men of half the world lies in the fact that the people of this Nation do not subscribe to the craven, whining, whimpering policy of fear of those who, because of an accident of history, are in a position of leadership. . . .

Questions for Study and Discussion

1. What sentence in paragraph 3 arouses the greatest suspicion of the Senator's credibility?

2. Which of the seven common propaganda devices are used in the first two pages of Senator McCarthy's speech?

3. What additional one of the seven propaganda devices is used in the paragraph beginning at the bottom of page 73?

4. Which sentence in paragraph 4, page 75, is the more obviously propagandistic than any others in the paragraph?

5. What makes paragraph 4, page 79, propagandistic rather than an expression of the whole truth?

6. Make a list of at least ten phrases in this speech which are highly emotional.

Vocabulary Study

Define the following words and phrases as used in this selection: alchemy, archives, enigmatic, strategist, paternity, nightmare, ambiguity, nominal, improvised, incarcerated, chicanery, ignominious, Kremlin, minions, charnel houses, satraps.

Writing Assignment

After reading brief biographical sketches of George C. Marshall, Dean Acheson, and President Truman, in a standard encyclopedia, write a composition expressing your reaction to Senator McCarthy's speech.

The Constitution Versus States Rights

Daniel Webster

[During the last week in January, 1830, one of the most stirring, significant, and famous debates in the history of American politics was carried on in the United States Senate between Senators Robert Y. Haynes of South Carolina and Daniel Webster of Massachusetts. The major theme was finally narrowed to a discussion of the conflicting claims of the supremacy of the Constitution versus States Rights. Although more than one hundred and thirty-five years have elapsed and a civil war has intervened, the question is still a live issue in some sections of the nation. Consequently, the final portion of Webster's three-hour speech is presented here for its timeliness as well as its propagandistic qualities.]

I must now beg to ask, sir, Whence is this supposed right of the States derived? Where do they find the power to interfere with the laws of the Union? Sir, the opinion which the honorable gentleman maintains is a notion founded in a total misapprehension, in my judgment, of the origin of this government, and of the foundation on which it stands. I hold it to be a popular government, erected by the people; those who administer it responsible to the people; and itself capable of being amended and modified, just as the people may choose it should be. It is as popular, just as truly emanating from the people, as the State government. It is created for one purpose; the State governments for another. It has its own powers; they have theirs. There is no more authority with them to arrest the operation of a law of Congress than with Congress to arrest the operation of their laws. We are there to administer a Constitution emanating immediately for the people, and trusted by them to our administration. It is not the creature of the State governments. It is of no moment to the argument that certain acts of the State legislatures are necessary to fill our seats in this body. That is not one of their original State powers, a part of the sovereignty of the State. It is a duty which the people, by the Constitution itself, have imposed on the State legislatures, and which they might have left to be performed elsewhere, if they had seen fit. So they have left the choice of President with electors; but all this does not affect the proposition that this whole government— President, Senate, and House of Representatives—is a popular government. It leaves it still all its popular character. The governor of a State (in some of the States) is chosen, not directly by the people, but by those who are chosen by the people for the purpose of performing, among other duties, that of electing a governor. Is the government of the State, on that account, not a popular government? This government, sir, is the independent offspring of the popular will. It is not the creature of State legislatures; nay, more, if the whole truth must be told, the people brought it into existence, established it, and have hitherto supported it for the very purpose, amongst others, of imposing certain salutary restraints on State sovereignties. The States cannot now make war; they cannot contract alliances; they cannot make, each for itself, separate regulations of commerce; they cannot lay imposts; they cannot coin money. If this Constitution, sir, be the creature of State legislatures, it must be admitted that it has obtained a strange control over the volitions of its creators.

The people, then, sir, erected this government. They gave it a Constitution, and in that Constitution they have enumerated the powers which they bestow on it. They have made it a limited government. They have defined its authority. They have restrained it to the exercise of such powers as are granted; and all others, they declare, are reserved to the States or the people. But, sir, they have not stopped here. If they had, they would have accomplished but half their work. No definition can be so clear as to avoid possibility of doubt; no limitation so precise as to exclude all uncertainty. Who, then, shall construe this grant of the people? Who shall interpret their will, where it may be supposed they have left it doubtful? With whom do they repose this ultimate right of deciding on the powers of the government? Sir, they have settled all this in the fullest manner. They have left it with the government itself, in its appropriate branches. Sir, the very chief end, the main design for which the whole Constitution was framed and adopted was to establish a government that should not be obliged to act through State agency, or depend on State opinion and State discretion. The people had had quite enough of that kind of government under the Confederation. Under that system, the legal action, the application of law to individuals, belonged exclusively to the States. Congress could only recommend; their acts were not of binding force till the States had adopted and sanctioned them. Are we in that condition still? Are we yet at the mercy of State discretion and State construction? Sir, if we are, then vain will be our attempt to maintain the Constitution under which we sit.

But, sir, the people have wisely provided, in the Constitution itself, a proper, suitable mode and tribunal for settling questions of constitutional law. There are in the Constitution grants of powers to Congress, and restrictions on these powers. There are, also, prohibitions on the States. Some authority must, therefore, necessarily exist, having the ultimate jurisdiction to fix and ascertain the interpretation of these grants, restrictions, and prohibitions. The Constitution has itself pointed out, ordained, and established that authority. How has it accomplished this great and essential end? By declaring, sir, that *"the Constitution, and the laws of the United States made in pursuance thereof, shall be the supreme law of the land, anything in the Constitution or laws of any State to the contrary notwithstanding."*

This, sir, was the first great step. By this the supremacy of the Constitution and laws of the United States is declared. The people so will it. No State law is to be valid which comes in conflict with the Constitution, or any law of the United States passed in pursuance of it. But who shall decide this question of interference? To whom lies the last appeal? This, sir, the Constitution itself decides also, by declaring *"that the judicial power shall extend to all cases arising under the Constitution and laws of the United States."* These two provisions cover the whole ground. These are, in truth, the keystone of the arch! With these it is a government; without them it is a confederation. In pursuance of these clear and express provisions, Congress established, at its very first session, in the judicial act, a mode for carrying them into full effect, and for bringing all questions of constitutional power to the final decision of the Supreme Court. It then, sir, became a government. It then had the means of self-protection; and but for this, it would, in all probability, have been now among things which are past. Having constituted the government and declared its powers, the people have further said that, since somebody must decide on the extent of these powers, the government shall itself decide; subject always, like other popular governments, to its responsibility to the people. And now, sir, I repeat, how is it that a State legislature acquires any power to interfere? Who or what gives them the right to say to the people, "We, who are your agents and servants for one purpose, will undertake to decide that your other agents and servants, appointed by you for another purpose, have transcended the authority you gave them!" The reply would be, I think, not impertinent,—"Who made you a judge over another's servants? To their own masters they stand or fall."

Sir, I deny this power of State legislatures altogether. It cannot stand the test of examination. Gentlemen may say that, in an extreme case, a State government might protect the people from intolerable oppression. Sir, in such a case the people might protect themselves without the aid of the State governments. Such a case warrants revolution. It must make, when it comes, a law for itself. A nullifying act of a State legislature cannot alter the case, nor make resistance any more lawful. In maintaining these sentiments, sir, I am but asserting the rights of the people. I state what they have declared, and insist on their right to declare it. They have chosen to repose this power in the general government, and I think it my duty to support it, like other constitutional powers.

For myself, sir, I do not admit the competency of South Carolina, or any other State, to prescribe my constitutional duty, or to settle, between me and the people, the validity of laws of Congress for which

I have voted. I decline her umpirage. I have not sworn to support the Constitution according to her construction of its clauses. I have not stipulated, by my oath of office or otherwise, to come under any responsibility, except to the people, and those whom they have appointed to pass upon the question whether laws supported by my votes conform to the Constitution of the country. And, sir, if we look to the general nature of the case, could anything have been more preposterous than to make a government for the whole Union, and yet leave its powers subject, not to one interpretation, but to thirteen or twenty-four interpretations? Instead of one tribunal, established by all, responsible to all, with power to decide for all, shall constitutional questions be left to four-and-twenty popular bodies, each at liberty to decide for itself, and none bound to respect the decisions of others; and each at liberty, too, to give a new construction on every new election of its own members? Would anything with such a principle in it, or rather with such a destitution of all principle, be fit to be called a government? No, sir. It should not be denominated a Constitution. It should be called, rather, a collection of topics for everlasting controversy; heads of debate for a disputatious people. It would not be a government. It would not be adequate to any practical good, or fit for any country to live under.

To avoid all possibility of being misunderstood, allow me to repeat again, in the fullest manner, that I claim no powers for the government by forced or unfair construction. I admit that it is a government of strictly limited powers; of enumerated, specified, and particularized powers; and that whatsoever is not granted is withheld. But notwithstanding all this, and however the grant of powers may be expressed, its limit and extent may yet, in some cases, admit of doubt; and the general government would be good for nothing, it would be incapable of long existing, if some mode had not been provided in which those doubts, as they should arise, might be peaceably but authoritatively solved.

And now, Mr. President, let me run the honorable gentleman's doctrine a little into its practical application. Let us look at his probable *modus operandi*. If a thing can be done, an ingenious man can tell *how* it is to be done, and I wish to be informed *how* this State interference is to be put in practice without violence, bloodshed, and rebellion. We will take the existing case of the tariff law. South Carolina is said to have made up her opinion upon it. If we do not repeal it (as we probably shall not), she will then apply to the case the remedy of her doctrine. She will, we must suppose, pass a law of her legislature declaring the several acts of Congress, usually called the tariff laws, null and void, so far as they respect South Carolina or the citizens thereof. So far, all is a paper transaction, and easy enough. But the collector at Charleston is collecting the duties imposed by these tariff laws. He, therefore, must be stopped. The collector will seize the goods if the tariff duties are not paid. The State authorities will undertake their rescue, the marshal, with his posse, will come to the collector's aid, and here the contest begins. The militia of the State will be called out to sustain the nullifying act. They will march, sir, under a very gallant leader; for I believe the honorable member himself commands the militia of that part of the State. He will raise the NULLIFYING ACT on his standard and spread it out as his banner! It will have a preamble, setting forth that the tariff laws are palpable, deliberate, and dangerous violations of the Constitution! He will proceed, with this banner flying, to the custom-house in Charleston,

"All the while,
Sonorous metal blowing martial sounds."

Arrived at the custom-house, he will tell the collector that he must collect no more duties under any of the tariff laws. This he will be somewhat puzzled to say, by the way, with a grave countenance, considering what hand South Carolina herself had in that of 1816. But, sir, the collector would not, probably, desist at his bidding. He would show him the law of Congress, the treasury instruction, and his own oath of office. He would say he should perform his duty, come what might.

Here would ensue a pause; for they say that a certain stillness precedes the tempest. The trumpeter would hold his breath awhile, and before all this military array should fall on the custom-house, collector, clerks, and all, it is very probable some of those composing it would request of their gallant commander-in-chief to be informed a little upon the point of law; for they have, doubtless, a just respect for his opinions as a lawyer, as well as for his bravery as a soldier. They know he has read Blackstone and the Constitution, as well as Turenne and Vauban. They would ask him, therefore, something concerning their rights in this matter. They would inquire whether it was not somewhat dangerous to resist a law of the United States. What would be the nature of their offense, they would wish to learn, if they, by military force and array, resisted the execution in Carolina of a law of the United States, and it should turn out, after all, that the law *was constitutional*? He would answer, of course, Treason. No lawyer could give any other answer. John Fries, he would tell them, had learned that some years ago. How, then, they would ask, do you propose to defend us? We are not afraid of bullets, but treason has a way of taking people off that we do not much relish. How do you propose to defend us? "Look at my floating banner," he would reply; "see there the *nullifying law*!" Is it your opinion, gallant commander, they would then say, that if we should be indicted for treason, that same floating banner of yours would make a good plea in bar? "South Carolina is a sovereign State," he would reply. That is true; but would the judge admit our plea? "These tariff laws," he would repeat, "are unconstitutional, palpably, deliberately, dangerously." That may all be so; but if the tribunal should not happen to be of that opinion, shall we swing for it? We are ready to die for our country, but it is rather an awkward business, this dying without touching the ground! After all, that is a sort of hemp tax worse than any part of the tariff.

Mr. President, the honorable gentleman would be in a dilemma like that of another great general. He would have a knot before him which he could not untie. He must cut it with his sword. He must say to his followers, "Defend yourselves with your bayonets;" and this is war,— civil war.

Direct collision, therefore, between force and force, is the unavoidable result of that remedy for the revision of unconstitutional laws which the gentleman contends for. It must happen in the very first case to which it is applied. Is not this the plain result? To resist by force the execution of a law, generally, is treason. Can the courts of the United States take notice of the indulgence of a State to commit treason? The common saying, that a State cannot commit treason herself, is nothing to the purpose. Can she authorize others to do it? If John Fries had produced an act of Pennsylvania annulling the law of Congress, would it have helped his case? Talk about it as we will, these doctrines go the length of revolution. They are incompatible with any peaceable administration of the government. They lead directly to disunion and civil commotion; and therefore it is that at their commencement, when they are first found to be maintained by respectable men and in a tangible form, I enter my public protest against them all.

The honorable gentleman argues that if this government be the sole judge of the extent of its own powers, whether that right of judging be in Congress or the Supreme Court, it equally subverts State sovereignty. This the gentleman sees, or thinks he sees, although he cannot perceive how the right of judging in this matter, if left to the exercise of State legislatures, has any tendency to subvert the government of the Union. The gentleman's opinion may be that the right *ought not* to have been lodged with the general government; he may like better such a Constitution as we should have under the right of State interference; but I ask him to meet me on the plain matter of fact. I ask him to meet me on the Constitution itself. I ask him if the power is not found there, clearly and visibly found there?

But, sir, what is this danger, and what are the grounds of it? Let it be remembered that the Constitution of the United States is not unalterable. It is to continue in its present form no longer than the people who established it shall choose to continue it. If they shall become convinced that they have made an injudicious or inexpedient partition and distribution of power between the State governments and the general government, they can alter that distribution at will.

If anything be found in the national Constitution, either by original provision or subsequent interpretation, which ought not to be in it, the people know how to get rid of it. If any construction unacceptable to them be established so as to become practically a part of the Constitution, they will amend it at their own sovereign pleasure. But while the people choose to maintain it as it is, while they are satisfied with it and refuse to change it, who has given, or who can give, to the State legislatures a right to alter it, either by interference, construction, or otherwise? Gentlemen do not seem to recollect that the people have any power to do anything for themselves. They imagine there is no safety for them any longer than they are under the close guardianship of the State legislatures. Sir, the people have not trusted their safety in regard to the general Constitution to these hands. They have required other security, and taken other bonds. They have chosen to trust themselves, first, to the plain words of the instrument and to such construction as the governments themselves, in doubtful cases, should put on their own powers, under their oaths of office, and subject to their responsibility to them: just as the people of a State trust their own State governments with a similar power. Secondly, they have reposed their trust in the efficacy of frequent elections, and in their own power to remove their own servants and agents whenever they see cause. Thirdly, they have reposed trust in the judicial power which, in order that it might be trustworthy, they have made as respectable, as disinterested, and as independent as was practicable. Fourthly, they have seen fit to reply, in case of necessity or high expediency, on their known and admitted power to alter or amend the Constitution, peaceably and quietly, whenever experience shall point out defects or imperfections. And, finally, the people of the United States have at no time, in no way, directly or indirectly, authorized any State legislature to construe or interpret *their* high instrument of government; much less, to interfere, by their own power, to arrest its course and operation.

If, sir, the people in these respects had done otherwise than they have done, their Constitution could neither have been preserved, nor would it have been worth preserving. And if its plain provisions shall now be disregarded, and these new doctrines interpolated in it, it will become as feeble and helpless a being as its enemies, whether early or more recent, could possibly desire. It will exist in every State, but as a poor dependent on State permission. It must borrow leave to be, and will be no longer than State pleasure or State discretion sees fit to grant the indulgence and to prolong its poor existence.

But, sir, although there are fears, there are hopes also. The people have preserved this, their own chosen Constitution, for forty years, and have seen their happiness, prosperity, and renown grow with its growth and strengthen with its strength. They are now, generally, strongly attached to it. Overthrown by direct assault it cannot be; evaded, undermined, NULLIFIED, it will not be, if we and those who shall succeed us here as agents and representatives of the people shall conscientiously and vigilantly discharge the two great branches of our public trust,—faithfully to preserve and wisely to administer it.

Mr. President, I have thus stated the reasons of my dissent to the doctrines which have been advanced and maintained. I am conscious of having detained you and the Senate much too long. I was drawn into the debate with no previous deliberation, such as is suited to the discussion of so grave and important a subject. But it is a subject of which my heart is full, and I have not been willing to suppress the utterance of its spontaneous sentiments. I cannot, even now, persuade myself to relinquish it without expressing once more my deep conviction that, since it respects nothing less than the Union of the States, it is of most vital and essential importance to the public happiness. I profess, sir, in my career hitherto, to have kept steadily in view the prosperity and honor of the whole country, and the preservation of our Federal Union. It is to that Union we owe our safety at home and our consideration and dignity abroad. It is to that Union that we are chiefly indebted for whatever makes us most proud of our country. That Union we reached only by the discipline of our virtues in the severe school of adversity. It had its origin in the necessities of disordered finance, prostrate commerce, and ruined credit. Under its benign influences these great interests immediately awoke as from the dead, and sprang forth with newness of life. Every year of its duration has teemed with fresh proofs of its utility and its blessings; and although our territory has stretched out wider and wider, and our population spread farther and farther, they have not outrun its protection or its benefits. It has been to us all a copious fountain of national, social and personal happiness.

I have not allowed myself, sir, to look beyond the Union, to see what might lie hidden in the dark recess behind. I have not coolly weighed the chances of preserving liberty when the bonds that unite us together shall be broken asunder. I have not accustomed myself to hang over the precipice of disunion, to see whether, with my short sight, I can fathom the depth of the abyss below; nor could I regard him as a safe counselor in the affairs of this government whose thoughts should be mainly bent on considering, not how the Union may be best preserved, but how tolerable might be the condition of the people when it shall be broken up and destroyed. While the Union lasts, we have high, exciting, gratifying prospects spread out before us for us and our children. Beyond that I seek not to penetrate the veil. God grant that in my day, at least, that curtain may not rise! God grant that on my vision never may be opened what lies behind! When my eyes shall be turned to behold for the last time the sun in heaven, may I not see him shining on the broken and dishonored fragments of a once glorious Union; on States dissevered, discordant, belligerent; on a land rent with civil feuds, or drenched, it may be, in fraternal blood! Let their last feeble and lingering glance rather behold the gorgeous ensign of the republic, now known and honored throughout the earth, still full high advanced, its arms and trophies streaming in their original lustre, not a stripe erased or polluted nor a single star obscured, bearing for its motto no such miserable interrogatory as "What is all this worth?" nor those other words of delusion and folly, "Liberty first and Union afterwards;" but everywhere, spread all over in characters of living light, blazing on all its ample folds, as they float over the sea and over the land, and in every wind under the whole heavens, that other sentiment, dear to every true American heart,—Liberty *and* Union, now and forever, one and inseparable!

Questions for Study and Discussion

1. In what paragraph of this speech does Webster first depart from an objective, educational approach to one with propagandistic overtones? Explain.

2. Point out the paragraph in which the speaker first admits that there is room for legitimate disagreement with his point of view.

3. Point out the three consecutive paragraphs in which the speaker makes his first extended and most powerful emotional appeal. Explain the specific bases of the most effective propagandistic appeals in these paragraphs.

4. Which is the most emotionally charged paragraph in the speech?

5. Point out the two most effective sentences in the paragraph designated and analyze the propagandistic elements within them.

Vocabulary Study

Define the following words and phrases as used in this speech: arrest, sovereignty, popular, imposts, confederation, transcended, impertinent, umpirage, disputations, *modus operandi,* subvert, efficacy.

Writing Assignment

Write a composition comparing and contrasting this Senate speech by Webster with the one by McCarthy.

The Man With the Hoe

Edwin Markham

(*Written after seeing Millet's famous painting.*)

God made man in His own image; in the image of God
made He him—Genesis

Bowed by the weight of centuries he leans
Upon his hoe and gazes on the ground,
The emptiness of ages in his face,
And on his back the burden of the world.
Who made him dead to rapture and despair,
A thing that grieves not and that never hopes,
Stolid and stunned, a brother to the ox?
Who loosened and let down this brutal jaw?
Whose was the hand that slanted back this brow?
Whose breath blew out the light within this brain?

Is this the Thing the Lord God made and gave
To have dominion over sea and land,
To trace the stars and search the heavens for power,
To feel that passion of Eternity?
Is this the Dream He dreamed who shaped the suns
And pillared the blue firmament with light?
Down all the stretch of hell to its last gulf
There is no shape more terrible than this—
More tongued with censure of the world's blind greed—
More filled with signs and portents for the soul—
More fraught with menace to the universe.

What gulfs between him and the seraphim!
Slave of the wheel of labor, what to him
Are Plato and the swing of Pleiades?
What the long reaches of the peaks of song,
The rift of dawn, the reddening of the rose?
Through this dread shape the suffering ages look;
Time's tragedy is in that aching stoop;
Through this dread shape humanity betrayed,
Plundered, profaned, and disinherited,
Cries protest to the Judges of the World,
A protest that is also prophecy.

O masters, lords, and rulers in all lands,
Is this the handiwork you give to God,
This monstrous thing distorted and soul-quenched?
How will you ever straighten up this shape,
Touch it again with immortality;
Give back the upward looking and the light;
Rebuild it in the music and the dream;
Make right the immemorial infamies,
Perfidious wrongs, immedicable woes?
O masters, lords and rulers in all lands,
How will the Future reckon with this Man?
How answer his brute question in that hour
When whirlwinds of rebellion shake the world?
How will it be with kingdoms and with kings—
With those who shaped him to the thing he is—
When this dumb Terror shall reply to God,
After the silence of the centuries?

Questions for Study and Discussion

1. What seems to be the poet's major purpose in this poem?

2. By what means does the author build up the emotional power of this poem?

3. Point out two of the most powerful lines in each stanza and explain the bases of their emotional power.

4. Analyze the propagandistic elements of the poem.

Vocabulary Study

Define the following words and phrases as used in this poem: rapture, portents, fraught, Pleiades, soul-quenched, immemorial, perfidious, immedicable.

Writing Assignment

Try converting this poem into prose that will include all of the basic ideas expressed by the poet. Then be able to tell why the prose version is not as good as the poem.

CHAPTER 2

RACIAL AND RELIGIOUS CONSIDERATIONS

The All-White World of Children's Books

Nancy Larrick

"Why are they always *white* children?"

The question came from a five-year-old Negro girl who was looking at a picture-book at the Manhattanville Nursery School in New York. With a child's uncanny wisdom, she singled out one of the most critical issues in American education today: the almost complete omission of Negroes from books for children. Integration may be the law of the land, but most of the books children see are all white.

Yet in Cleveland, 53 per cent of the children in kindergarten through high school are Negro. In St. Louis, the figure is 56.9 per cent. In the District of Columbia, 70 per cent are Negro. Across the country, 6,340,000 nonwhite children are learning to read and to understand the American way of life in books which either omit them entirely or scarcely mention them. There is no need to elaborate upon the damage—much of it irreparable—to the Negro child's personality.

But the impact of all-white books upon 39,600,000 white children is probably even worse. Although his light skin makes him one of the world's minorities, the white child learns from his books that he is the kingfish. There seems little chance of developing the humility so urgently needed for world cooperation, instead of world conflict, as long as our children are brought up on gentle doses of racism through their books.

For the past ten years, critics have deplored the blatant racial bias of the textbooks. Last August, Whitney Young, r., executive director of the National Urban League, attacked the trade books as well. In a nationally syndicated column, he berated American trade book publishers for omitting Negroes from their books for children. As an example, he singled out a Little Golden Book, entitled *A Visit to the Zoo,* which pictures New York's Central Park Zoo in realistic detail except that no dark face is shown. "The entire book-publishing industry is guilty of this kind of omission," charged Mr. Young.

Are the publishers guilty as charged? To find the answer, I undertook a survey of more than 5,000 trade books published for children in 1962, 1963, and 1964. Surely the effect of Little Rock, Montgomery, and Birmingham could be seen by this time, I reasoned.

As a start, I turned to the seventy members of the Children's Book Council who published trade books for children in each of these three years. Sixty-three of them—90 per cent—completed my questionnaire; many gave anecdotal information as well.

Analysis of the replies and examination of several hundred books led to the discouraging conclusion that the vast majority of recent books are as white as the segregated zoo of Golden Press. Of the 5,206 children's trade books launched by the sixty-three publishers in the three-year period, only 349 include one or more Negroes—an average of 6.7 per cent. Among the four publishers with the largest lists of children's books, the percentage of books with Negroes is one-third lower than this average. These four firms (Doubleday, Franklin Watts, Macmillan, and Harper & Row) published 866 books in the three-year period, and only 4.2 per cent have a Negro in text or illustration. Eight publishers produced only all-white books.

Of the books which publishers report as "including one or more Negroes," many show only one or two dark faces in a crowd. In others, the litho-pencil sketches leave the reader wondering whether a delicate shadow indicates a racial difference or a case of sunburn. It would be easy for some of these books to pass as all-white if publishers had not listed them otherwise.

The scarcity of children's books portraying American Negroes is much greater than the figure of 6.7 per cent would indicate, for almost

60 per cent of the books with Negroes are placed outside of continental United States or before World War II, an event as remote to a child as the Boston Tea Party. There are books of African folk tales, reports of the emerging nations of Africa, stones laid in the islands of the Caribbean, biographies of Abraham Lincoln and Jefferson Davis and historical stories about the Underground Railroad. Most of them show a way of life that is far removed from that of the contemporary Negro and may be highly distasteful to him. To the child who has been involved in civil rights demonstrations of Harlem or Detroit, it is small comfort to read of the Negro slave who smilingly served his white master.

Over the three-year period, only four-fifths of one per cent of the children's trade books from the sixty-three publishers tell a story about American Negroes today. Twelve of these forty-four books are the simplest picturebooks, showing Negroes in the illustrations but omitting the word from the text. Examples are *Benjie* by Joan M. Lexau (Dial Press); *Tony's Birds* by Millicent Selsam (Harper & Row); *The Snowy Day* and *Whistle for Willie* by Ezra Jack Keats (Viking).

Those for readers of twelve and up mention the word Negro, and in several the characters tackle critical issues stemming from school integration, neighborhood desegregation, and nonviolent demonstrations. But these books are usually so gentle as to be unreal. There are no cattle prods, no bombings, no reprisals. The white heroine who befriends a Negro in high school enjoys the support of at least one sympathetic parent and an admiring boy friend.

Several books do have outstanding literary merit. Among them are *Roosevelt Grady*, by Louise Shotwell (World), the story of a Negro boy whose parents are migratory workers; *I Marched with Hannibal*, by Hans Baumann (Henry Z. Walck), a boy's report of the brilliant Carthaginian general; *Forever Free: The Story of the Emancipation Proclamation*, by Dorothy Sterling (Doubleday); *The Peoples of Africa*, by Colin M. Turnbull (World); and *The Peaceable Revolution*, by Betty Schechter (Houghton Mifflin), a beautifully written report of three phases of the nonviolent revolution as seen in the work of Thoreau, Gandhi, and the American Negro today.

But these notable titles are the exceptions. "Really fine books are still scarce," says Augusta Baker, coordinator of Children's Services in the New York Public Library. Most of the books depicting Negroes are mediocre or worse. More than one-third have received unfavorable reviews or been ignored by the three major reviewing media in the juvenile book field—*The Horn Book, School Library Journal,* and *Bulletin of the Children's Book Center* of the University of Chicago.

How well do recent children's books depict the Negro? To answer this question I enlisted the help of four Negro librarians who work with children in New York, Chicago, and Baltimore. They rated 149 of the books "excellent" and thirteen "objectionable" in their portrayal of Negroes either through illustration or text.

Among those listed as "objectionable" are three editions of *Little Black Sambo.* Another is *The Lazy Little Zulu,* which a reviewer in *School Library Journal* rated as "Not recommended" because it "abounds in stereotypes."

The identification of Negro stereotypes in adult fiction is vividly spelled out in the unpublished doctoral dissertation (1963) of Catherine Juanita Starke at Teachers College, Columbia University. By analyzing the work of popular American novelists of the past hundred years—from James Fenimore Cooper to James Baldwin and Ralph Ellison—Dr. Starke shows how the Negro in fiction has changed from the ridiculous stock character to the emerging individual who is first a human being and second a Negro.

Early novelists called the Negro "gorilla-like," gave him a name that ridiculed his servile status (Emperor, Caesar, or Brutus, for example), and made his dark skin and thick lips the epitome of the ludicrous. The Negro mother was described as uncomely and ungraceful, clothing her stout body in gaudy calico.

Concurrently there were protest novels which showed the "counter stereotype"—the Negro of unsurpassed grace and beauty, poetic language, great wisdom, and unfaltering judgment.

In the 1920s *The Saturday Evening Post* was building circulation on the Irvin S. Cobb stories of Jeff, the comic Negro menial. Twenty years later, the *Post* was still doing the same with stories by Octavius Roy Cohen and Glenn Allan, who wrote of Negroes who ridiculed themselves and their race.

Perhaps the public opinion which applauded this kind of adult fiction in the forties was responsible also for the 1946 Caldecott Medal award to *The Rooster Crows: A Book of American Rhymes and Jingles,* illustrated by Maud and Miska Petersham and published by Macmillan. Apparently the librarians who selected this book as "the most distinguished American Picture Book for Children published in the United States" in 1945 were not bothered by four pages showing Negro children with great buniony feet, coal black skin, and bulging eyes (in the distance, a dilapidated cabin with a black, gun-toting, barefoot adult). White children in this book are nothing less than cherubic, with dainty little bare feet or well-made shoes. After eighteen years enough complaints had been received to convince the publisher that the book would be improved by deleting the illustrations of Negro children. In the new edition of *The Rooster Crows* (1964) only white children appear.

The 1964 Caldecott Award went to *The Snowy Day*, written and illustrated by Ezra Jack Keats and published by Viking. The book gives a sympathetic picture of just one child—a small Negro boy. The Negro mother, however, is a huge figure in a gaudy yellow plaid dress, albeit without a red bandanna.

Many children's books which include a Negro show him as a servant or slave, a sharecropper, a migrant worker, or a menial.

On the other hand, a number of books have overtones of the "counter stereotype" observed by Dr. Starke—the Negro who is always good, generous, and smiling in the face of difficulties. The nine-year-old hero of *Roosevelt Grady* is one of these. Cheerfully and efficiently he looks out for the younger children or works alongside his parents in the fields, does well at school when there is a school to go to, never loses his temper, and in the end finds a permanent home for the family. The book won the Nancy Bloch Award for the Best Intercultural Children's Book for 1963, although it includes no whites except the teacher, the social worker, and the owner of the trailer camp. Only the pictures indicate that the Gradys and their friends are Negroes.

When the Cleveland Board of Education recommended *Roosevelt Grady* for children's reading, a Negro newspaper deplored this choice because one picture shows a workgang leader grappling with a fat knife-toting Negro who has threatened a young boy. "This is a gross stereotype," was the objection. "But the main story shows beautiful family life among Negroes," was the reply, and *Roosevelt Grady* remains on the Cleveland list.

It is not unusual for critics to disagree as to the effectiveness of the picture of the Negro in a book for children. For example, one of the librarians who helped me gave *Tolliver*, by Florence Means (Houghton Mifflin), a rating of "excellent" for its picture of the Negro. Another criticized it as a modern story set in Fisk University as it was twenty-five years ago. "There has been a revolution down there since then," she wrote. "As a result the book seems somewhat condescending."

Whispering Willows, by Elizabeth Hamilton Friermood (Doubleday), also brought mixed response. It tells of the friendship of a white girl who is a high school senior in the class of 1911 and a Negro girl who works as a domestic in a white home. One librarian gave the book top rating. Another objected to the stereotype of the gentle Negro serving-girl who "knows her place."

These divergent opinions point up the dilemma faced by publishers of children's books. As Albert R. Leventhal, president of Golden Press, explains it, "Golden Press has been criticized from both sides.... Almost every time we reissue *Little Black Sambo* we receive mail deploring it. When it is not available in our Little Golden Book series, we have had letters asking why we do not keep this classic in print!"

One irate Mississippi mother (white) denounced a Little Golden Book of Mother Goose rhymes in a long letter to the Jackson *Clarion-Ledger.* She was aroused by the old rhyme, "Three babes in a basket/And hardly room for two/And one was yellow and one was black/And one had eyes of blue."

"I bought one of the Little Golden Books entitled *Counting Rhymes,*" she wrote. "I was horrified when I was reading to my innocent young child, and, behold, on page 15 there was actually the picture of three small children in a basket together.... and one was a little Negro! I put my child and the book down and immediately called the owner of the drugstore and told him he would not have any more of my business (and I buy a lot of drugs, for I am sick a lot) if he didn't take all the rest of his copies of that book off his shelves."

The illustration shows the Negro baby looking down at a mouse. Determined to get the whole truth about basket integration, the Mississippi mother said she got in touch with the author, presumably Mrs. Goose herself. She said the author gave this explanation of the black child: "He was aware he didn't belong there, and he was looking down in shame because somebody (a symbol for the outside meddling yankees) has placed him in the same basket with the white child, where he didn't really want to be. Also he was looking down at the mouse as if he recognized some kinship to animals."

It's an amusing story. But the sad fact is that many publishing houses are catering to such mothers of the South and of the North. As one sales manager said, "Why jeopardize sales by putting one or two Negro faces in an illustration?"

Caroline Rubin, editor of Albert Whitman, tells of three books brought out in the 1950s: *Denny's Story*, by Eunice Smith, which shows Negro children in illustrations of classroom activity; *Fun for Chris*, by Blossom Randall, with Negro and white children playing together; and *Nemo Meets the Emperor*, by Laura Bannon, a true story of Ethiopia. "The books won favorable comment," writes Mrs. Rubin, "but the effect on sales was negative. Customers returned not only these titles but all stock from our company. This meant an appreciable loss and tempered attitudes toward further use of Negro children in illustrations and text."

Jean Poindexter Colby, editor of Hastings House, faced similar opposition in 1959 when she told her salesmen about plans for *A Summer to Share*, by Helen Kay, the story of a Negro child from the city who visits a white family in the country on a Fresh-Air-Fund vacation. "Galleys on the book had been set and art work was in preparation," Mrs. Colby wrote in the April 1965 issue of *Top of the News*, published by the American Library Association. "I told the salesmen present about the book and immediately encountered such opposition that I felt we either had to cancel the book entirely or change the book to an all-white cast. I wrote apologetically to the author and artist, explaining the situation. They were both cooperative and the racial switch was made." *A Summer to Share* came out in 1960 with the Negro child turned into another white one.

Mrs. Colby's experience with *New Boy in School*, by May Justus (1963), was quite different. This is a simple story for second and third graders about a Negro boy who enters an all-white class. "We had a great deal of trouble selling *New Boy in School* in the South," she writes. "Ed Jervis, our southern salesman, reported that one big jobber would neither stock nor sell it. Another one would only fill special orders." But then favorable reviews began to come in—from *School Library Journal*, the *New York Times*, the Chattanooga *Times*, the Savannah *News*, the Raleigh *Observer*, and the Tulsa *World*, among others. "Now it is a real best seller!" she reports.

Mrs. Colby is also feeling pressure from those who deplore a story that shows the Negro as a slave, a servant, a railroad porter. "Slavery has been practically taboo for many years now as a subject for children's literature," she writes, "and depicting the Negro as anything but perfect is not welcome either. White children and adults can be bad but Negroes cannot. So my job has been to tone down or eliminate such people and situations. . . . But when can we lift the shroud from the truth?"

Not all editors speak as frankly as Mrs. Colby. One, who asks to remain anonymous, says it took her two years to get permission to bring out a book about children in a minority group. Another reports a leading children's book club rejected a 1961 book "especially because Southern subscribers would not like the way this heroine tackled the problem of prejudice." Although no other publisher commented on book-club selection, this is undoubtedly an important influence in editorial decisions.

When the directors of eight children's book clubs were questioned about the books they have distributed since September 1962, they listed only a tiny fraction that includes Negroes. Four hard-cover book clubs offered 230 books of which only six mention Negroes. Four paperback book clubs distributed 1,345 titles with Negroes included in fifty-three.

Not one of the fourteen Negro books on the ALA list of Notable Children's Books in 1962, 1963, and 1964 won the more lucrative award of book-club selection.

In the two Negro books distributed by the Weekly Reader Children's Book Club—*Long Lonesome Train*, by Virginia Ormsby (Lippincott), and *Skinny*, by Robert Burch (Viking)—the Negro characters are Aunt Susan, her son Matt, a fireman, and the handyman, Roman. Richard R. RePass, director of this hard-cover book club, says, "These I would consider neither germane to the plot, nor particularly flattering to our Negro citizens. The main reason why there are not more books with Negro characters among our book club selections is the general dearth of good candidates."

It should be explained that the hard-cover book clubs send the same book to every child while the paperback book clubs ask each member to choose one title from a list of ten to a dozen. Perhaps for this reason the paperback clubs have distributed certain titles which the hard-cover book clubs would not take a chance on. One of these is *Mary Jane*, by Dorothy Sterling, published by Doubleday in hard cover and given a two-star rating by *School Library Journal*. It also received the Nancy Bloch Award for 1959. This is the realistic story of a Negro girl who is the first to enter an all-white junior high school that bristles with prejudice.

Mary Jane has not been selected for hard-cover book club distribution.

But after several years of deliberation, the Arrow Book Club, one of the paperbook clubs, offered *Mary Jane* to its fifth- and sixth-grade members. By December 1964, 159,895 copies had been sold. "Only six letters of complaint were received," reports Lilian Moore, Arrow Book Club editor, "all from adults in the South. And many warm comments have come in from the children who read *Mary Jane*."

By March 1965, *Mary Jane* had been published in Swedish, Dutch, Czech, German, and Russian editions. According to *Publishers' Weekly*, the Children's Literature House of Moscow reports 100,000 copies of *Mary Jane* have been printed there and are stirring up "lively interest."

Obviously not all children's books can or should include Negroes. The story of a family in Plymouth Colony or in modern Sweden would be distorted if Negro faces were shown. Certainly no author or artist should be required to follow any formula for integration.

But, consciously or unconsciously, most writers and artists have long been following the formula for pure white books. Some of the distortions caused by this formula are ludicrous. For example, *We Live in the City*, a simple picture-book by Bert Ray (Children's Press, 1963), tells of Laurie and Gregg looking over the city of Chicago—a city that apparently has no Negroes.

Only white people appear in *Your Brain*, by Margaret O. Hyde (McGraw-Hill, 1964). In books of science experiments, it is usually a white hand that holds the thermometer, a white arm reaching for a test tube, white children feeding the guinea pig. In books of poetry it is a white face smiling over the first stanza.

While making a survey of G. P. Putnam's books of the past three years, Putnam's juvenile editor Tom MacPherson came upon an Illustrated novel about professional football, with not a single Negro player among the professionals. "That embarrassed us considerably," he wrote.

Several juvenile editors expressed similar concern. "I was surprised," wrote Virginia Fowler, editor of Knopf's Borzoi Books for Young People, "to realize how few books we have on our list that accept an integrated society.... as I look at my titles and think of the books [I realize] in many instances they could easily have been books about a Negro child or could have been shared books of child and friend."

Executives at Golden Press analyzed the Little Golden Books of 1962, 1963, and 1964 and decided that thirteen of their all-white books could have included Negroes in a perfectly natural, realistic way. One of these is *A Visit to a Children's Zoo*, cited by Whitney Young, Jr. ("He is certainly right," said the Golden Press editor. "A missed opportunity for a natural handling of the situation.")

In the meantime, the Negro market has expanded to at least $25 billion in consumer purchasing power, according to John H. Johnson, publisher of *Ebony*. The Negro school population and the number of Negro teachers are growing rapidly, particularly in the large urban centers. With vastly increased funds available through government sources, a huge economic force is building up for integrated schools and integrated reading materials.

Lacking good children's books about Negro history, many school libraries are purchasing the $5.95 adult book, *A Pictorial History of the Negro in America*, by Langston Hughes and Milton Meltzer (Crown). Boards of education in both New York and Detroit have written and published their own paperback Negro histories for young readers.

The integrated readers produced by the Detroit Board of Education and published in 1964 by Follett for in-school use are now being sold in paperback in the book stores—where parents are reported to be buying eagerly.

The market that most publishers are avoiding is being cultivated by— of all corporations—the Pepsi-Cola Company, which has produced an excellent LP recording *Adventures in Negro History*. This has been made available to schools through local soft-drink distributors. The first pressing of 10,000 copies was grabbed up almost immediately, according to Russell Harvey, director of Special Market Services. After a year, 100,000 copies had been distributed and a second record is being made. (The first record, filmstrip, and script may be purchased for $5 through the Special Markets Division of Pepsi-Cola, 500 Park Avenue, New York, N.Y. 10022).

What about the children's books coming out in 1965? According to reports from editors, about 9 per cent of their 1965 books will include one or more Negroes. This is 1.5 per cent above the average for 1964.

In addition, there will be a continuing trend to up-date or reissue earlier books that include Negroes. Among those reissued in the past three years: *My Dog Rinty*, by Ellen Tarry and Marie Hall Ets (Viking) ; *Black Fire: A Story of Henri Christophe*, by C. Newcomb (McKay) ; *Famous Women Singers*, by Ulrich (Dodd, Mead) ; *The Story of the Negro*, by Arna Bontemps (Knopf) ; and *The Barred Road*, by Adele DeLeeuw (Macmillan). *Ladder to the Sky*, by Ruth Forbes Chandler

(Abelard), which went out of print for several years, has returned in 1965.

This year Doubleday is launching its new Zenith Books, "to explain America's minorities." These books are planned for supplementary reading in high school English and social studies classes. The accompanying Teacher's Manual puts them more definitely with textbooks than with trade books.

Many juvenile editors who state determination to present a completely fair picture of Negroes in our multiracial society add the reservation: "where it seems natural and not forced."

"We don't set about deliberately to do these things," writes Margaret McElderry, editor of children's books at Harcourt, Brace & World, "but take them as they seem natural and right."

"We plan to continue to introduce Negroes where it can be handled in context and illustrations in a normal way," says Margaret E. Braxton, vice president of Garrard Publishing Company. "Artificial books forcing the racial issue are *not* a part of our future plans."

"Most publishers are eagerly looking for manuscripts that deal with integration and the problems faced by Negroes in our country," writes Mrs. Esther K. Meeks, children's book editor of Follett Publishing Company. "If we found twice as many publishable books that included Negroes in a natural and sympathetic manner, we should be happy to publish them." (*South Town*, by Lorenz Graham, winner of the Follett Award of 1958, is one of the few books for young people that tells a realistic story of the violence resulting from racial prejudice.)

Fabio Coen, editor of Pantheon Books for children, makes this comment: "A book even remotely discussing racial problems has to deal with the subject with the same spontaneity and honesty that is basically required of any book. To my mind, it is therefore impossible to commission one."

The newly formed Council for Interracial Books for Children operates on the principle that, given encouragement, authors and artists will create good children's books that include nonwhites, and that given the manuscripts, publishers will produce and market them. The Council, sponsored by a group including Benjamin Spock, Ben Shahn, Langston Hughes, Mary Gaver, Alex Rosen, Harold Taylor, Harry Golden, and Sidonie M. Gruenberg, will offer prizes for outstanding manuscripts and will negotiate with editors for their publication.

The crisis that brought the Council into being is described by one of its organizing members, Elinor Sinnette, district school librarian for the Central and East Harlem Area of New York: "Publishers have participated in a cultural lobotomy. It is no accident that Negro history and Negro identification have been forgotten. Our society has contrived to make the American Negro a rootless person. The Council for Interracial Books for Children has been formed to relieve this situation."

Whether the Council gets many books into print or not, it can accomplish a great deal simply by reminding editors and publishers that what is good for the Ku Klux Klan is not necessarily good for America —or for the book business. White supremacy in children's literature will be abolished when authors, editors, publishers, and booksellers decide that they need not submit to bigots.

Questions for Study and Discussion

1. According to this report, what Negro stereotypes are often found in children's books?

2. What stereotypes of white people sometimes appear in children's books?

3. What Negro stereotypes often appear in adult fiction?

4. What counter stereotypes of Negroes occasionally appear in literature?

5. Why do some publishers use stereotypes in their books?

6. By what means do most publishers avoid the use of stereotypes?

Vocabulary Study

Define the following words as used in this report: racism, blatant, berated, anecdotal, litho-pencil, media, cherubic, bandanna, condescending, dilemma, jeopardize, galleys, taboo, lucrative, germane, dearth, lobotomy.

Writing Assignment

Write a composition expressing your reaction to the information presented in this report.

What the Historian Owes the Negro

Benjamin Quarles

Emergence of long-obscured facets of Negro history brings with it the challenge to develop new perspectives on this nation's past.

Just as the Negro's place in American life is now changing, so is his place in American history. The true role of the Negro in our country's past is emerging from the shadows. Like other aspects of our national life, history is now being desegregated; old outlooks are giving way to new.

The role of Negro brawn in the physical building of America is not an unfamiliar story, but today's readers are prepared to go further—to reflect, for example, upon Margaret Just Butcher's carefully considered statement that "some of the most characteristic features of American culture are derivatives of the folk life and spirit of this darker tenth of the population." It is no longer somewhat unsettling to come across a book that credits the Negro with enlarging the meaning of freedom in America, giving it new expressions. In today's schools, a youngster would react more receptively than ever to finding out, for example, that the first non-Indian to explore portions of Arizona and New Mexico was a Negro; that a Negro was the first to die at the Boston Massacre; that a Negro wrote the second book of verse published by any woman in colonial America; that a Negro was the first Chicagoan; that a Negro was one of the three commissioners who laid out the city of Washington; that a Negro preached the first Protestant sermon heard west of the Mississippi; that a Negro invented a vacuum cap that revolutionized the sugar industry; that another Negro invented the shoe-lasting machine that had a similar effect in the shoe industry; that a Negro accompanied Peary at the discovery of the North Pole; and that the first American fatality in World War II was a Negro.

Negro history's coming of age springs from no single cause. In recent decades anthropology and related fields have exploded racial myths.

Thoughtful people have sensed the peril inherent in the kind of racist dogma that helped to spawn a Hitler and to create a Dachau. And the Negro's own stepped-up drive for equal status since World War II has called for a revitalized study of our country's past. In the larger cities— New York, Washington, Detroit, and Los Angeles, among others—colored parents have requested that social studies books used in the public schools deal adequately and fairly with minorities. Because they now know their past better, Negroes are no longer ashamed of it. Gone is the defensive, apologetic tone.

Another reason for the new Negro history is the changing historical image of Africa. "The existence of African history has, in recent years, achieved widespread recognition," writes Robert I. Rotberg of Harvard, in his authoritative *Political History of Tropical Africa.* No longer is it tenable to believe that when the Europeans first ventured down the African coastline in the mid-1400s, they found the natives living in barbarism and savagery. No longer can it be said that when the ancestor of the American Negro arrived in the New World he was "culturally naked."

In the last twenty-five years a growing number of white historians have viewed the Negro from new and fresh angles. These include Dwight L. Dumond, an authority on the abolition movement and the ante bellum free Negro; Kenneth M. Stampp, who portrayed slavery and the slave somewhat differently from the traditional viewpoint; James M. McPherson, who saw the Civil War Negro as a participant rather than as a spectator; and C. Vann Woodward, whose *The Strange Career of Jim Crow* gave us a new perspective on race relations in the South. The number of articles on the Negro submitted to *The American Historical Review* also is multiplying, according to Henry R. Winkler, managing editor. To write or to read Negro history is now no longer to venture into *terra incognita* or to take an excursion, at one's own risk, through history's underworld.

Why has Negro history been so late in coming into its own, and why in so many quarters are the shores still only dimly seen?

"The use of history is to tell us what we are, for at birth we are merely vessels, and we become what our traditions pour into us," Learned Hand has written. But this phrase, trenchant as it is, requires one major modification: We become what our *traditionalists, i.e.,* our historians, pour into us. Events of the past do not exist of themselves, but only as they reach us via their chroniclers.

Much of history is interpretation. Its most trusted interpreter is, of course, the professionally trained historian, his name trailed by clusters of letters. Guardian of the sacred word, he knows that he is expected to bring an objective intelligence to his work—to winnow and sift sensitively and then to relate what it was that actually happened. This is a tall order. For despite his professional training, the historian's own values and beliefs are likely to be intrusive. His own social outlook may give a "personal equation" to his reconstructions of the past. This tendency, however natural, poses a real problem. One who works from what Oliver Wendell Holmes called an "inarticulate major premise" may well wind up with something less than the whole truth. History then becomes image-making with footnotes, its brush strokes blurred by what logicians call the fallacy of initial predication.

Such historical introspectionism has inevitably worked to the detriment of the various minority groups in America—the Asiatics, the Spanish-speaking peoples, and immigrants from southern Europe—all of whom have been treated as "out-groups." Negroes, especially, have been the objects of this narrow-mindedness on the part of historians. Speaking in 1840, Henry Highland Garnet, then beginning a long career as a militant clergyman, clearly stated the problem: "All other races are permitted to travel over the wide fields of history and pluck the flowers that blossom there—to glean up heroes, philosophers, sages, and poets, and put them into a galaxy of brilliant genius; but if a black man attempts to do so, he is met at the threshold by the objection, 'You have no ancestry behind you.' "

A researcher is often engaged in a subconscious mission, his conclusions already lodged in the back of his head. He has, in Herbert Butterfield's words, "a magnet in his mind," one that impels him to extract from the documents such data as fit into a framework already fashioned. When, as he combs the sources, this researcher comes across a reference to Negroes, he turns the page as though it were blank. When one goes fishing for facts, writes historian Edward Hallett Carr, what he catches will depend partly on chance, but primarily upon other factors, such as "the part of the ocean he chooses to fish in," the kind of tackle he selects, and the kind of fish he wants to catch. And, to take Carr's figure a step further, an unwanted specimen is likely to be quickly thrown back into the water.

As often as not this mind-set of the historian takes the form of glorifying his own. Historians are not immune to ancestor worship. To puff up one's own ethnic group is not the exclusive province of a Hitler (whose favorite subject was history). As practitioners of the dictum, "Be to her faults a little blind, / Be to her virtues very kind," historians tend to reflect rather than to correct the group mores. This ethnocentric attitude has had serious implications for the Negro. Since American history has been written, in the main, by men of old English stock, the role of the Negro could hardly come in for a rounded appraisal. Such a historian felt no kinship with the colored people, no identity. To glorify one's own is certainly no sin, but in a many-faceted culture such as America's this in-group emphasis may amount to a denigration of other component population elements.

Four years ago the American Historical Association and two of its counterparts in Great Britain—the Historical Association of England and Wales, and the British Association for American Studies—agreed to launch a joint Anglo-American study entitled, "National Bias in the School Books of the United Kingdom and the United States." History teachers had long been strongly suspicious that a strong national slant characterized the textbooks of both America and England; it hardly need be added that the joint committee of historians found (in their recently published book, *The Historian's Contribution to Anglo-American Misunderstanding**) this to be true to some degree in every one of the thirty-six works put under examination. If two nations as close as these have reason to be concerned about the textbook bias each shows against the other, imagine, if you will, the kind of attitudes that English and American textbook writers might exhibit toward peoples of another color, peoples with whom they discerned few ties and felt no sense of community.

An almost complementary refrain to group glorification has been the historian's tendency to take his cue from the civilization or culture that is currently dominant. For the past five centuries the dominant peoples and nations have been of Germanic-tribes origin and have been located in Europe. Nobody can touch the historian for hindsight—he knows to begin with "where the bodies are buried." He knows that for half a millennium the nations of Western Europe were destined to predominate. Thus, it is natural for him to have a Europocentric view of the modern world, to believe that non-Western cultures were below par if not permanently inferior. Less blatantly, but no less surely,

*See Chapter 3, "Nationalistic Bias in History Textbooks." [Editor's note.]

writers of history have shared Tennyson's belief, "Better fifty years of Europe than a cycle of Cathay."

The fact that these dominant nations of Europe were white was bound to make a deep impression on observers. Europe was equated with white, which in turn was equated with civilization and progress. Non-European was equated with non-white, which in turn meant outside the pale—stagnant if not primitive, lesser breeds standing in long-time tutelage to Western man. These assumptions, reflected in the writings of generation after generation of historians, certainly did the Negro no service.

The belief in white superiority has been fully shared by historians. No less than other Americans, they have found it possible to subscribe simultaneously to the all-men-are-created-equal dictum of the Declaration of Independence and the theory of "divine-right white." Hence, the historian's treatment of the Negro has been more of a conditioned reflex than of an examined premise.

It follows, then, that the great majority of historians have operated under the assumption that the role of the Negro in American life was hardly worth considering. They believed that the Negro contributed very little to our country's history, and, if asked whether on the whole the Negro has been an asset or a liability, they would have answered quickly, as if no reflection were required. Basically an "unperson," the Negro was viewed by the historian as part of a monolithic mass that was to be classified as the cause of something or the effect on something—with causes and effects, however varied, being alike in one respect: their threat to the general welfare, the common good.

Moreover, the sources used by historians reflected the currently unflattering attitude toward the Negro. No concept was more deeply rooted in American thought than that of Negro inferiority. Whites who crossed the color line were publicly punished. Within a dozen years after the first Negroes landed at Jamestown, the Virginia court ordered one Hugh Davis to be whipped for "defiling his body in lying with a Negro." From the beginning Negroes were not thought to be assimilable; they were not considered fellow parishioners in the church or even fellow roisterers at the tavern.

This conviction of Negro inequality was strong throughout colonial America. Even in New England, with its sparse colored population, the free Negro was placed on a different footing from others, reflecting the view that he was inferior. Phillis Wheatley, bred in Boston although born in Africa, took note, on the eve of the Revolutionary War, of the prevailing attitude toward the Negro:

> Some view our sable race with scornful eye,
> "Their colour is a diabolic die."

The Founding Fathers, revered by historians for over a century and a half, did not conceive of the Negro as part of the body politic. Theoretically, these men believed in freedom for everyone, but in actuality they found it hard to imagine a society in which Negroes were of equal status to whites. Jefferson, who was far more liberal than the run of his contemporaries, was nevertheless certain "that the two races, equally free, cannot live in the same government."

In the eighteenth and early nineteenth centuries, most of the people of the United States were tolerant of slavery. Southern spokesmen assured all who would listen that the Negro, by color, culture, and nature, was peculiarly fitted for slavery. Indeed, it was for him an upward step in civilization, plus a sheltered way of life. Writing as late as 1929, the authoritative U. B. Phillips stated that "the home of a planter or of a well-to-do townsman was likely to be 'a magnificent Negro boarding-house,' at which an indefinite number of servants and their dependents and friends were fed."

The corrosive race issue inevitably entered into the historian's treatment of the Civil War and Reconstruction. Most historians, having an aristocratic conception of tragedy, were more deeply moved by the suffering of the rich than that of the poor. Hence, it is not surprising that the misfortunes of the bankrupt and ruined planters would evoke a sympathetic response. The race issue emerged more pointedly in the historian's assessment of the trying Reconstruction decade. He tended to identify with the defeated and stricken white Southerner, rather than with the newly freed Negro people. Therefore, he was prepared to accept at face value the appraisal of Reconstruction formulated by fellow guildsmen such as William A. Dunning, Walter L. Fleming, and John W. Burgess.

Southern sympathizers to the core, these writers made the Negro the whipping boy of Reconstruction. Their charges were familiar: Negro legislators wasted money or stole it; the Negro was given the ballot but he didn't know what to do with it. To an ex-Confederate soldier such as Burgess, who exerted a strong influence on Reconstruction historiography, nothing good could come from the Negro. "A black skin," he wrote, "means membership in a race of men which never of itself succeeded in subjecting passion to reason."

Turn-of-the-century historians shared the Burgess viewpoint. The new imperialism of the Western powers, starting in the 1870s, reached this country in the 1890s with the Spanish-American War. With it came the concept of the "white man's burden"—the mission to spread Anglo-Saxon civilization to backward peoples in far-away places. Applying the Darwinian theory of evolution to social development, historians now discovered added support for their belief in the basic inequality of dark-skinned peoples.

For the next third of a century—down to the eve of World War II— American historical thought and expression were pervaded by a justification of Jim Crow, whether by a Virginian such as Philip A. Bruce or a Californian such as H. H. Bancroft, historian of the West. Like their predecessors, these interpreters of the past would have scoffed at the charge that they were prejudiced. To them the inferiority of the Negro was an undeniable fact, not an assumption, and certainly not a manifestation of bigotry.

The prejudgment of the scholar has not been the only hurdle for Negro history. There were more conscious considerations, such as the paucity of source materials. John Chavis of the Detroit Historical Museum has posed the problem of the researcher in Negro history. "Where are the diaries, the family Bibles, the correspondence in fancy script tied in dusty bundles? Where are the silver services, the porringers, the samplers, the furniture dark and glossy, the oil portraits of awesome ancestors?"

History is written from the viewpoint of the articulate, of those who had the foresight to put their thoughts on paper. Unless records of an event or a person exist in sufficient supply, the historian is handicapped, his emphasis may lack balance, and his conclusions must be that much more tentative.

Much of the historical information about Negroes must be dug out; it is not readily available in printed form as are papers of the Presidents or other men of great place—the Hamiltons, Clays, and Calhouns. The Negro has not been articulate in a literary sense; indeed, he was relatively unlettered and hence lacking in a literary tradition. And those Negroes who could read and write were not fully aware of the importance of preserving records—minutes, letters, and fugitive publications. The problem, too, of Negro history is that the Negro, unlike many of the later arrivals in America, never had a foreign press; his past has been so interwoven with the American past as to make it difficult to separate the strands. [See "The Racial News Gap," *Saturday Review*, August 13.]

Another conscious consideration in Negro history-writing is the matter of dollars and cents. A historian likes to feel that his manuscript will attract publishers and readers; he may shy from a topic that would seem to present abnormal difficulties in getting attention. The questions that run in the mind of the historian are down-to-earth: "If I were to tackle subject X, who would finance research on this kind of topic? Who would publish it? Who would buy it?" A manuscript with a limited sales potential may never see print, no matter how meritorious or path-breaking.

Negro history manuscripts have been prominent among those lacking pocketbook appeal. Manuscripts that challenged deeply held beliefs about the Negro have not been welcomed by publishers, who have not wished to antagonize potential white buyers, particularly in the sensitive South. Even in more liberal centers booksellers have been skittish about Negro-history titles, feeling that the demand would be small.

This hesitancy by white publishers and authors concerning Negro history had the predictable effect of making Negroes bestir themselves. As early as 1883 this desire to bring to public attention the untapped material on the Negro prompted George Washington Williams to publish his two-volume *History of the Negro Race in America from 1619 to 1880*. A many-sided man—soldier, theologian, lawyer, public office-holder—Williams was hailed as a "Negro Bancroft." His effort was a worthy one, although his style was grandiloquent.

The first formally trained Negro historian was W. E. B. DuBois, whose doctoral dissertation, published in 1895 (*The Suppression of the African Slave-Trade to the United States of America 1638–1870*), became the first title to be published in the Harvard Historical Studies. DuBois was not destined to give independent scholarship his chief devotion; turning to civil rights, he became one of the founders of the NAACP, and editor of its organ, *The Crisis*.

It was with Carter G. Woodson, another Harvard Ph.D., that Negro history took a quantum leap. Convinced that unless something were done to rescue the Negro from history's oversight, he would become "a negligible factor in the thought of the world," Woodson, in 1915, founded the Association for the Study of Negro Life and History. During the preceding twenty years an American Negro Academy had been founded in Washington, and a Negro Society for Historical Research had appeared in New York. But these organizations had lacked a Woodson. In 1916, he began publication of a scholarly quarterly, *The Journal of Negro History.* To bring out book-length studies, Woodson, in 1920, organized the Associated Publishers, with himself as president of the board of trustees.

Writers for Woodson's publication strove for objectivity, to avoid chauvinism or overstatement. They knew that their books and articles would be received with some puzzlement by Negro glorifiers—black supremacists who, in the words of A. A. Schomburg, "glibly tried to prove that half of the world's geniuses have been Negroes and to trace the pedigree of nineteenth-century Americans from the Queen of Sheba." ("Lord, forgive me if my need / Sometimes shapes a human creed," wrote the Negro poet, Countee Cullen.)

Negro historians had to be careful because they knew that the data they presented often seemed incredible to the reader, being so unexpected. But the care exercised by the professionally trained Negro historian was no guarantee that he would be read. This problem of a slim audience for histories written by Negroes was eloquently stated by George A. Myers, a Cleveland barbershop proprietor who personally knew the great historian, James Ford Rhodes, and asked him to give credit in his widely read writings to the valor of the Negroes who had fought in the Civil War. "Negro historians might write until their hands palsied, and all they might write would not be given the credence of one chapter in your history," wrote Myers, a Negro himself. "Plainly speaking, it makes a difference who says it." Rhodes ignored Myers's Macedonian cry in 1915. But since then, as has been noted, the picture has changed.

The new emphasis on the Negro as a contributing participant to American life since he arrived on these shores does not require that historians undergo professional retraining. Historians will continue to view the past from the vantage point of the present (as if there were any other way) and they will continue to take pride in their own country or group (as if there were anything wrong with this, within reason). Nor, as desirable as it might be, can we expect most historians to enter into the thinking and the feelings of people they regard as different from themselves.

But the careful reader, of whatever hue himself, has a right to expect that the historian recognize that the record of the colored American has something to add to the knowledge and understanding of our country's past, something to add to the story of human collaboration and interdependence. Readers have a right to expect that the historian be led to examine more closely anti-minority assumptions that may have crept into his thinking.

To say that the historian is morally accountable would be gratuitous. But to the extent that he helps to shape the national character in a pluralistic land such as ours, to that extent a special responsibility may inescapably be his.

Questions for Study and Discussion

1. What makes the tone of the first five paragraphs of this essay more educational than propagandistic?

2. What personal problems expose the historian to the temptation of propagandizing history?

3. Show how Lippmann's discussion of "Stereotypes" explains Quarles' contention in the ninth paragraph.

4. What is the author's aim in this essay?

5. To what extent has the author used propagandistic devices to achieve his aim? Cite specific examples.

6. Cite evidence to show that the author has consciously tried to be unbiased in his arguments.

Vocabulary Study

Define the following words and phrases as used in this essay: anthropology, *terra incognita*, trenchant, intrusive, galaxy, group mores, ethnocentric, denigration, pale, tutelage, conditioned reflex, monolithic, guildsmen, bigotry, quantum, chauvinism, gratuitous, pluralistic.

Writing Assignment

Write a composition expressing your reaction to this essay.

Types of Anti-Catholicism

Robert McAfee Brown

As the nation at large has been reminded during the recent spate of "Reformation Sunday" sermons, addresses and rallies, Protestants claim that their faith is "positive" (a term which has no connection, incidentally, with the booming cult of "positive thinking"). The term "protestant," we have again been reminded, is not as negativistic as it sounds. The real meaning of the word *pro-testari* is to testify on behalf of something, to make positive affirmations, to witness for, rather than against. This theme is picked up each fall, as Protestants celebrate the nailing of the Ninety-Five Theses on the chapel door by Martin Luther, and then in most quarters it is tucked away in spiritual mothballs for another fifty-one Sundays.

So that if one is going to be factually honest, one is forced to report that a great many Protestant laymen, abysmally ignorant of their own Protestant heritage, tend to define their faith in negative terms: to be a "protestant" is *not* to be a "catholic." If they are uneasy about this, they are even more uneasy about the fact that they do not know what the positive affirmations should be, and if they know what the positive affirmations should be, they are inclined to be slightly embarrassed by them. Their ministers should, and often do, know better, but in these days of the "return to religion," the religion to which many Protestant churches are "returning" is a far cry from the Reformation, let alone the New Testament. The result is that in this kind of situation, it is a lot easier (and more fun) to throw stones at the Catholics, than to use those stones to build a solid edifice of faith.

There are many varieties of anti-Catholicism in Protestant circles today. Some are petty. Some are vicious. Some are significant. And although every Catholic must have encountered some of them, a brief roster is called for.

1. *The "if-they're-for-it-I'm-agin'-it" type.* This is the kind of "protestant" (the quotation marks are used advisedly) who uses all his energy being against Catholicism. His creed is entirely negative. He does

not believe in the Pope. He does not believe in the saints. He does not believe in Purgatory. He does not believe in "priests" (said with an inflection to indicate horror) or "priestcraft" (which carries sufficient connotation without inflection). He is against an ambassador to the Vatican. He is against parochial schools. He is against Catholics who run for public office.

At any point where you are in doubt about his position, it can be clarified simply by telling him where the Catholics stand, and he will instinctively jump to the other pole of the argument. He doesn't know much about the place of Mary in Christian thought, for example, but when he discovers how highly she is regarded by Catholics, that settles the matter. No "feminine deities" for him, thank you.

It is difficult to pin him down on the content of his own Protestant faith. He feels that it has something to do with "freedom" and "the right of private judgment," and he may even talk vaguely about freedom of conscience, or freedom of worship, or (what has recently become quite popular) freedom to believe in whatever god you please. But this is all very hazy. He's on much firmer ground describing the things in which he does not believe.

2. *The Protestant "bigot" approach.* The word "bigot" is used loosely and spitefully and sometimes gleefully in Protestant–Catholic exchanges. It may seem a poor word to introduce into the present discussion. The breed does exist, however, and neither group is without its accomplished exemplars.

In the present writer's book, the Protestant bigot is one who cultivates the art of knowing all the dirt about the Catholics. All he does is give you the "facts," the positive information. No negativist, he! He can give you detailed accounts of the immoralities of all the Renaissance Popes, he has a mass of data about the Spanish Inquisition, he keeps a file of all the unwise things that members of the hierarchy unwisely allow to get into print, he can furnish you with a running account of the publicity maneuvers of every Cardinal who has ever been near a helicopter. (He seems to miss the times when members of the hierarchy condemn segregated Catholic worship and receive commendation from Rome.) He can tell you all about the Knights of Columbus "oath," and a dozen other things, each more blood-curdling than the last. He knows all the worst, and he will not listen to the best. His favorite word to describe fellow-Protestants who have good things to say about Catholicism is "naive." His next favorite word is "misinformed."

It is in this category that most Catholics seem to put what they call "Blanshardism," a term springing from the very vigorous attacks on Catholicism by Paul Blanshard. (I have discovered that among Catholics the term carries about the same emotional and moral connotations that the term "McCarthyism" carries for political liberals.) The present writer does not mean to include Mr. Blanshard himself among the front-line bigots. But if another term may be coined, the "Blanshardites" often are in the front lines.

With regard to Mr. Blanshard himself, there are areas where he has amassed some impressive documentation. Even some Catholic reviewers were not totally unkind to his book on the Irish and Catholic power. But Mr. Blanshard presents his material in a tone and manner which are usually so ardently "anti-Catholic" that the force of his argument is often lost. If his facts were as watertight as he claims, it would seem that they could be presented in a dispassionate enough way to speak for themselves. One sometimes wonders whether it would be worse to live in a country dominated by the Catholic mentality Mr. Blanshard describes, or the Blanshard mentality which he embodies. Protestants and Catholics should be aware that Mr. Blanshard writes from an almost completely "secularist" viewpoint, rather than from a distinctively Protestant one, and that technically he does not belong in a description of *Protestant* types of anti-Catholicism. But actually he does belong, since so many Protestants make undiscriminating use of his material.

3. The *"when-they-get-to-be-the-majority-they'll-destroy-our-freedom"* angle. The advocate of this position has accumulated a great deal of data on the situation in predominantly Catholic countries like Spain, Italy, Colombia and Argentina. He points out that in these countries Protestants are not only denied many rights which are granted to Catholics, but also that they are often persecuted if they try to evangelize. The conclusion is reached that if Catholics ever become the predominant group in America the same thing will happen here.

Now unfortunately, among thinking Protestants, this line of reasoning cannot be dismissed quite so easily as those we have looked at so far. For there *is* considerable evidence that in some predominantly Catholic countries, Protestants often do suffer for their minority status. Churches have been burned. Protestant ministers have been attacked. Priests have incited anti-Protestant riots. Furthermore there are plenty of extant writings by Catholics indicating their avowal of democracy when in the minority, and of authoritarianism when in the majority. And there is the passage so well-known to Protestants in Ryan and Boland's *Catholic Principles of Politics,* which indicates that if Catholics were an overwhelming majority in America, they would have to deny certain rights to Protestants. No rapport can be reached as long as Catholics simply deny that these things are so.

There is, of course, another side to the picture, a side about which most Protestants know very little, and no rapport can be reached so long as Protestants simply deny that this side of the picture exists. This is the dimension in *American* Catholic thought which is concerned about civil liberties for minorities, which insists that the pattern in Spain should not be normative for other countries, which publicly disavows the "grab for secular power" which Protestants fear, and so forth. It finds its voice in such periodicals as *America* and *The Commonweal,* and in the writings of such men as Father John Courtney Murray.

However, to be descriptively honest about Protestantism, it must further be pointed out that to cite this kind of evidence (as, for example Will Herberg does in his *Protestant-Catholic-Jew*) is not to convince most Protestants, who simply respond that such voices are only a tiny minority in present American Catholicism, and that they would be swallowed up, stifled or destroyed come the day of an America eighty-five per cent Catholic. As a result, the misgivings remain.

4. *The vast-monolithic-structure-apprehension.* The representative of this position has a curious, and often envious, way of looking at Roman Catholicism. He sees it as one vast structure, totally alike in every part. He is sure that there are no matters on which Catholics disagree, and that if they do, a word from the priest will set matters straight. He talks about the "Catholic vote," the "Catholic mind," and looks with fear on the phenomena of Catholic organizations paralleling most of the "regular" organizations in American life. He sees Catholic war veterans, Catholic schools, Catholic hospitals, Catholic charities, ad infinitum. All of these, he is sure, are ruled in hierarchical fashion in a vast pyramid of power culminating in the Pope.

Part of this apprehension springs from what may be an unarticulated and even unacknowledged fear of institutions which are "undemocratic" in their structure. Democracy equals freedom, Catholicism is undemocratic, therefore Catholicism equals un-freedom or tyranny: this is one way the syllogism might run.

It is difficult to allay this apprehension in principle and the difficulty must be faced by Catholics. It is a little easier, perhaps, to allay it in fact, for it is patently observable that "thought control" does not exist within Catholicism in the way the Protestant tends to fear. There are Catholics who are Republicans and Catholics who are Democrats, Catholics who like the Giants and Catholics who like the Dodgers, Catholics who send their children to parochial schools, Catholics who are Irish and Catholics who (if truth be told, and may they seek forgiveness for it) hate the Irish.

5. *The "Catholicism-is-clericalism" belief.* Discussion of the "monolith" leads inevitably to Protestant apprehensions about "clericalism." The position is found in both sophisticated and unsophisticated forms. The latter type is roughly equivalent to "Catholicism-is-like-the-local-priest-in-our-community." The Protestant knows that the local priest (a) promotes bingo games, (b) uses wine in the Mass, (c) believes that Roman Catholicism is the only true Church, and (d) is raising funds for a parochial school. So he reasons from such data to the unwarranted conclusion that *all* Catholics respectively (a) are gamblers, (b) are drunkards, (c) think all Protestants are going to Hell, and (d) oppose American democracy.

However, in its sophisticated form, the position has more substance than this. It is voiced by many leading Protestants, running the gamut of theological profundity from the *Christian Century* (a completely independent but nevertheless significant voice in Protestant thought) to such men as Dr. John Mackay, who, whatever Catholics may think of his uncompromising attitude toward Catholicism, is one of the ablest and most respected voices in the Protestant theological world.

The concern of these people is that the Catholic hierarchy has become a very disturbing "power bloc" in modern American life. They see the hierarchy making far-reaching decisions which can be implemented by the total disciplined structure of the Church, with its millions (both of men and money), its cohesiveness, and its acceptance of the principle that those who speak in the name of the Church speak pretty nearly in the name of God. They feel that power corrupts in the realm of the spirit even more unfortunately than elsewhere, and that those voices in the hierarchy with power are quite ready to use it for the ends of their Church, to the detriment of others. An example of this would be the pressures continually brought upon the State Department to deny passports to Protestant missionaries going to South America, on the grounds that these countries are "Catholic countries." It is in terms of this fear of "clericalism" that many of the bitterest fights are fought in America—over public vs. parochial schools, federal aid to education, an ambassador to the Vatican, dissemination of birth control information, and so forth. And one unfortunate outburst by a Cardinal can do as much harm to Protestant-Catholic relations here as can a dozen books by Paul Blanshard.

Through it all, the Protestant sounds reasonably tolerant. He has no quarrel with Catholic laymen. In fact, some of his best friends are Catholics, and he does not find their motives suspect. But the "hierarchy," that is a different matter . . . .

These types of anti-Catholicism represent varying degrees of significance and depth, and the reader must make his own assessment. But there is still one further type of Protestant opposition to Catholicism. This is on a deeper level yet, and it is very important for Roman Catholics to try to understand it. It comes from the Protestant who feels that Protestantism is a religion of affirmation rather than a series of polemics against Rome, and who tries to take this seriously not only on Reformation Sunday, but on the other fifty-one Sundays as well, with the week days thrown in for good measure.

This Protestant feels, however wrong the Catholic may think him, that he stands within the heritage of the church of Jesus Christ, and that it is his duty to maintain that heritage. He sees the Reformation, for example, not as an individualistic "revolt," but as an attempt to recover the gospel which Christ not only proclaimed but enacted, the redemption of the world through His death and resurrection. He believes redemption or salvation to be the work of God, a gift which men must receive in repentance, gratitude and newness of life in the Holy Spirit.

And the point is, that it is in the name of such convictions as these that he feels bound to take issue with certain aspects of Roman Catholicism. It is *because* of his Christian convictions, rather than through lack of them, that part of his difficulty with Catholicism arises. Thus, to take only one example, when this Protestant takes exception to the Dogma of the Assumption, he would assert that he does so not because he believes *less* than the Catholic, but because he wants to assert unqualifiedly and without possibility of diminution, the sole efficacy of *Christ's* redemptive work for his salvation. He sees Catholic doctrine leading in the direction of making Mary the co-redeemer, and he feels that this is a point of view which endangers the Biblical understanding of Christ as sole mediator and savior.

Without minute elaboration, then, let it be reiterated that there is a kind of Protestant attitude toward Catholicism which must take issue with it, not out of bigotry, not out of political fears, not out of jealousy, but out of an attempt by the Protestant to be faithful to the gospel of Jesus Christ as he understands it. From that basis, he sees areas of Catholic thought, belief and practice, which seem to him to do less than justice to, or even to distort, Biblical faith. No Catholic reader is particularly going to appreciate such a contention, but let him at least try to understand Protestant motives at this point, and see that the Protestant is acting out of concern for the faith, rather than in denial of it.

The main purpose of the preceding paragraphs has been descriptive. Perhaps in conclusion, a tentative foray into the realm of the hortatory is permissible. A great need, if Protestant-Catholic relations are to be improved, is a genuine attempt at understanding, by both sides. It is noteworthy that on the Catholic side, there have recently been some really significant atempts to assess the Protestant Reformation afresh, as Karl Adam's little book *One and Holy,* and the massive historical studies by Lortz, bear testimony. These are heartening to Protestants who had come to expect Catholic treatments of the subject to be full of the vilification found in the writings of Grisar and Denifle. And it is encouraging to note that a recent Protestant book attempting to explain Roman Catholicism to Protestants was greeted by the Catholic press as so fair that one publisher recommended it to priests as helpful in converting Protestants to Catholicism!

The plea for understanding, while it may not produce many conversions, is always important as a safeguard against distortions of the opposing position and the building up of straw men. If most Protestants misunderstand the area and extent of papal infallibility, most Catholics have no notion of what Protestants mean when they talk about "the priesthood of all believers." (Nor do most Protestants, if truth be told.) To whatever extent Catholics are permitted, they should seek to understand Protestant faith in something other than sheerly polemical terms. Their priests are quite at liberty to point out the shortcomings of Protestantism, but it could be done more constructively if a position which actually exists were to be exposed, rather than a distorted caricature which exists nowhere save in the debunker's mind.

But two further pleas must be made, beyond that of understanding. These are pleas for charity and firmness. Let each side espouse both. Various types of Protestant "anti-Catholicism have been under discussion, and an attempt has been made to indict a number of them. The shoe must fit on the other foot as well. For there are types of Catholic "anti-Protestantism" just as bigoted and unenlightened, and also just as significant in terms of deep commitment to the Church. Perhaps the most important thing, the greatest gift of charity for which we can hope in this situation, is not to cease disagreeing, but to make sure that we disagree about the right things. We can do this only as we are firm in holding to those things which comprise the essentials of our faith. And we can do it only as charity motivates our discussion and defines the areas of our disagreements. If these ingredients are present, it may be that the Holy Spirit can lead us closer to one another than we have yet come.

Questions for Study and Discussion

1. Which type of anti-Catholicism seems to be most vicious? why?
2. Why did the author not list and discuss the sixth type of anti-Catholicism in the manner of the first five?
3. In what sense are these anti-Catholic types propagandistic?
4. What makes the author's treatment of the subject more educational than propagandistic?

Vocabulary Study

Define the following words as used in this essay: Reformation, authoritarianism, rapport, patently, clericalism, hortatory.

Writing Assignment

Write a composition discussing religious stereotypes that you know about other than those pertaining to Catholicism.

The State

Adolf Hitler

[The following selection is taken from Volume II, Chapter 2, of Adolph Hitler's *Mein Kampf* (My Struggle). Volume I, published in 1925, was written during the author's imprisonment for political activities and, together with Volume II published the following year, explains the basic philosophy of the founder of Germany's Nazi Party.]

Since Nationality or rather race does not happen to lie in language but in the blood, we would only be justified in speaking of a Germanization if by such a process we succeeded in transforming the blood of the subjected people. But this is impossible. Unless a blood mixture brings about a change, which, however, means the lowering of the level of the higher race. The final result of such a process would consequently be the destruction of precisely those qualities which had formerly made the conquering people capable of victory. Especially the cultural force would vanish through a mating with the lesser race, even if the resulting mongrels spoke the language of the earlier, higher race a thousand times over. For a time, a certain struggle will take place between the different mentalities, and it may be that the steadily sinking people, in a last quiver of life, so to speak, will bring to light surprising cultural values. But these are only individual elements belonging to the higher race, or perhaps bastards in whom, after the first crossing, the better blood still predominates and tries to struggle through; but never final products of a mixture. In them a culturally backward movement will always manifest itself.

Today it must be regarded as a good fortune that a Germanization as intended by Joseph II in Austria was not carried out. Its result would probably have been the preservation of the Austrian state, but also the lowering of the racial level of the German nation induced by a linguistic union. In the course of the centuries a certain herd instinct would doubtless have crystallized out, but the herd itself would have become inferior.

A state-people would perhaps have been born, but a culture-people would have been lost.

For the German nation it was better that such a process of mixture did not take place, even if this was not due to a noble insight, but to the shortsighted narrowness of the Habsburgs. If it had turned out differently, the German people could scarcely be regarded as a cultural factor.

Not only in Austria, but in Germany as well, so-called national circles were moved by similar false ideas. The Polish policy, demanded by so many, involving a Germanization of the East, was unfortunately based on the same false inference. Here again it was thought that a Germanization of the Polish element could be brought about by a purely linguistic integration with the German element. Here again the result would have been catastrophic; a people of alien race expressing its alien ideas in the German language, compromising the lofty dignity of our own nationality by their own inferiority.

How terrible is the damage indirectly done to our Germanism today by the fact that, due to the ignorance of many Americans, the German-jabbering Jews, when they set foot on American soil, are booked to our German account. Surely no one will call the purely external fact that most of this lice-ridden migration from the East speaks German a proof of their German origin and nationality.

What has been profitably Germanized in history is the soil which our ancestors acquired by the sword and settled with German Peasants. In so far as they directed foreign blood into our national body in this process, they contributed to that catastrophic splintering of our inner being which is expressed in German super-individualism—a phenomenon, I am sorry to say, which is praised in many quarters....

The *state* in itself does not create a specific cultural level; it can only preserve the race which conditions this level. Otherwise the state as such may continue to exist unchanged for centuries while, in consequence of a racial mixture which it has not prevented, the cultural capacity of a people and the general aspect of its life conditioned by it have long since suffered a profound change. The present-day state, for example, may very well simulate its existence as a formal mechanism for a certain length of time, but the racial poisoning of our national body creates a cultural decline which even now is terrifyingly manifest.

Thus, the precondition for the existence of a higher humanity is not the state, but the nation possessing the necessary ability.

This ability will fundamentally always be present and must only be aroused to practical realization by certain outward conditions. Culturally and creatively gifted nations, or rather races, bear these useful qualities latent within them, even if at the moment unfavorable outward conditions do not permit a realization of these latent tendencies. Hence it is an unbelievable offense to represent the Germanic peoples of the pre-Christian era as cultureless, as barbarians. That they never were. Only the harshness of their northern homeland forced them into circumstances which thwarted the development of their creative forces. If, without any ancient world, they had come to the more favorable regions of the south, and if the material provided by lower peoples had given them their first technical implements, the culture-creating ability slumbering within them would have grown into radiant bloom just as happened, for example, with the Greeks. But this primeval culture-creating force itself arises in turn not from the northern climate alone. The Laplander, brought to the south, would be no more culture-creating than the Eskimo. For this glorious creative ability was given only to the Aryan, whether he bears it dormant within himself or gives it to awakening life, depending whether favorable circumstances permit this or an inhospitable Nature prevents it.

From this the following realization results:

The state is a means to an end. Its end lies in the preservation and advancement of a community of physically and psychically homogeneous creatures. This preservation itself comprises first of all existence as a race and thereby permits the free development of all the forces dormant in this race. Of them a part will always primarily serve the preservation of physical life, and only the remaining part the promotion of a further spiritual development. Actually the one always creates the precondition for the other.

States which do not serve this purpose are misbegotten, monstrosities in fact. The fact of their existence changes this no more than the success of a gang of bandits can justify robbery.

We National Socialists as champions of a new philosophy of life must never base ourselves on so-called 'accepted facts'—and false ones at that. If we did, we would not be the champions of a new great idea, but the coolies of the present-day lie. We must distinguish in the sharpest way between the state as a vessel and the race as its content. This vessel has meaning only if it can preserve and protect the content; otherwise it is useless.

Thus, the highest purpose of a folkish state is concern for the preserva-

tion of those original racial elements which bestow culture and create the beauty and dignity of a higher mankind. We, as Aryans, can conceive of the state only as the living organism of a nationality which not only assures the preservation of this nationality, but by the development of its spiritual and ideal abilities leads it to the highest freedom.

Questions for Study and Discussion

1. Point out four words or phrases in the first paragraph that reveal the propagandistic tone of this essay.

2. Point out five statements in this essay that have the unmistakable characteristics of "bad" propaganda.

3. Which paragraph of this essay represents the most offensive elements of propaganda?

4. Compare and contrast the effectiveness of the emotional appeal of this essay with that of Webster's "The Constitution Versus States Rights" in Chapter 1.

Vocabulary Study

Define the following words and phrases as used in this essay: mongrels, linguistic, compromizing, German-jabbering, simulate, latent, barbarians, primeval, Aryan, inhospitable, dormant, coolies.

Writing Assignment

Write a composition on one of the following topics:

1. My Reaction to Hitler's Propaganda

2. The Contrasting Concepts of the State as Presented by Hitler and Daniel Webster

CHAPTER 3

IN PURSUIT OF EDUCATIONAL GOALS

Liberty of the Press

John Milton

[More than three hundred years ago John Milton, in *Areopagitica*, addressed himself to a problem in his own country similar to that attacked recently by the American Library Association and the American Book Publishers Council in their statement of principles. Because of this similarity, excerpts from Milton's speech to the Parliament of England in 1644 are presented for comparative purposes as well as for the significance of the arguments in themselves.

The Order of Parliament (June 14, 1643) against which Milton's arguments were directed contained, among others, the following key provisions: "It is therefore ordered by the Lords and Commons in Parliament," (1) that no Order "of both or either House shall be printed" except by command; (2) *that no book, etc., "shall from henceforth be printed or put on sale, unless the same be first approved of and licensed by such person or persons as both or either of the said Houses shall appoint for the licensing of the same"*; that no book, of which the copyright has been granted to the Company* . . . be printed by any person or persons "without the license and consent of the Master, Warden, and assistants of the said Company." . . .]

*The Stationers' Company, a company or guild of the city of London, incorporated in 1556, comprising booksellers, printers, bookbinders, and dealers in writing materials.

131

... I deny not, but that it is of greatest concernment in the Church and Commonwealth, to have a vigilant eye how books demean themselves as well as men; and thereafter to confine, imprison, and do sharpest justice on them as malefactors. For books are not absolutely dead things, but do contain a potency of life in them to be as active as that soul was whose progeny they are; nay, they do preserve as in a vial the purest efficacy and extraction of that living intellect that bred them. I know they are as lively, and as vigorously productive, as those fabulous dragon's teeth; and being sown up and down, may chance to spring up armed men. And yet, on the other hand, unless wariness be used, as good almost kill a man as kill a book. Who kills a man kills a reasonable creature, God's image; but he who destroys a good book, kills reason itself, kills the image of God, as it were in the eye. Many a man lives a burden to the earth; but a good book is the precious life-blood of a master spirit, embalmed and treasured up on purpose to a life beyond life. 'Tis true, no age can restore a life, whereof perhaps there is no great loss; and revolutions of ages do not oft recover the loss of a rejected truth, for the want of which whole nations fare the worse.

We should be wary therefore what persecution we raise against the living labors of public men, how we spell that seasoned life of man, preserved and stored up in books; since we see a kind of homicide may be thus committed, sometimes a martyrdom, and if it extend to the whole impression, a kind of massacre; whereof the execution ends not in the slaying of an elemental life, but strikes at that ethereal and fifth essence, the breath of reason itself, slays an immortality rather than a life....

Good and evil we know in the field of this world grow up together almost inseparably; and the knowledge of good is so involved and interwoven with the knowledge of evil, and in so many cunning resemblances hardly to be discerned, that those confused seeds which were imposed on Psyche as an incessant labour to cull out and sort asunder, were not more intermixed. It was from the rind of one apple tasted that the knowledge of good and evil, as two twins cleaving together, leaped forth into the world. And perhaps this is that doom which Adam fell into of knowing good and evil; that is to say, of knowing good by evil. As therefore the state of man now is, what wisdom can there be to choose, what continence to forbear, without the knowledge of evil? He that can apprehend and consider vice with all her habits and seeming pleasures, and yet abstain, and yet distinguish, and yet prefer that which is truly better, he is the true wayfaring Christian.

I cannot praise a fugitive and cloistered virtue, unexercised and unbreathed, that never sallies out and sees her adversary, but slinks out of the race, where that immortal garland is to be run for, not without dust and heat. Assuredly we bring not innocence into the world, we bring impurity much rather: that which purifies us is trial, and trial is by what is contrary. The virtue therefore which is but a youngling in the contemplation of evil, and knows not the utmost that vice promises to her followers, and rejects it, is but a blank virtue, not a pure; her whiteness is but an excremental whiteness; which was the reason why our sage and serious poet Spenser, whom I dare be known to think a better teacher than Scotus or Aquinas, describing true temperance under the person of Guyon, brings him in with his palmer through the cave of Mammon, and the bower of earthly bliss, that he might see and know, and yet abstain. Since therefore the knowledge and survey of vice is in this world so necessary to the constituting of human virtue, and the scanning of error to the confirmation of truth, how can we more safely, and with less danger, scout into the regions of sin and falsity than by reading all manner of tractates, and hearing all manner of reason? And this is the benefit that may be had of books promiscuously read....

They are not skillful considerers of human things, who imagine to remove sin by removing the matter of sin; for, besides that it is a huge heap increasing under the very act of diminishing, though some part of it may for a time be withdrawn from some persons, it cannot from all, in such a universal thing as books are; and when this is done, yet the sin remains entire. Though you take from a covetous man all his treasure, he has yet one jewel left, ye cannot bereave him of his covetousness. Banish all objects of lust, shut up all youth into the severest discipline that can be exercised in any hermitage, ye cannot make them chaste, that came not thither so....

Questions for Study and Discussion

1. Which sentence in the first paragraph is the most effective emotionally?

2. Which sentence in the third paragraph best summarizes the main thought of that paragraph and the one that follows?

3. Which sentence in the last paragraph best summarizes the thought of the paragraph?

4. What rhetorical devices does Milton use to make his arguments most effective?

5. Point out the similarities between the arguments in this essay and in "The Freedom to Read."

Vocabulary Study

Define the following words and phrases as used in this essay: malefactors, potency, progeny, dragon's teeth, wary, ethereal, Psyche, cloistered, excremental, palmer, tractates, promiscuously, covetousness, chaste.

Writing Assignment

Write a composition expressing in your own words the major ideas in Milton's essay.

The Freedom to Read

A Statement by the American Library Association and the American Book Publishers Council

The freedom to read is essential to our democracy. It is under attack. Private groups and public authorities in various parts of the country are working to remove books from sale, to censor textbooks, to label "controversial" books, to distribute lists of "objectionable" books or authors, and to purge libraries. These actions apparently rise from a view that our national tradition of free expression is no longer valid; that censorship and suppression are needed to avoid the subversion of politics and the corruption of morals. We, as citizens devoted to the use of books and as librarians and publishers responsible for disseminating them, wish to assert the public interest in the preservation of the freedom to read.

We are deeply concerned about these attempts at suppression. Most such attempts rest on a denial of the fundamental premise of democracy: that the ordinary citizen, by exercising his critical judgment, will accept the good and reject the bad. The censors, public and private, assume that they should determine what is good and what is bad for their fellow-citizens.

We trust Americans to recognize propaganda, and to reject obscenity. We do not believe they need the help of censors to assist them in this task. We do not believe they are prepared to sacrifice their heritage of a free press in order to be "protected" against what others think may be bad for them. We believe they still favor free enterprise in ideas and expression.

We are aware, of course, that books are not alone in being subjected to efforts at suppression. We are aware that these efforts are related to a larger pattern of pressures being brought against education, the press, films, radio, and television. The problem is not only one of actual censorship. The shadow of fear cast by these pressures leads, we suspect, to an even larger voluntary curtailment of expression by those who seek to avoid controversy.

Such pressure toward conformity is perhaps natural to a time of uneasy change and prevading fear. Especially when so many of our apprehensions are directed against an ideology, the expression of a dissident idea becomes a thing feared in itself, and we tend to move against it as against a hostile deed, with suppression.

And yet suppression is never more dangerous than in such a time of social tension. Freedom has given the United States the elasticity to endure strain. Freedom keeps open the path of novel and creative solutions, and enables change to come by choice. Every silencing of a heresy, every enforcement of an orthodoxy, diminishes the toughness and resilience of our society and leaves it the less able to deal with stress.

Now as always in our history, books are among our greatest instruments of freedom. They are almost the only means for making generally available ideas or manners of expression that can initially command only a small audience. They are the natural medium for the new idea and the untried voice from which come the original contributions to social growth. They are essential to the extended discussion which serious thought requires, and to the accumulation of knowledge and ideas into organized collections.

We believe that free comunication is essential to the preservation of a free society and a creative culture. We believe that these pressures towards conformity present the danger of limiting the range and variety of inquiry and expression on which our democracy and our culture depend. We believe that every American community must jealously guard the freedom to publish and to circulate, in order to preserve its own freedom to read. We believe that publishers and librarians have a profound responsibility to give validity to that freedom to read by making it possible for the reader to choose freely from a variety of offerings.

II

The freedom to read is guaranteed by the Constitution. Those with faith in free men will stand firm on these constitutional guarantees of essential rights and will exercise the responsibilities that accompany these rights.

We therefore affirm these propositions:

1. *It is in the public interest for publishers and librarians to make available the widest diversity of views and expressions, including those which are unorthodox or unpopular with the majority.*

Creative thought is by definition new, and what is new is different. The bearer of every new thought is a rebel until his idea is refined and tested. Totalitarian systems attempt to maintain themselves in power by the ruthless suppression of any concept which challenges the established orthodoxy. The power of a democratic system to adapt to change is vastly strengthened by the freedom of its citizens to choose widely from among conflicting opinions offered freely to them. To stifle every non-conformist idea at birth would mark the end of the democratic process. Furthermore, only through the constant activity of weighing and selecting can the democratic mind attain the strength demanded by times like these. We need to know not only what we believe but why we believe it.

2. *Publishers and librarians do not need to endorse every idea or presentation contained in the books they make available. It would conflict with the public interests for them to establish their own political, moral, or esthetic views as the sole standard for determining what books should be published or circulated.*

Publishers and librarians serve the educational process by helping to make available knowledge and ideas required for the growth of the mind and the increase of learning. They do not foster education by imposing as mentors the patterns of their own thought. The people should have the freedom to read and consider a broader range of ideas than those that may be held by any single librarian or publisher or government or church. It is wrong that what one man can read should be conformed to what another thinks is proper.

3. *It is contrary to the public interest for publishers or librarians to determine the acceptability of a book solely on the basis of the personal history or political affiliations of the author.*

A book should be judged as a book. No art or literature can flourish if it is to be measured by the political views or private lives of its creators. No society of free men can flourish which draws up lists of writers to whom it will not listen, whatever they may have to say.

4. *The present laws dealing with obscenity should be vigorously enforced. Beyond that, there is no place in our society for extra-legal efforts to coerce the taste of others, to confine adults to the reading matter deemed suitable for adolescents, or to inhibit the efforts of writers to achieve artistic expression.*

To some, much of modern literature is shocking. But is not much of life itself shocking? We cut off literature at the source if we prevent serious artists from dealing with the stuff of life. Parents and teachers have a responsibility to prepare the young to meet the diversity of experiences in life to which they will be exposed, as they have a responsibility to help them learn to think critically for themselves. These are affirmative responsibilities, not to be discharged simply by preventing them from reading works for which they are not yet prepared. In these matters taste differs, and taste cannot be legislated; nor can machinery be devised which will suit the demands of one group without limiting the freedom of others. We deplore the catering to the immature, the retarded or the mal-adjusted taste. But those concerned with freedom have the responsibility of seeing to it that each individual book or publication, whatever its contents, price, or method of distribution, is dealt with in accordance with due process of law.

5. *It is not in the public interest to force a reader to accept with any book the prejudgment of a label characterizing the book or author as subversive or dangerous.*

The idea of labeling presupposes the existence of individuals or groups with wisdom to determine by authority what is good or bad for the citizen. It presupposes that each individual must be directed in making up his mind about the ideas he examines. But Americans do not need others to do their thinking for them.

6. *It is the responsibility of publishers and librarians, as guardians of the people's freedom to read, to contest encroachments upon that freedom by individuals or groups seeking to impose their own standards or tastes upon the community at large.*

It is inevitable in the give and take of the democratic process that the political, the moral, or the esthetic concepts of an individual or group will occasionally collide with those of another individual or group. In a free society each individual is free to determine for himself what he wishes to read, and each group is free to determine what it will recommend to its freely associated members. But no group has the right to take the law into its own hands, and to impose its own concept of politics or morality upon other members of a democratic society. Freedom is no freedom if it is accorded only to the accepted and the inoffensive.

7. *It is the responsibility of publishers and librarians to give full meaning to the freedom to read by providing books that enrich the quality of thought and expression. By the exercise of this affirmative responsibility, bookmen can demonstrate that the answer to a bad book is a good one, the answer to a bad idea is a good one.*

The freedom to read is of little consequence when expended on the trivial; it is frustrated when the reader cannot obtain matter fit for his purpose. What is needed is not only the absence of restraint, but the positive provision of opportunity for the people to read the best that has been thought and said. Books are the major channel by which the intellectual inheritance is handed down, and the principal means of its testing and growth. The defense of their freedom and integrity, and the enlargement of their service to society, require of all bookmen the utmost of their faculties, and deserve of all citizens the fullest of their support.

III

We state these propositions neither lightly nor as easy generalizations. We here stake out a lofty claim for the value of books. We do so because we believe that they are good, possessed of enormous variety and usefulness, worthy of cherishing and keeping free. We realize that the application of these propositions may mean the dissemination of ideas and manners of expression that are repugnant to many persons. We do not state these propositions in the comfortable belief that what people read is unimportant. We believe rather that what people read is deeply important; that ideas can be dangerous; but that the suppression of ideas is fatal to a democratic society. Freedom itself is a dangerous way of life, but it is ours.

Questions for Study and Discussion

1. To what extent is this statement by the American Library Association and the American Book Publishers Council propagandistic?

2. What one word that has great emotional and propagandistic overtones is used most often throughout the statement? Explain.

3. In your opinion, to what extent do the views embodied in this statement represent those of the average parent, teacher, politician, or religious leader?

Vocabulary Study

Define the following words as used in this statement: dissident, orthodoxy, resilience, totalitarian, mentor, obscenity, subversive, encroachments, esthetic, repugnant.

Writing Assignment

Write a paragraph effectively presenting arguments supporting the opposite side of one of the seven principles recommended in this statement.

Nationalistic Bias in History Textbooks

Stephen E. Ambrose

[This is a review of *The Historian's Contribution to Anglo-American Understanding: Report of a Committee on National Bias in Anglo-American History Textbooks,* by Ray Allen Billington, et al. The review was published in the *Baltimore Sunday Sun,* May 15, 1966.]

Who was the first man to split the atom? It all depends on whose textbook you read. In the British version, the creative genius was Lord Rutherford, of Cambridge. Danish texts award the honor to Niels Bohr. In Germany credit goes to Otto Hahn and Lise Meitner. Italian historians mention Enrico Fermi and no one else. Americans say it was Ernest Lawrence and the team of physicists at the University of Chicago during World War II.

All textbooks are, in short, nationalistic, most of them to the point that they distort history to give young readers the impression that their nation has monopolized progress, "single-handedly turned back the enemies of civilization, and is alone equipped to lead the world along the path to a righteous future." Scholarly sophistication, so evident in the current historical monographs, has not yet come to the textbooks. Even more serious, the distortions usually come at the expense of other nations. Far from helping students to understand the world in which they live, textbooks promote old stereotypes.

For the last three years a team of American and British historians has worked on one aspect of the problem—the way in which nationalistic bias in history textbooks in England and the United States has contributed to Anglo-American misunderstanding. The team dealt primarily with books that are read by the 6 through 18 age group.

The study was concerned with both nations' textbooks. The authors make no explicit statement as to whose texts are more objective, more devoted to truth, but it is obvious from the examples that the Americans are far behind the British.

Perhaps this is because of the differences in the educational philosophies. In Great Britain the teachers are specialists in their fields; in America they are specialists in the science of teaching and often know little or nothing about the subject matter. British teachers select their own textbooks; in America the selection of a textbook is a tortuous process in which a whole hierarchy of committees and groups—but never the teacher—is involved. Historians write textbooks in order to make money, and they gear their works to the people who will select and adopt them. If the local P.T.A. is dominated by a pressure group, the writer will write for that group, not for the student or for the sake of objective truth.

There is a final, most important difference. The "vast majority" of British history teachers see the value of their subject in the "contribution it can make to the development of the individual human being... in the cultivation of the whole man." In the United States teachers, and most of the public, "view instruction in the nation's history as a practical, pragmatic means of protecting and preserving the American way of life." Or, more directly, to instill patriotism.

As the authors point out, "When the *purpose* of a textbook is nationalistic, its tone will mirror that purpose. Yet loyalty to one's country can be taught without breeding dislike of other nations, and of this textbook authors in the United States have been guilty."

The team that made this examination concentrated on three events, the Revolutionary War, the War of 1812, and the first World War. They found five basic forms of nationalistic bias:

The failure of textbook writers to keep abreast of current scholarly findings and their tendency to repeat outworn legends constitutes Bias of Inertia. Writing only from the point of view of one's own nation leads to Unconscious Falsification. Discussing only the battles the author's countrymen won and neglecting all those that they lost makes for Bias by Omission. Calling your statesman "skilled" and those of another country "grasping" is Bias in Use of Language. Constantly extolling your people's virtues and accomplishments while ignoring those of others is clearly Bias by Cumulative Implication.

All these faults are present in American treatments of the Revolutionary War. The textbooks concentrate on the Boston Massacre, George III's supposed insanity, British stupidity, the use of Hessian troops and

American victories in the war. They make no attempt to understand British problems and never mention the defeats George Washington suffered.

Most American junior high school and high school texts give a large portion of their discussion of the War of 1812 to the burning of parts of Washington, D.C., but none mention that the British did it in retaliation for the American burning of Toronto, Canada. Textbook treatment of World War I is so poor that the student is given the impression that it began in 1917, when America entered the conflict. The worst of these books, which are often the most popular and widely adopted, imply "that the American expeditionary force began fighting a year before it did, turned the tide of victory, and suffered casualties out of all proportion to their numbers." No mention is made of British and French contributions or losses.

The authors reproduce a number of illustrations from secondary school textbooks, along with the captions. These are even more biased than the material in the text. A page from a leading American high school textbook shows three scenes dealing with the War of 1812. The first shows the British about to burn Washington, the second an American sea victory, and the last the scene that inspired "The Star-Spangled Banner." The arrangement, the authors note, is "obviously designed to stimulate patriotism rather than understanding."

Prime Minister Nehru once wondered about the future of a world in which "all peoples and all nations believe that in some way they are a chosen race." In a world in which we can all be destroyed in a few seconds, possibly because some world leader read the wrong textbook and came to the wrong conclusion about another nation, we can no longer afford to believe in "one invincible nation, forever right, forever triumphant, and forever superior."

This is a book that should be read by all those who are involved in the process of selecting textbooks for the schools, or indeed by all those who have children in school.

Questions for Study and Discussion

1. Name and explain the meaning of each of the five kinds of bias listed by the reviewer.

2. According to the reviewer, what unfortunate consequences may result from the study of biased history texts?

3. According to the reviewer, how do the majority of British history teachers differ from the majority of teachers in the United States in their attitudes toward the objectives and value of their subject?

Vocabulary Study

Define the following words as used in this review: sophistication, monographs, nationalistic, hierarchy, pragmatic, inertia.

Writing Assignment

Write a composition comparing and contrasting this review with the essay by Benjamin Quarles in Chapter 2.

A Letter to Johnny's Mother

Rudolph Flesch

DEAR MARY:

I have decided to start this book with a letter to you. You know that the idea came to me when I offered to help Johnny with his reading. It's really his book—or yours. So the only proper way to start it is with the words "Dear Mary."

You remember when I began to work with Johnny half a year ago. That was when he was twelve and they put him back into the sixth grade because he was unable to read and couldn't possibly keep up with the work in junior high. So I told you that I knew of a way to teach reading that was altogether different from what they do in schools or in remedial reading courses or anywhere else. Well, you trusted me, and you know what has happened since. Today Johnny can read—not perfectly, to be sure, but anyone can see that in a few more months he will have caught up with other boys of his age. And he is happy again: You and I and everyone else can see that he is a changed person.

I think Johnny will go to college. He has a very good mind, as you know, and I don't see why he shouldn't become a doctor or a lawyer or an engineer. There is a lot in Johnny that has never come to the surface because of this reading trouble.

Since I started to work with Johnny, I have looked into this whole reading business. I worked my way through a mountain of books and articles on the subject, I talked to dozens of people, and I spent many hours in classrooms, watching what was going on.

What I found is absolutely fantastic. The teaching of reading—all over the United States, in all the schools, in all the textbooks—is totally wrong and flies in the face of all logic and common sense. Johnny couldn't read until half a year ago for the simple reason that nobody ever showed him how. Johnny's only problem was that he was unfortunately exposed to an ordinary American school.

You know that I was born and raised in Austria. Do you know that there are no remedial reading cases in Austrian schools? Do you know that there are no remedial reading cases in Germany, in France, in Italy, in Norway, in Spain—practically anywhere in the world except in the United States? Do you know that there was no such thing as remedial reading in this country either until about thirty years ago? Do you know that the teaching of reading never was a problem anywhere in the world until the United States switched to the present method around about 1925?

This sounds incredible, but it is true. One of the articles on reading that I found was by a Dr. Ralph C. Preston, of the University of Pennsylvania, who reported on his experiences on a trip through Western Germany in the April, 1953, *Elementary School Journal*. Dr. Preston visited a number of classrooms in Hamburg and Munich. "After the experience of hearing these German children reading aloud," he says, "I began to attach some credence to a generally expressed opinion of German teachers that before the end of Grade 2 almost any child can read orally (without regard to degree of comprehension) almost anything in print!"

Of course, Dr. Preston, being an American educator, didn't draw the obvious conclusion from what he saw. The explanation is simply that the method used over there works, and the method used in our schools does not. We too could have perfect readers in all schools at the end of the second grade if we taught our children by the system used in Germany.

Now, what is this system? It's very simple. Reading means getting meaning from certain combinations of letters. Teach the child what each letter stands for and he can read.

Ah, no, you say, it can't be that simple. But it is. Let me give you an illustration.

I don't know whether you know any shorthand. Let's suppose you don't. Let's suppose you decide to learn how to read English shorthand.

Right away you say that nobody learns how to *read* shorthand. People who want to know shorthand learn how to *write* it; the reading of it comes by the way.

Exactly. That's why shorthand is such a good illustration of this whole thing. It's just a system of getting words on paper. Ordinary writing is another such system. Morse code is the third. Braille is a fourth. And so it goes. There are all sorts of systems of translating spoken words into a series of symbols so that they can be written down and read back.

Now the way to learn any such system is to learn to write and to read it at the same time. And how do you do that? The obvious answer is, By taking up one symbol after another and learning how to write and how to recognize it. Once you are through the whole list of symbols, you can read and write; the rest is simply practice—learning to do it more and more automatically.

Since the dawn of time people have learned mechanical means of communication in this way—smoke signals and drums in the jungle and flag language and I don't know what all. You take up one item after another, learn what it stands for, learn how to reproduce it and how to recognize it, and there you are.

Shorthand, as I said, is an excellent example. I don't know any English shorthand myself, but I went to a library and looked up the most widely used manual of the Gregg system, the *Functional Method* by L. A. Leslie. Sure enough, it tells you about the symbols one after the other, starting out with the loop that stands for the long *a* in *ache, make,* and *cake*. After a few lessons, you are supposed to know the shape of all the shorthand "letters," and from there on it's just a matter of practice and picking up speed.

Our system of writing—the alphabet—was invented by the Egyptians and the Phoenicians somewhere around 1500 B.C. Before the invention of the alphabet there was only picture writing—a picture of an ox meant "ox," a picture of a house meant "house," and so on. (The Chinese to this day have a system of writing with symbols that stand for whole words.) As soon as people had an alphabet, the job of reading and writing was tremendously simplified. Before that, you had to have a symbol for every word in the language—10,000, 20,000 or whatever the vocabulary range was. Now, with the alphabet, all you had to learn was the letters. Each word stood for a certain sound, and that was that. To write a word—any word—all you had to do was break it down into its sounds and put the corresponding letters on paper.

So, ever since 1500 B.C. people all over the world—wherever an alphabetic system of writing was used—learned how to read and write by the simple process of memorizing the sound of each letter in the alphabet. When a schoolboy in ancient Rome learned to read, he didn't learn that the written word *mensa* meant a table: that is, a certain piece of furniture with a flat top and legs. Instead, he began by learning that the letter *m* stands for the sound you make when you put your lips together, that *e* means the sound that comes out when you open your mouth about halfway, that *n* is like *m* but with the lips open and the teeth together, that *s* has a hissing sound, and that *a* means the sound made by opening your mouth wide. Therefore, when he saw the written word *mensa* for the first time, he could read it right off and learn, with a feeling of happy discovery, that this collection of letters meant a table. Not only that, he could also write the word down from dictation without ever having seen it before. And not only *that,* he could do this with practically every word in the language.

This is not miraculous, it's the only natural system of learning how to read. As I said, the ancient Egyptians learned that way, and the Greeks and the Romans, and the French and the Germans, and the Dutch and the Portuguese, and the Turks and the Bulgarians and the Esthonians and the Icelanders and the Abyssinians—every single nation throughout history that used an alphabetic system of writing.

Except, as I said before, twentieth century Americans—and other nations in so far as they have followed our example. And what do we use instead? Why, the only other possible system of course—the system that was in use before the invention of the alphabet in 1500 B.C. We have decided to forget that we write with letters and learn to read English as if it were Chinese. One word after another after another after another. If we want to read materials with a vocabulary of 10,000 words, then we have to memorize 10,000 words; if we want to go to the 20,000 word range, we have to learn, one by one, 20,000 words; and so on. We have thrown 3,500 years of civilization out the window and have gone back to the Age of Hammurabi.

You don't believe me? I assure you what I am saying is literally true. Go to your school tomorrow morning—or if Johnny has brought home one of his readers, look at it. You will immediately see that all the words in it are learned by endless repetition. Not a sign anywhere that letters correspond to sounds and that words can be worked out by pronouncing the letters. No. The child is told what each word means and then they are mechanically, brutally hammered into his brain. Like this:

> "We will look," said Susan.
> "Yes, yes," said all the children.
> "We will look and find it."
>
> So all the boys and girls looked.
> They looked and looked for it.
> But they did not find it.

Or this:

> "Quack, quack," said the duck.
> He wanted something.
> He did not want to get out.
> He did not want to go to the farm.
> He did not want to eat.
> He sat and sat and sat.

All the reading books used in all our schools, up through fourth and fifth and sixth grade, are collections of stuff like that. Our children learn the word *sat* by reading over and over again about a duck or a pig or a goat that sat and sat and sat. And so with every word in the language.

Every word in the language! You know what that means? It means that if you teach reading by this system, you can't use ordinary reading matter for practice. Instead, all children for three, four, five, six years have to work their way up through a battery of carefully designed readers, each one containing all the words used in the previous one plus a strictly limited number of new ones, used with the exactly "right" amount of repetition. Our children don't read Andersen's *Fairy Tales* any more or *The Arabian Nights* or Mark Twain or Louisa May Alcott or the Mary Poppins books or the Dr. Doolittle books or *anything* interesting and worth while, *because they can't*. It so happens that the writers of these classic children's books wrote without being aware of our Chinese system of teaching reading. So *Little Women* contains words like *grieving* and *serene,* and *Tom Sawyer* has *ague* and *inwardly,* and Bulfinch's *Age of Fable* has *nymph* and *diety* and *incantations.* If a child that has gone to any of our schools faces the word *nymph* for the first time, he is absolutely helpless because nobody has ever told him how to sound out *n* and *y* and *m* and *ph* and read the word off the page.

So what does he get instead? He gets those series of horrible, stupid, emasculated, pointless, tasteless little readers, the stuff and guff about Dick and Jane or Alice and Jerry visiting the farm and having birthday parties and seeing animals in the zoo and going through dozens and dozens of totally unexciting middle-class, middle-income, middle-I.Q. children's activities that offer opportunities for reading "Look, look" or "Yes, yes" or "Come, come" or "See the funny, funny animal." During the past half year I read a good deal of this material and I don't wish that experience on anyone.

Who writes these books? Let me explain this to you in detail, because there is the nub of the whole problem.

There are one or two dozen textbook houses in America. By far the most lucrative part of their business is the publication of readers for elementary schools. There are millions of dollars of profit in these little books. Naturally, the competition is tremendous. So is the investment; so is the sales effort; so is the effort that goes into writing, editing, and illustrating these books.

Now, with our Chinese word-learning system you can't produce a series of readers by printing nice, interesting collections of stuff children of a certain age might like to read. Oh no. Every single story, every single sentence that goes into these books has to be carefully prepared and carefully checked to make sure that each word is one of the 637 that the poor child is supposed to have memorized up to that point—or if it's the 638th word, that it appears in just the right context for optimum guesswork and is then repeated seventeen times at carefully worked-out intervals.

Naturally, the stupendous and frighteningly idiotic work of concocting this stuff can only be done by tireless teamwork of many educational drudges. But if the textbook house put only the drudges on the title page, that wouldn't look impressive enough to beat the competition. So there has to be a "senior author"—someone with a national reputation who teaches how to teach reading at one of the major universities.

And that's why each and every one of the so-called authorities in this field is tied up with a series of readers based on the Chinese word-learning method. As long as you use that method, you have to buy some $30 worth per child of Dr. So-and-so's readers; as soon as you switch to the common-sense method of teaching the sounds of the letters, you can give them a little primer and then proceed immediately to anything from the *Reader's Digest* to *Treasure Island.*

I have personally met some of the leading authorities in the field of reading. They are all very nice ladies and gentlemen, and obviously sincere and well meaning. But they *are* firmly committed to the application of the word method, and it would be inhuman to expect from them an objective point of view.

Consequently it's utterly impossible to find anyone inside the official family of the educators saying anything even slightly favorable to the natural method of teaching reading. Mention the alphabetic method or phonetics or "phonics" and you immediately arouse derision, furious hostility, or icy silence.

For instance, in the May 1952 *Catholic Educator,* Monsignor Clarence E. Elwell published an article "Reading: The Alphabet and Phonics." Monsignor Elwell is Superintendent of Schools of the Diocese of Cleveland and knows what he is talking about. He says: "In a language based on an alphabetic (that is, phonetic) method of coding the spoken word, the only sensible way to teach how to decode the written symbols is (1) *by teaching the phonetic code,* that is, the alphabet, and (2) the manner of coding—letter by letter, left to right. It is nonsensical to use a whole word method for beginning reading as it would be to teach the Morse code on a whole word basis. . . . A child who has been taught the code and how to use it . . . gains a confident habit in attacking words. Instead of guessing when he comes to a new word, as he did when taught by the sight word method, he now works through a word and to the surprise of the teachers usually comes up with the right answer. . . . After four years' experiment with the introduction of a strong program of phonics at the very beginning of grade one, the experimenter finds teachers convinced and children apparently happier in their success."

What do you think happened when Monsignor Elwell said publicly that our whole system of teaching reading is nonsense? Absolutely nothing. So far as I know, none of the reading "experts" has paid the slightest attention to the Cleveland experiment.

Or take the case of the late Dr. Leonard Bloomfield, professor of linguistics at Yale. Dr. Bloomfield wasn't just any scholar in the field of language; he was universally recognized as the greatest American linguist of modern times. His masterpiece was a book simply called *Language* published in 1933.

In the last few pages of that book, Bloomfield dealt with the teaching of English and reading in our schools. "Our schools," he wrote, "are utterly benighted in linguistic matters. . . . Nothing could be more discouraging than to read our 'educationalists' treatises on methods of teaching children to read. The size of this book does not permit a discussion of their varieties of confusion on this subject."

Several years later, Bloomfield took time out to prepare an alphabetic-phonetic primer, based on strictly scientific principles. It was an excellent piece of work, carefully designed to teach children quickly and painlessly. After Bloomfield's death in 1949 his literary executor offered the manuscript to every single elementary textbook publisher in the United States. Not one of them considered it. As I am writing, the book is still unpublished.

The introduction of this Bloomfield primer was, however, published as an article in the *Elementary English Review* in April and May, 1942. I ran across that article eight or ten years ago and that's what started me on this whole business. Taking the ideas of that article and applying them in homemade fashion, I taught my eldest daughter Anne to read when she was five years old. Well, you know Anne: she's ten now and reads anything and everything, all the time. Here is what Bloomfield told the country's elementary English teachers twelve years ago: "The most serious drawback of all the English reading instruction known to me. . . . is the drawback of the word-method. . . . The child who fails to grasp the content of what he reads is usually a poor reader in the mechanical sense. . . . If you want to play the piano with feeling and expression, you must master the keyboard and learn to use your fingers on it. The chief source of difficulty in getting the content of reading is imperfect mastery of the mechanics of reading. . . . We must train the child to respond vocally to the sight of letters. . . ."

And what did the teachers and reading experts do after the greatest scientist in the field had explained to them their mistake? Absolutely nothing. Except that several years later, in 1948, Dr. William S. Gray, of the University of Chicago, published a book, *On Their Own in Reading*. There, in the first chapter, was a lengthy quotation from Bloomfield's paper, followed by this statement: "The recent trend toward . . . the old alphabetic or phonic methods is viewed with alarm by educators. . . ."

The most conspicuous example of this deadly warfare between the entrenched "experts" and the advocates of common sense in reading is the reception of the primer *Reading With Phonics* by Hay and Wingo, published by the J. B. Lippincott Company. By some miracle, this textbook company decided to jump into the fray and publish the Hay-Wingo book, the only primer on the market today that is based firmly on the alphabetic-phonetic principle. Well, the book was duly reviewed in *Elementary English* magazine by Dr. Celia B. Stendler of the University of Illinois. I quote: *"Reading With Phonics* does not fit the modern conception of the place of phonics in a reading program. . . . One wonders at the naivete of the authors. . . . One wonders, too, whether the authors have ever had the thrill of seeing a group of children learn to read by the use of modern methods. The zest with which these children approach reading and the zeal with which they read will almost certainly be lost if we turn the clock back twenty years with *Reading With Phonics.*" (This from someone who is all for turning the clock back 3,500 years!)

I'll have more to say later in this book about the Hay-Wingo primer which produces first-graders reading news items from the daily papers —and the zest and zeal with which our children read:

> Jack ran out to see the truck.
> It was red and it was big—
> very, very big.
>
> It had come to take Jack
> far away to his new home—
> far away to his new home—
> on a big farm.

In doing research for this book, I ran into exactly the same kind of hostility. I wrote a letter to the National Council of Teachers of English, asking for information on the phonetic method of teaching reading. I got a brief reply, referring me to Dr. Paul Witty of Northwestern University (one of the top word-method people) and to a pamphlet "What About Phonics?" by Dr. Alvina Treut Burrows of New York University, which turned out to be violently anti-phonics. I also wrote the U.S. Office of Education. That time I got a somewhat longer reply, referring me to Dr. Edward W. Dolch of the University of Illinois (another well-known word-method man) and to the same biased pamphlet by Dr. Burrows.

At a later stage in my research I found an excellent paper by a Dr. Agnew who had compared the results of teaching reading in the schools of Durham and Raleigh, North Carolina. The monograph was published in 1939, at which time the schools in Durham produced splendid results by teaching phonics. So I wrote to the Superintendent of Schools in Durham, asking for information. The answer was that the teaching of phonics there had been discontinued seven years ago.

Then I ran across a book by the Italian educator Dr. Maria Montessori, published way back in 1912. Dr. Montessori, who was a world-famous progressive kindergarten teacher, taught her little Italian four-year-olds (!) the shapes and sounds of the letters of the alphabet and had them reading within weeks. I found that there was a Child Education Foundation in New York City carrying on Dr. Montessori's work. I wrote to them, asking about their method of teaching reading. The answer came back: "For a number of years we have found other methods to be more effective, so have not used Montessori."

Now that I have gone through dozens and dozens of books on reading, I know well it all fits together. The primers and readers are keyed to the textbooks on how to teach reading, and the textbooks are all carefully written so that every teacher in the land is shielded from any information about how to teach children anything about letters and sounds.

It's a foolproof system all right. Every grade-school teacher in the country has to go to a teachers' college or school of education; every teachers' college gives at least one course on how to teach reading; every course on how to teach reading is based on a textbook; every one of those textbooks is written by one of the high priests of the word method. In the old days it was impossible to keep a good teacher from following her own common sense and practical knowledge; today the phonetic system of teaching reading is kept out of our schools as effectively as if we had a dictatorship with an all-powerful Ministry of Education.

And how do you convince thousands of intelligent young women that black is white and that reading has nothing to do with letters and sounds? Simple. Like this:

First, you announce loudly and with full conviction that our method of writing English is *not* based on pronunciation. Impossible, you say? Everybody knows that all alphabetic systems are phonetic? Oh no. I quote from page 297 of *Reading and the Educative Process* by Dr. Paul Witty of Northwestern University: "English is essentially an unphonetic language."

This is so ridiculous that it should be possible to just laugh about it and forget it. But the reading "experts" have created so much confusion that it's necessary to refute this nonsense. Well then: *All* alphabetic systems are phonetic; the two words mean the same thing. The only trouble is that English is a little more irregular than other languages. Now much more has been established by three or four independent researchers. They all came up with the same figure. About 13 per cent of all English words are partly irregular in their spelling. The other 87 per cent follow fixed rules. Even the 13 per cent are not "unphonetic," as Dr. Witty calls it, but usually contain just one irregularly spelled vowel: *done* is pronounced "dun," *one* is pronounced "wun," *are* pronounced "ar" and so on.

So our English system of writing is *of course* phonetic, but has a few more exceptions to the rules than other languages.

The next step in this great structure of nonsense and confusion is careful avoidance of the teaching of the letters:

"Current practice in the teaching of reading does not require a knowledge of the letters," says Dr. Donald D. Durrell of Boston University. "In remedial work, such knowledge is helpful."

"The skillful teacher will be reluctant to use any phonetic method with all children," says Dr. Witty.

"The child should be allowed to 'typewrite' only after he has a certain degree of ability in reading," says Dr. Guy L. Bond of the University of Minnesota. "Otherwise he is apt to become too conscious of the letter-by-letter elements of words."

And Dr. Roma Gans of Teachers College, Columbia University, tells us simply and starkly: "In recent years phonetic analysis of words at any level of the reading program fell into disrepute."

If they have their way, our teachers would never tell the children that there are letters and that each letter represents a sound. However, that isn't quite possible for the simple reason that a good many children are bright enough to find this out for themselves. So, if systematic phonetics or phonics from the outset is taboo, there has to be some sort of an answer when a child in second or third grade begins to notice that the first letter in *cat* is different from the first letter in *sat*. This is called "phonetic analysis" and—lo and behold!—it does get mentioned in the textbooks. For instance, if you turn to the index in *Learning to Read: a Handbook for Teachers* by Carter and McGinnis of the Psycho-Educational Clinic of the Western Michigan College of Education, you will find *one* lonely page reference to "phonetic analysis." Turning back to that page, you will learn that phonetic analysis "grows out of the fact that words are made up of letters or letter combinations that have known sounds. Phonetic analysis, then, is the process of associating the appropriate sounds with the printed forms. At this stage of development [third and fourth grade] emphasis should be placed upon beginning consonant sounds."

Otherwise, phonics is usually discussed in this literature as something that stupid and ignorant parents are apt to bring up. Yes, I am not joking: Our teachers are carefully coached in what to answer parents who complain about the abandonment of phonics.

For instance, let me quote from an "official" pamphlet on *Teaching Reading* by Dr. Arthur I. Gates (of Teachers College, Columbia University) published by the National Education Association. "When a mother storms to the school," writes Dr. Gates, "to protest delaying the starting of the child to read or what she imagines is the failure to teach good old phonics, it is likely that things have already happened in the home which are having a disadvantage—indeed, sometimes a disastrous—influence on the pupil's efforts to learn. Had the mother understood the school's policy, provided it is a good one, the home life might have been organized in such a way as to assist the pupil greatly." In other words, if a parent complains that you don't teach her child the sounds of the letters, tell her the child can't read because she has made his home life unhappy.

That's what you get on the subject of phonetics in our literature on the teaching of reading. And what do the books contain instead? With what do they fill all those fat volumes with hundreds of pages if they don't mention the letters and sounds of the alphabet? Very simple: Those books are not about reading at all but about word guessing.

Because, you see, if a child isn't taught the sounds of the letters, then he has absolutely nothing to go by when he tries to read a word. All he can do is guess.

Suppose a child tries to read the sentence: "I saw a kangaroo." Suppose he has never seen the word *kangaroo* before. If he has been trained in phonics, he simply "sounds out" the *k*, the *a*, the *ng*, the *a*, the *r*, and the *oo*, and reads "kangaroo" as easy as pie. ("Ah, kangaroo!" he says. Of course he has known the meaning of the word for years.) But if he has no training in phonics, if the meaning of the letters has been carefully hidden from him, he can only guess. How can he guess? Well, the educators say, he can guess from context. With the sentence "I saw a kangaroo" that is extremely difficult, however, because it could just as easily mean "I saw a giraffe" or "I saw a flea" or "I saw a piano." So, the next thing, the child looks at the top of the page to see whether there is a picture. Usually in those factory-produced readers, when an animal is mentioned there is a picture of it somewhere on the page, so ten to one he'll find that the word means "kangaroo." And what if there isn't any picture? Well, then he has to rely on the sound of the first letter *k* if he knows *that*—or the length of the word—or its general shape—or just sheer luck. He might guess "kangaroo" or he might guess "plumber" or he might guess "forget-me-not" or—most likely—he might just sit there with a vacant look, waiting for the teacher to tell him what the word is. He knows very well she'll tell him eventually. Learning to read, he knows, is guessing or waiting until you are told what the word means.

You think I exaggerate? On the contrary: I am describing exactly what I saw in one classroom after another and what is detailed endlessly in all the textbooks on how to teach reading. Listen to them:

"Little is gained by teaching the child his sounds and letters as a first step to reading. More rapid results are generally obtained by the direct method of simply showing the word to the child and telling him what it is." (Irving H. Anderson and Walter F. Dearborn, *The Psychology of Teaching Reading.* Anderson is at the University of Michigan, Dearborn is a professor emeritus of Harvard.)

"The simplest solution when a child does not know a word is to *tell him what it says*." (*Teaching Primary Reading* by Professor Edward A. Dolch, University of Illinois. The triumphant italics are by Dr. Dolch.)

"If the word is *daddy*, the pupil may give the word *father*, or *papa*, or *man*, since the basal meaning is the same. If the word is the noun *drink*, the pupil may say *water* or *milk* or some other fluid. Similarily, words related to a common situation or to a general topic, such as *cow, horse, pig, sheep, chicken*, are likely to be mistaken for each other.

"Errors of this type are frequently regarded as evidence of carelessness on the part of the pupil. In some instances he may be reprimanded for having made a 'wild guess,' when in fact, from the point of view of meaning the guess is not at all wild. In the early stages of learning to read frequent errors of this type are to be expected. They are . . . evidence of keen use of the device of guessing words from context." (Professor Arthur I. Gates, *The Improvement of Reading*, pp. 184–185. This is generally considered the most authoritative text of them all.)

And finally, here is a perfect summary of the situation from *Teaching the Child to Read* by Bond and Wagner. Professor Guy L. Bond is at the University of Minnesota.

The usual unit of reading material is short and simple, rarely running more than four or five pages and introducing but few words. It is concerned with the common experiences of boys and girls of first-grade age whose activities are to be followed throughout the first year. Usually the boy and girl are introduced and some little story or incident told about them, mainly through the pictures with but little reading material. The pictures in the initial unit carry the story, and the words are so closely allied to the picture story that they usually can be guessed by the children. The teacher's major tasks during this time are to introduce the words in a meaningful fashion so that the children have contextual clues to aid them in "guessing" the word and to give repetition of the words so that those words may become the nucleus of a sight vocabulary. The words should be recognized as whole words. It is detrimental indeed to have the children spell or sound out the words at this stage.

Most of the modern readers have carefully worked out vocabulary so that the child will not encounter many new words in comparison to the number of words he actually reads. In various ways, which have been mentioned, the child is prepared for reading those words. In fact, he has been either given the name of the word or has been led to recognize the word before he meets it in his purposeful reading activity. When, however, he does have trouble with a word, that difficulty should not be focused upon as a difficulty. The teacher should at this stage tell him the word or lead him to guess it from the context.

What does all this add up to? It means simply and clearly that according to our accepted system of instruction, reading isn't taught at all. Books are put in front of the children and they are told to guess at the words or wait until Teacher tells them. But they are *not* taught to read —if by reading you mean what the dictionary says it means, namely, "get the meaning of writing or printing."

Now you will say that all this applies only to first grade. Not at all. If you think that after this preparatory guessing game reading begins in earnest in second grade, or in third, or in fourth, you are mistaken. Reading *never* starts. The guessing goes on and on and on, through grade school, through high school, through college, through life. It's all they'll ever know. They'll never really learn to read.

When I started to work with Johnny, I didn't quite realize all this. In my innocence, I gave him what I thought was an easy word for a twelve-year-old: *kid*. He stared at it for quite some time, then finally said "*kind*."

I tell you, it staggered me. Nobody born and raised on the continent of Europe can easily grasp the fact that *anyone* can mistake *kid* for *kind*.

Later on, when I had done a good deal of phonics work with Johnny, I gave him, as an exercise, the word *razzing*. He hesitated, then read it as *realizing*. I said, "Don't guess, Johnny." I don't know how many hundreds of times I must have said to him, "Don't guess, Johnny." To my mind, a remedial reading case is someone who has formed the habit of guessing instead of reading.

You see, remedial reading cases are harder to teach than first-graders for the simple reason that they already have four or five or six years of guessing behind them. It usually takes at least a year to cure them of the habit. There wouldn't *be* any remedial reading cases if we started teaching reading instead of guessing in first grade. (Did I say this before? Forgive me. I have fallen into the habit of telling people the simple fact about reading over and over again. It seems to be the only way.)

And how do the educators explain all the thousands and thousands of remedial reading cases? This is what really got me mad. To them, failure in reading is *never* caused by poor teaching. Lord no, perish the thought. Reading failure is due to poor eyesight, or a nervous stomach, or poor posture, or heredity, or a broken home, or undernourishment, or a wicked stepmother, or an Oedipus complex, or sibling rivalry, or God knows what. The teacher or the school is never at fault. As to the textbook or the method taught to the teacher at her teachers' college—well, that idea has never yet entered the mind of anyone in the world of education.

In the book *How to Increase Reading Ability* by Professor Albert J. Harris of Queens College, New York, there are long descriptions of remedial reading cases with all sorts of supposed causes and reasons—except the fact that Jimmie "confused *m* and *n*, *u* and *v*, *b* and *d*, *p* and *q*, *k* and *f*, and *y* and *w*," and Bruce "was unfamiliar with all of the short vowel sounds and some consonant sounds." Fortunately Dr. Harris hit upon a phonics book, the Hegge-Kirk *Remedial Reading Drills,* and that was enough in most cases to bring those unhappy children up to par in their reading. (The Hegge-Kirk drills are what I finally used with Johnny. I'll come back to that book later on.)

There are also detailed case descriptions in *The Improvement of Reading* by Dr. Arthur I. Gates, the widely used text that I mentioned before. For instance, he tells about a ten-year-old girl who "often confused the sounds of *m* with *n* and had difficulty sounding the letter *y*. She also confused *l* with *i*." A seven-year-old boy, in a "test of ability to give sounds for individual letters, did not know the following: *f, d, z, r, m, l, q, u, w, h, n* and *y*." An eight-year-old girl "in a test where she was asked to give the sounds for individual letters, missed the following: *e, x, z, q,* and *g*."

And how does Dr. Gates account for all this? He obliges us by giving each of his cases a simple explanatory label. The first of these cases is labeled

Good Intellect, Poor Reading Techniques; Sibling Rivalry a Causal Factor.

The second case is headed

Reading Difficulties Resulting From Parental Interference.

The third case is of

Poor Reading Resulting Largely From Parental Anxiety and Family Conflicts.

Dr. Gates, in contrast to Dr. Harris, didn't give his remedial cases phonics and consequently didn't help them; apparently he just gave the parents a good bawling out and let it go at that.

Most educators, however, don't go quite as far as that. They do use phonics in remedial cases—in dribs and drabs, testily, and rather furtively. Ordinary children, they say, shouldn't be deprived of the privilege of guessing words; but those poor unfortunate ones who didn't catch on to the guessing game—well, let's teach them the sounds of the letters as a last resort, purely as an emergency measure. (Remember the dictum by Dr. Durrell: "Current practice in the teaching of reading does not require a knowledge of the letters. In remedial work, such knowledge is helpful.") And so you find phonics discussed, if at all, tucked away in a section dealing with remedial reading with a careful explanation that this rather nasty medicine shouldn't be given to nice, average children who can guess the few hundred words contained in the "basal series."

The irony is that phonics is also recognized when it comes to the children *above* average—those that somehow learn to read properly and effectively *in spite of the way they were taught*. Those boys and girls, the reading experts tell us, have unusual phonic ability—which means that they managed to figure out by themselves which letter stands for which sound. Of course, you can't really read at all if you don't know that; but for our reading teachers it's a miraculous achievement, only to be explained by special gifts and extraordinary graces.

Not long ago, in January, 1954, Dr. Ruth Strang of Teachers College, Columbia University, published an article on the "Reading Development of Gifted Children" in *Elementary English*. "It may be," she wrote, "that the phonetic approach is more appropriate for the quick-learning than for the slow-learning child because of the former's greater analytical ability." (How she reconciled this observation with the fact that phonic methods are the only thing that works with retarded children I don't know.)

The article was based on statements by gifted boys and girls in junior high school. Here are some of them:

"How did I learn to read? First my grandmother taught me, then I caught on to certain words and got accustomed to sounding out words."

"By very small words and sentences. Also by syllables and the letter's sound."

"In first grade the teacher was dismissed for teaching phonetics, but I think phonetics has helped me very much in sounding out new words."

It seems clear to me that those bright twelve- and thirteen-year-olds know more about reading than all the faculties, students, and alumni of all our teachers' colleges and schools of education taken together. And I *don't* think that those children are a bit more gifted than your Johnny. They were just luckier. Just lucky enough to find out in time that learning to read means to sound out words.

Questions for Study and Discussion

1. What sentences in paragraph 5 and paragraph 6 seem strongly propagandistic? Explain.

2. What methods used by the author make the discussion of the problem seem highly objective and reliable?

3. What methods cause the reader to doubt the author's reliability?

4. In what sense is the letter primarily educational?

5. Cite three paragraphs other than 5 and 6 that are strongly propagandistic. Explain.

6. What is the author attempting to prove?

Vocabulary Study

Define the following words and phrases as used in this letter: Age of Hammurabi, emasculated, middle class, nub, phonics, benighted, educationalists, entrenched, naivete, nucleus, Oedipus complex, sibling rivalry, irony.

Writing Assignment

On the basis of your own experience in learning to read, write a composition defending or refuting Dr. Flesch's point of view.

———

The Tyranny of Multiple-Choice Tests

Banesh Hoffman

There is no escaping the testers with their electrical scoring machines. They measure our IQs at regular intervals and assess our scholastic achievement throughout our school days. They stand guard at the gateway to National Merit Scholarships, and they tell admissions officers how many points' worth of college aptitude we possess. They pass on our qualifications for graduate study and entry to professional schools. They classify us *en masse* in the Army. They screen us when we apply for jobs—whether in industry or government. They are even undertaking to certify our worth when we come up for promotion to positions far outranking their own.

The nation, in short, is placing enormous reliance on machine-graded multiple-choice tests as a measure of ability. But, unhappily, it can be shown that they have grave defects. Our confidence in them can have dangerous consequences, not only for education but for the strength and vitality of the nation. The whole question of multiple-choice testing needs thorough reexamination—and it is not getting it.

Few of the people who take these tests give much thought to where they come from. For the most part, they are not made up by the schools and other organizations that administer them. They are bought or rented. Test-making has developed into a large, lucrative, and increasingly competitive business—some of the test publishers employ traveling salesmen to promote their wares. If you have a valid reason for giving a test, you can probably find an appropriate one already in stock. Or you can commission a test-making organization to construct one to suit your special needs—although the cost may run to many thousands of dollars. (Though some tests may be purchased outright, many of the more important ones are available only for rent and under pledge of stringent secrecy; all copies must be returned immediately after use.)

The most recent edition of the *Mental Measurements Yearbook,* a compendium of information used throughout the testing industry, reviews 957 different tests (most of them of the multiple-choice type) produced by some 173 organizations, of which 28 issue catalogues of the tests they have for sale or hire. It is difficult to estimate how many millions of machine-graded multiple-choice tests are administered each year; the National Merit Scholarship Tests alone now account for half a million.

Of all these test-producing organizations, five are generally recognized as the most important:

Educational Testing Service, of Princeton, New Jersey, a nonprofit organization concentrating mainly on academic tests, among them being the well-known College Entrance Board Examinations;

Psychological Corporation, of New York City, a business organization owned and operated by professional psychologists, and devoting a larger proportion of its activities to nonacademic tests;

Science Research Associates, Inc., of Chicago, a business organization which, among other things, now publishes the Iowa Tests widely used in schools;

California Test Bureau, of Los Angeles, a business organization, one of whose best-known products is the California Test of Mental Maturity.

World Book Company, better known to the general public as a publisher of educational books (recently merged with Harcourt, Brace to form the firm of Harcourt, Brace & World, Inc.).

All five organizations are highly reputable, and together they produce the bulk of the tests used in this country. Their work is not simple. The very concept of multiple-choice tests is the result of years of research by test psychologists seeking ever more precise ways of measuring human abilities. A test emerges from an intricate collaboration. First an expert on test-making, usually one trained in psychology, maps out the test with experts in the subject to be tested and then calls on these, or other, subject experts to submit questions which can be graded by scoring machines. Test experts and subject experts reject many of the questions and reword others. The surviving questions are then "pretested" on people comparable to those for whom the test is intended, and a statistical dossier is compiled for each question. If a question is answered correctly mainly by the "better" examinees it is a good question. If it is answered correctly mainly by the "poorer" ones it is a bad question. If a fair number of the "better" examinees favor one answer and a comparable number another answer, the question is probably ambiguous. If everyone gets it right, it is useless. And so on.

In the light of the pretest statistics, still further questions are rejected or rewritten, and ultimately a rigorously screened version of the test emerges. It is now ready to be given to the people for whom it was constructed, but the process is by no means over. The test is given a preliminary tryout and the results receive elaborate statistical analysis. This yields a variety of important technical information—for example, a numerical measure of the test's success in fulfilling the purposes for which it was constructed.

The test-makers put this information into a "manual" which accompanies the test. And even now the process is not necessarily at an end, for the manual may be revised in the light of statistics accumulated during actual use of the test; and sometimes the test itself is revised.

MELANCHOLY FLAWS

The services of the test-makers understandably have been in heavy demand. They aim to meet urgent and large-scale needs: to sort out millions of servicemen; to give reliable information to college admissions officers about the abilities of candidates for entrance; to deal with increasingly large groups of job candidates in private business. Busy executives—especially those who secretly lack confidence in their own judgment—are only too happy to hand over to professional testers the job of deciding who is worthy and who is not.

For such clients, the multiple-choice test has strong and obvious appeal. It combines efficiency and economy with the splendid advantage of being labeled "objective": it can be graded quickly by machine or with a scoring stencil that even a child can use. No subjective element enters the *process* of grading. (Of course, highly subjective judgments may enter the test-makers' decisions as to which answers are to be counted as right and which wrong.)

The great question that the public must ask of the multiple-choice testing industry is not how quick and economical its products are but, simply, how good the tests are themselves. Significant flaws in the tests we use so widely should certainly be of vital concern. The test-makers, by their impressive scientific ritual of psychological expertise, pretesting, and statistical analysis, have created a widespread impression that their products must surely be free of such flaws, an impression especially prevalent among people with unshakable confidence in scientific routines, no matter how or by whom applied. Yet there is melancholy evidence to the contrary.

How would you feel, for example, if on applying for a responsible position, you were given a test with questions like this:

You are an editor forced to turn down a scholarly book which you think is a good piece of work but which will not sell. Which one of the following statements would best inform the author of your decision without discouraging him?

(A) You'll probably think me grossly mercenary when I tell you that, good though I think it is, I must turn down your book because it would have very little commercial success.

(B) You are obviously unfamiliar with the requirements of the publishing business—through no fault of your own. The point is that your book would have a very limited sale, and therefore we cannot accept it.

(C) Having read your book with great care, I must admit that it is a creditable effort. However, we doubt that it would have a great enough sale to justify our publishing it.

(D) We feel that your book is an important contribution in its field. But, since so few readers are interested in that field, we find that we cannot fit the book into our publishing program.

You cannot, of course, ask your examiner what he meant by "would best inform the author of your decision *without discouraging him.*" You are not allowed to ask questions; nor even to explain your answer. You must simply pick a letter—A, B, C, or D; you will be judged right if you pick the one the tester wants, wrong if you do not. If you fail to pick the wanted answer, and thereby jeopardize your chances of getting the job, it will be small consolation to you to know that neither one of the two editors on whom I tried this question picked the right answer.

This question is a product of the Educational Testing Service. It is taken verbatim from a booklet, *Sample Questions from the Foreign Service Officer Examination*, put out by the U.S. State Department, and is quoted here with permission. It is intended to test "the candidate's ability to recognize the appropriateness of certain forms of expression to specific situations."

I tried it on several of my colleagues. Here are their choices (I omit their various cogent reasons) : a professor of classics—D; a public relations man—C; a personnel director—C; a professor of music widely known for his writing ability—A; a professor of English—A; a professor of anthropology—C; two professors of anthropology acting in concert (after long wavering between A and D)—A; a professor of English—D; a dean—C. And not one of them had a kind word to say for the question. (The test-makers happen to consider answer D the best.)

Do questions of this sort really test what is claimed? Do they not rather test ability to fathom what is in the mind of the examiner?

When a question is merely ambiguous, like the one above, you have at least a sporting chance. But there are some questions that load the dice against you if your ability is far above the average. These occur far too frequently.

Suppose you were up for promotion to an executive position and were ordered to take the *Watson-Glaser Critical Thinking Appraisal*. Your career may be at stake. In the part of the test called "Recognition of Assumptions," you read that you are *"to decide for each assumption whether it necessarily is taken for granted in the statement."* You then read the sample question, reproduced below, that is intended to show what you are required to do; neither you nor the tester, of course, would provide parenthetical explanations of the choices if this were an actual instead of a sample question. The marks at the right, used for machine scoring, indicate that the "correct" answer is that Assumptions 1 and 2 are MADE, while Assumption 3 is NOT MADE.

Passing over the doubly faulty English in the phrase "greater speed of a plane over other means of transportation," look at the second proposed assumption, bearing in mind what the test is supposed to test, and note the force of the word *"necessarily"* in the italicized part of the instructions. In order to save time by plane it must indeed be possible to go by plane. But not necessarily "to our destination." Nor are plane "connections" essential. Therefore, the correct answer ought to be "not made."

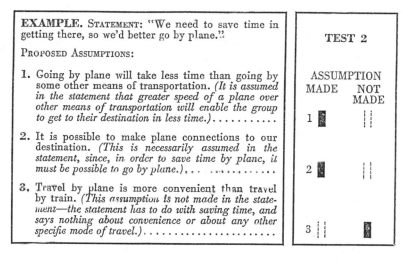

EXAMPLE. STATEMENT: "We need to save time in getting there, so we'd better go by plane."

PROPOSED ASSUMPTIONS:

1. Going by plane will take less time than going by some other means of transportation. *(It is assumed in the statement that greater speed of a plane over other means of transportation will enable the group to get to their destination in less time.)* . . . .

2. It is possible to make plane connections to our destination. *(This is necessarily assumed in the statement, since, in order to save time by plane, it must be possible to go by plane.)* . . . .

3. Travel by plane is more convenient than travel by train. *(This assumption is not made in the statement—the statement has to do with saving time, and says nothing about convenience or about any other specific mode of travel.)* . . . .

TEST 2

ASSUMPTION
MADE   NOT
            MADE

1

2

3

Sample Question from the "Watson-Glaser Critical Thinking Appraisal" (Copyright 1951–2 by Harcourt, Brace & World, Inc.; reproduced by permission): "Recognition of Assumptions"

But the test-maker says it is "made." Thus, with your future at stake, and with resentment mounting inside you, you must now abandon logic and embark instead on the hazardous task of trying to guess what other blunders the tester has made. You dare not assume he has made none. No matter how transparent a question may seem, you must stalk it warily, wondering what possible mental quirk may have influenced the test-maker's choice of answer. And while you are agonizing over the answers, less capable competitors in the promotion race who failed to spot the error are going blithely ahead, quite possibly picking wanted answers, and certainly confident that they are taking an objective test.

What would happen if you protested? Judging by what has happened in the past when individual questions have been criticized, I believe the test experts might deny that the question was bad. Certainly, they would point out that in all the years the test had been in use nobody else had complained about the question and that, in any case, statistics proved the test to be an excellent instrument for determining who is able to think critically and who is not.

In effect, you would be told that you must pay a penalty for being exceptional. You are a statistical misfit in an age of mechanized judgment.

DUBIOUS NATIONAL MERIT

Those who produce and administer tests have strong interests in defending their effectiveness, and they often cite statistics to show that the high scores of those who did well on the tests were confirmed by their later performance. Consider, for example, the National Merit Scholarship Corporation, which each year awards many millions of dollars' worth of college scholarships all over the nation and gives valuable testimonials in the form of certificates of merit to many thousands of runners-up. In its latest annual report, it speaks with pride of the accomplishments of the National Merit Scholars in college. Among other things, it says "about 82 per cent [of the scholars] rank in the top quarter of their classes even though many have selected colleges of very high academic standing."

This is a curious boast. In 1959, out of 478,991 candidates for the Merit Scholarships, all but 10,334 were eliminated from further consideration because of their scores on a qualifying test, and ultimately a mere 920 received Merit Scholarships. In four years, out of 959,683 candidates only 3,465 were awarded scholarships. The scholars are certainly a select group. Yet we gather from the Corporation's statement that not all of this presumed elite went to colleges of very high academic standing and that nevertheless, almost 20 per cent of them failed to rank even in the first quarter of their classes. Do these facts encourage faith in the screening process?

Again, the Corporation says in its report that "the national examinations have been praised as among the best available for determining aptitude and readiness to profit from a college education," and nowhere does it make any adverse remarks about these tests (except inadvertently, as in the above boast.)

The Corporation cannot always have been satisfied with its qualifying test, for in 1958 it not only made an abrupt change in the nature of the test but took the contract away from the Educational Testing Service and gave it to Science Research Associates.

What of the new National Merit Tests? There are two reviews of the April 1958 tests in the *Fifth Mental Measurements Yearbook*. One of them is, on the whole, favorable, though it does not give the glowing impression that the Corporation's words might convey to the unwary reader. The reviewer characterizes the quality of the individual questions as "acceptable," and he is by no means convinced that the new type of test is an improvement over the old. Of course, it is natural for the Corporation to put its case in as favorable light as possible. Foundations and industrial corporations have entrusted it with the distribution of enormous sums of money for scholarships and it has become, willingly or not, a by no means negligible force in the affairs of the nation. So it is understandable that the Corporation did not take public notice of the other critic, who complains that data supplied along with the test by Science Research Associates "exhibited characteristics suggestive of too much emphasis on salesmanship," and cites "as a wholesome contrast" the literature prepared by Educational Testing Service for their earlier form of the test.

The critic goes on to point out, among other things, that the test "was not suited to its task of identifying potential scholarship recipients" because it was not difficult enough for the superior candidates, and that "considerable psychometric naivete is exhibited in several sections of the Technical Manual," a charge he documents by pointing out significant flaws in the interpretation of statistics. He remarks briefly that "some of the [questions] are poorly written." He says that the parts of the test that deal with social studies and natural science "measure almost entirely reading ability and general verbal aptitude," and in this connection he points out that the statistics cited by Science Research Associates show scores on the social studies part to be about as good a measure of ability in natural science as they are of ability in social studies, and vice versa. He ends with the following words:

"In conclusion, the [qualifying test] and the literature distributed about it did not seem to be a step forward. The reviewer is concerned that assessment psychology has been retarded and may have lost ground through the production and use of this test. He is amazed and disturbed that such inferior work can be conducted and tolerated on such a large scale. It is hoped that it will not be repeated." The people who take the tests, of course, know nothing of such criticisms and the tests go merrily on.

STATISTICS SHOW : : :

Can anything be done about the multiple-choice tests? Must we simply accept them passively? It is not difficult to find prominent educators and other commentators who have launched wide-ranging *general* protests against them. William H. Whyte in *The Organization Man* and Professor Jacques Barzun in *The House of Intellect* are but two of the more recent.

These writers and others have made many charges against the tests. For example:

The tests deny the creative person a significant opportunity to demonstrate his creativity, and favor the shrewd and facile candidate over the one who has something of his own to say.

They penalize the candidate who perceives subtle points unnoticed by less able people, including the test-makers.

They are apt to be superficial and intellectually dishonest, with questions made artificially difficult by means of ambiguity because genuinely searching questions do not readily fit into the multiple-choice format.

They too often degenerate into subjective guessing games in which the candidate does not pick what he considers the best answer out of a bad lot, but rather the one he believes the unknown examiner would consider the best.

They neglect skill in disciplined expression.

They have, in sum, a pernicious effect on education and the recognition of merit.

But such criticisms do not seem to disturb the test-makers, who, well entrenched and growing more powerful every day, have developed a strikingly effective routine for dealing with their critics.

When confronted with general criticisms, they make a show of patient reasonableness. Of course they welcome concerned criticism, they say. But the critic is just an amateur offering mere opinion, not scientific fact. After all, they are experts, and they know. Having said this, they go on to extol the virtues of their product. They speak proudly of the professional competence of the people who make their tests—recently the president of the Educational Testing Service boasted of "hundreds of outstanding teachers from schools and colleges" who work with his organization. They point to the elaborate scientific ritual they follow in constructing and evaluating their tests. Insisting that "statistics show . . . !" they surround themselves with such an aura of scientific infallibility that few people realize that they have avoided answering the criticism aimed at them.

There is, I suggest, a way to penetrate this defense. Instead of making general criticisms, one should exhibit specific test questions, such as the two I have presented above; declare that they are defective; and challenge the test-makers to defend these questions *specifically*.

The test-makers intensely dislike this sort of challenge because it puts them in a quandary. They have to be wary of conceding that the questions are bad and claiming that they are rare exceptions, for they do not know how many more examples the challenger has in reserve. On the other hand, if they defend a bad question by their "statistics show . . ." maneuver, they risk the implication that their use of statistics is improper or that their statistics are untrustworthy. If they defend the question by referring to the scientific ritual used in constructing their tests, they undermine faith in the efficacy of that ritual. If they defend it by pointing to the high caliber of their staff experts and consultants, they may well start people wondering whether the caliber is high enough. Therefore, a sharply focused challenge of specific questions seems the one *effective* means by which the quality of multiple-choice tests can be called into question.

It is important to point out, however, that no matter how many defective sample questions one could find, no more than a *prima facie* case could be made against the testers because most of the important tests used for competitive selection purposes are kept secret. Even if the sample questions are found to be defective, we still have no way of knowing whether they fairly reflect the tests themselves. In short, there is at present no way for a comprehensive and independent judgment of the tests to be made in the public interest.

One solution to this dilemma could be the formation of a completely independent board of eminent educators and scholars which could have access to the whole range of questions produced by the testing organizations. Committee members could examine the actual tests and the statistical evidence concerning them, consult with experts and their critics, and form an opinion as to the real worth of current tests. The scope of their critique should extend far beyond the technical reviews of tests now published in the *Mental Measurements Yearbooks*. The committee could open up the question whether the multiple-choice format is really suited to measuring the various kinds of ability tested today. If they found the tests wanting, they might recommend alternative approaches to testing to supplement or supplant the multiple-choice method. And they could consider the merits of the rather hesitant steps already being taken within the testing industry to augment the role of essay questions in certain testing programs.

If, however, they found that present tests are doing a generally effective job, we would have the assurance that this was a conclusion arrived at not merely by the test-makers and their clients but by a distinguished independent board acting in the public interest. ...*

TOO CRUCIAL FOR TRUST

In view of the above, most of us would agree with the College Board that the question is "difficult." But with us this is merely a matter of opinion. With the test experts it is an objective, scientific, no-nonsense fact based on statistics. Of course, the statistics do not reveal that the wording of the question is vague. Nor that, if the wanted answer is a correct one, so are three others. Nor that the examiners have chosen the most immediate and superficial answer, thus penalizing the candidates with more probing minds, as they so often do. Can we be complacent when we know that such questions are used by so many of our colleges to assess scientific talent?

As I have pointed out, my first published challenges of two sample questions from the Scholastic Aptitude Test elicited no public defense of the questions themselves from the College Entrance Examination Board. Will the Board now come forward and defend the two additional science questions I have cited above, and defend them *specifically*? Will the organizations that produced the two other questions quoted in the first part of this article defend those questions—their own samples—and defend them *specifically*? And if the criticisms I have made remain unchallenged, will there not be a *prima-facie* case for a full-scale inquiry into the whole question of testing for aptitude and ability? If an outstanding organization like the Educational Testing Service can, after twice filtering its questions, come up with such defective specimens, would there not seem to be legitimate cause for concern about the methods and products of other test-making organizations?

Admittedly there is no easy solution to the problem of testing. That is why the committee I advocated earlier should include creative people of commanding intellectual stature who could bring fresh vision to the testing situation, especially as it affects those gifted young people whose

---

*With the author's permission we have omitted the citation and discussion of two sample questions taken from two booklets published by the College Entrance Examination Board. The author's purpose in the omitted material is to demonstrate that the superior student is at a disadvantage in arriving at the normally expected answer to the most difficult questions in multiple-choice tests. For further discussion, see Chapters 16 and 17 of the author's book, *The Tyranny of Testing*.

talents do not conform to the statistically based norms of the multiple-choice testers. Only a minority of such a committee should consist of test psychologists or professional test-makers. Perhaps one way to bring such a group into being would be through appointment—with or without foundation help—by scholarly organizations of the highest repute—for instance, the American Council of Learned Societies, the National Academy of Sciences, and the Modern Language Association.

It would be premature to anticipate the conclusions of such a committee. Certainly there is a case for the usefulness of multiple-choice tests, properly constructed, in a limited range of testing. It is possible that their quality can be much improved. But if it is decided that their very format makes them inappropriate for broader testing purposes, their tight grip on our educational system should be broken. Testing in this country is too crucial an activity to be accepted on trust.

Questions for Study and Discussion

1. What is the author attempting to prove in this selection?
2. By what means does the author establish a certain degree of objectivity in his arguments?
3. What are the propagandistic elements in the selection?
4. What makes it more educational than propagandistic?
5. Point out the major similarities in methods of this selection and "A Letter to Johnny's Mother."

Vocabulary Study

Define the following words and phrases as used in this selection: compendium, reputable, dossier, ambiguous, melancholy, mercenary, inadvertently, facile, aura, quandary.

Writing Assignment

Write a composition defending multiple-choice tests.

Education and Democracy

Robert M. Hutchins

Only the other day I read for what seemed to me the hundredth time that one more distinguished educator had said that the University of Chicago, or at least its chancellor, stood for limiting education to an intellectual elite. The conclusion was, of course, that the University of Chicago, or at least its chancellor, was undemocratic. I should like to try this morning to make clear the relationship between education and democracy. Confusion about this issue lies, I think, at the bottom of most of the confusion about education.

Consider the case of Thomas Jefferson. He was a celebrated democrat. He proposed that all children in Virginia should receive three years' free instruction in reading, writing, arithmetic, and geography. He said, "The mass of our citizens may be divided into two classes—the laboring and the learned. . . . At the discharging of the pupils from the elementary schools, the two classes separate—those destined for labor will engage in the business of agriculture, or enter into apprenticeships to such handicraft art as may be their choice; their companions, destined to the pursuits of science, will proceed to the college. . . ."

Three years of free education for all was doubtless a notable contribution to democratic practice in Jefferson's day. But the notion that it is possible to separate human beings at the age of nine or ten into those destined for labor and those destined for learning surpasses the fondest hopes of the psychological testers of our own time and seems to be an oligarchical notion. It seems to be based, not on the differences in the abilities of individuals, but on the differences in their social and economic background. Those destined for labor were destined for it primarily because they were the children of laboring men. Those destined for learning were destined for it because their fathers had wealth and leisure, and it was supposed that they would have wealth and leisure, too. These were the men who were to rule the commonwealth. They, and they alone, needed a liberal education.

Jefferson, great as he was, seems to have suffered from the limitations of his time. The foundation of democracy is universal suffrage. Universal suffrage makes every man a ruler. If every man is a ruler, every man needs the education that rulers ought to have. If liberal education is the education of rulers, then every man needs a liberal education. If Jefferson did not see this, it may be because in his day the right to vote, and hence to rule, was still regarded as the privilege of the few who had inherited or acquired property.

In America the oligarchs have lost the battle. We have, or are on the way to having, universal suffrage. We have, or are on the way to having, universal education. Every man is now a ruler. But in the changes of the past 150 years the idea of an education appropriate to rulers has got lost somewhere.

It seems to have got lost because, though we are for universal suffrage and universal education, we have not noticed the connection between the two. The kind of education we accept now when everybody is destined to rule is fundamentally an extension of the kind that in Jefferson's time was thought suitable for those destined to labor but not to rule. When we talk of our political goals, we admit the right of every man to be a ruler. When we talk of our educational program, we see no inconsistency in saying that only a few have the capacity to get the education that rulers ought to have. We believe that the people are qualified to rule; many among us do not believe that the people are qualified for the education of rulers. The popular syllogism—and it is popular in the highest educational circles—runs like this: everybody has the right to education. But only a few are qualified for a good education. Those who are not qualified for a good education must be given a bad education, because everybody has the right to education. Anybody who favors a good education must, therefore, be antidemocratic, because only a few are qualified for a good education. The paradoxical consequence is that those who believe in the capacity of the people are called reactionary and antidemocratic, whereas those who doubt the capacity of the people revel in the name of democrats and liberals.

Because of our belief in the extension of education, the educational system has been swamped with steadily increasing numbers. Merely to supply custodial care for the tremendous flood of pupils that has inundated the system would have put a serious strain on the intelligence of any country. The preposterous grading and credit methods in general use in the United States owed their origin rather more to the difficulty of dealing with vast hordes of students than to the fact, upon which Thorstein Veblen insisted, that we live in an accountant's world and have to have a scheme of educational accountancy to keep education in tune with the times.

The education of rulers is a hard education to give. Uneducated or half-educated teachers, teachers who did not have this education themselves, could hardly be expected to know or to have time to find out how to give this education to boys and girls who descended on them in enormous quantities, who did not always look or act like future rulers, and who showed few signs of wanting to take the long, hard path toward learning how to rule. Since many pupils did not seem to want a good education, since many teachers could not help them get it even if they did want it, the impression was naturally created that the mass of the people were not capable of getting a good education.

If you want all young people in school, because you believe in universal education, and if you don't know what to do with them when you get them in school, because it seems impossible to give them the kind of education they ought to have, you must think up all kinds of reasons for having them in school other than the one good reason, which would be that you proposed to help them get the kind of education they ought to have. And all kinds of reasons have been thought up. But I think it fair to say that most attempts at rationalization have now been abandoned. For example, the Report of the President's Commission on Higher Education takes the position that it is a good thing to have all young people in school at least until the age of twenty and that it is immaterial what they do there. It is simply a good thing for them to be there. This is a logical consequence of their assumed inability to do what they ought to be doing there. We want them to be in school because we believe in universal education. We cannot give them the education of rulers because they have not the ability to acquire it.

But surely there is no magic about merely being in school. I hold that everybody can learn; but this does not mean that it makes no difference what he learns. A bad education may be worse than none. We cannot define education as whatever goes on in educational institutions. The most obvious fact about education is the one most often overlooked, and that is that formal education is a practical enterprise. As such, it must be carried out within a certain time and with certain means; and that time and those means must be spent with a view to achieving the purpose of the enterprise.

It follows that irrelevant or insignificant activities must be excluded, because they consume the time and means needed to achieve the main purpose, and because they confuse the institution about what its main purpose is. If the main purpose of a democratic educational system is the education of rulers, then everything that does not contribute to the achievement of that purpose must be excluded, or at least postponed until that purpose has been achieved.

If all men are to be rulers, then the educational system must avoid any kind of education that is based on the assumption that some are to rule and others to be ruled. As Medford Evans and George Clark said in *Harper's Magazine* not long ago,

> In every society where there is a ruling class there is one kind of education for the rulers and another for the ruled. Vocational training, which confines itself to teaching skills, tends to limit the individual's interest in general social problems and to discourage intelligent participation in political life. As such it is the ideal education for the servants of the ruling class. . . . There is no more radical and democratic idea afloat in educational circles today than that of providing liberal education for everyone. Conversely, there is no group more anti-democratic than those who believe that for the majority of people vocational training is enough.

Here the authors echo the words of John Dewey in his book, "Democracy and Education," written more than thirty years ago,

> To split the system, and give to others, less fortunately situated, an education conceived mainly as specific trade preparation, is to treat the schools as an agency for transferring the older division of labor and leisure, culture and service, mind and body, directed and directive class, into a society nominally democratic.
>
> I embrace the radical and democratic idea of liberal education for all. I reject the notion that some of our rulers are incapable of being educated for their task of ruling. I insist that, if some of them act as though they were incapable, it is because we have not found out how to teach them, not because they cannot learn.

Of course, rulers do not spend all their time ruling. In our society they have to support themselves. But as Mr. Dewey said, "The only adequate training *for* occupations is training *through* occupations." There are a great many things citizens have to do that education cannot help them do; if it tries to help them to do them, it will merely fail in its own task. And it will be found, I think, that those arts and sciences which ruling requires are not altogether useless in the ordinary business of life. Those arts and sciences are clearly most useful in that expanding area of our lives which is known as leisure. Education regarded as preparation for some future occupation loses such value as it may have in direct proportion as the share of a person's life devoted to earning a living decreases. The steady decline in the hours of labor means a steady decline in the significance of vocational training and a steady increase in the significance of the arts and sciences that are thought to prepare the student to rule.

Leisure is something more than relaxation. The Greek word for leisure is the origin of our word for school. Leisure means intellectual and moral growth, which Mr. Dewey described as the dominant vocation of all human beings at all times, and it means activity on behalf of the common good rather than one's selfish advancement. Education for leisure in a democratic society is not distinguishable from education for ruling. Hence your university has sponsored on a national scale a program of education for adults, and it is intended for all adults, that is, as nearly as possible, an extension of the program of liberal education conducted for younger students on the campus.

Liberal education in a society built on slavery was the education of free men. In a society divided into a class that ruled and a class that was ruled it was education of the ruling class. Liberal education was an aristocratic education. It was so because the society in which it developed was aristocratic. When society becomes democratic, should the citizens have the education of free men or the education of slaves? Should they have the education of the ruling class or of the class that was to be ruled? It has never been suggested, as far as I know, that liberal education was not a good education for the purpose for which it was intended, namely, the education of rulers. It has been stigmatized as undemocratic because it was formulated in an era when only the few were rulers, when only the few had power and leisure. When every citizen is a ruler, when every citizen has power and leisure, the education that was good for the few becomes a good education for every citizen. To attack liberal education as aristocratic is to mistake its origins for its content.

The way to determine who is to have a liberal education is to ask who are to be the rulers of your society. If the answer is everybody, then the conclusion follows that everybody must have a liberal education. If you do not like this conclusion, you do not like democracy; you do not like universal suffrage, and you should move to abandon democracy and universal suffrage. The one thing you cannot do is to say at one and the same time that everybody has the right to vote and only the few have the right to liberal education.

In my view the educational system is not a housing project designed to keep young people off the labor market until we are ready to have them go to work. It is not a combination sanitarium, dancing class, and reformatory. Nor is it a place in which the whims of the public, of parents, of students, or of special interests are to find their gratification. The slogan, "Education for All," cannot mean merely that all young people must go to school. It cannot mean that the educational system has done its duty if everybody is in school up to the age of twenty, regardless of what he is doing there. Education for all, if it means anything, must mean that everybody is to be educated.

It must mean that everybody is to have that education, to experience that moral and intellectual growth, which will fit him for his dominant vocation of democratic citizenship. It does not mean that he may remain indefinitely in the educational system at public expense. When the system has helped the student get started on liberal education—it is a process that should go on through the whole of life, and by the time a young person is 19 or 20—then specialized education, education for individual interests and special callings, may begin. Access to such specialized education is not a right in the same sense in which access to liberal education is. It may properly be limited to those who have demonstrated their capacity to profit by it. In the case of liberal education no such limitation can be permitted. Our political system and our political ideals require us to find out how to give that education to everybody, no matter what we assume his capacity to be.

The usual answer is that it cannot be done. I say that it must be done and that there is no evidence that it cannot be done. Liberal education consists fundamentally in learning how to use the mind so that it can operate well in all fields and deal with new problems as they arise. Men are rational animals, and though the fact that they are animals should never be forgotten, the fact that they are rational is equally well established and infinitely more important, for the rationality of men gives us some hope that they may ultimately learn how to control their animality. The object of the educational system is the development of the rational powers of men.

It is impossible to use the mind without knowing how to read, write, and figure. It is impossible to use the mind to operate well in all fields and to be prepared for new problems as they arise without having studied the models of greatness in all fields and without having some understanding of the way in which the great issues that have concerned mankind have been met by the best minds of the past. Although the methods of liberal education may vary and their application may be proportioned to individual differences among students, the aim of liberal education remains constant from epoch to epoch. It is the education of rulers in the use of their minds.

Failure to educate the rulers of a democratic society cannot be excused by saying that they have no minds, or that all of them do not always care to learn how to use them. The blame for failure must be placed where it belongs, first, on the educational system, which has found it easier to say that the students cannot do the work than to find out how to help them do it; and, second, on the community, which has been satisfied to cherish the illusion that the educational problem is solved through numbers—numbers of pupils, numbers of buildings, numbers of teachers, and numbers of dollars.

To propose liberal education for all is certainly not proposing to limit education to an intellectual elite. It is proposing that every citizen have the education that used to be limited to an intellectual elite. This is what it means to take democratic education seriously.

In the past there has been no particular reason why we should take democratic education seriously. We could afford to trifle away our time in any way we liked. Now America is the most powerful nation in the world; and it is not the least dangerous. The whole world knows of our riches, our resources, our scientific knowledge, our technical skill. The question is, will they be used for good or ill? The fate of the whole world—and the whole world knows it very well—depends upon the answer. The fate of the whole world depends from minute to minute on the intelligence and character that the American people bring to their common task of democratic citizenship. The time for trifling in American education is past.

Questions for Study and Discussion

1. What is the author's thesis in this essay?

2. Does any sentence in the fifth paragraph cast doubt on either the author's sincerity or his knowledge about the facts with which his thesis deals?

3. On what basis can the fifth sentence in the sixth paragraph be classified as propagandistic?

4. Point out five additional sentences in this essay that have propagandistic overtones.

5. What are the educational values of this essay?

Vocabulary Study

Define the following words and phrases as used in this essay: elite, oligarchical, universal suffrage, syllogism, revel, custodial, inundated, preposterous, rationalization, stigmatized, rationality.

Writing Assignment

Write a paragraph strongly refuting one important contention in Mr. Hutchins' argument.

CHAPTER 4

EFFECTIVE ADVERTISING: THE ART OF HIDDEN PERSUASION

Whispers for Sale: Verbal Advertising

Robert Littell and John J. McCarthy

Whether you like it or not—and few people do—you will now please imagine yourself to be sitting among the tired commuters on a certain five-fifteen Philadelphia suburban train. It is a dreary, uninteresting scene, and we apologize. We could have demonstrated our discovery—a new and sinister variation in an ancient human activity—by taking you to a movie cathedral or a department store, or by whisking you up and down in an office building elevator; but this commuters' train is more suitable, for reasons which will soon appear.

The train is crowded. Those of the commuters who were lucky enough to find seats are hidden behind the evening newspapers. The aisle is jammed with others who were not so lucky. Two of them are standing right beside you: a moderately prosperous-looking business man with octagonal spectacles, and a younger man in the uniform of a chauffeur. They are talking, but what they are trying to say is drowned out as the train roars into a tunnel.

Did we say this scene was uninteresting, commonplace, uneventful? Only to those who have no imagination. It may strike you merely as a jolting interval between work and home, but actually it is much more than that. It is a battlefield, a marketplace, a hunting ground. From one end of the car to the other, near the ceiling, runs a double line of advertising posters. The passengers are not looking at them; they are reading the newspapers. The newspapers are also full of advertising. The passengers have seen so many thousands of car cards and newspaper advertisements that they are to some extent immune.

But never wholly immune. When they leave this train some of these commuters will have a desire to buy, and to buy something, which they did not have when they got on.

Americans spend a great deal of their time thinking about things and about buying them. Those two men beside you for instance. The one in the chauffeur's uniform is now saying, to the business man with the octagonal glasses: "Yes, Mr. Bradley, those God-sent tires are the best I ever put on the boss's car."

"You don't say, John," answers the business man; "how many thousand miles do you get out of them?"

They have good ringing voices, these two, and some of the commuters nearest to them glance up, automatically, and seem to be listening to them. . . .

Did we say that this train was an invisible marketplace? It is also a hunting ground. The advertisements—in the newspapers and along the top of car—are the hunters. They are spraying the commuters with the fine shot of their sales appeal. But the commuters have tough hides, and not many of the pellets that manage to hit them sink in. The hits are few for all the shot and powder expended. There ought to be some cheaper, quicker, surer method.

The train is running through open country now (the landscape, as well as the inside of this car, is full of advertising matter). There is less noise, and several dozen commuters are listening, perhaps for lack of anything better to do, perhaps because they are really interested, to the loud voices of the chauffeur and the business man. The former is saying:

"Those God-sent Tires have gone twenty-two thousand miles, and are just as good as ever. Why, the tread is hardly worn."

"Is that so?" answers the business man; "I guess I'll get a set for my bus; they sound good to me, and you ought to know, John. What did you say their name was?"

"God-sent," says the chauffeur, "God-sent Non-Skid Four-Ply Balloons."

The chauffeur speaks with the confidence of experience, and the business man nods assent. He is impressed, he will probably buy some God-sent Tires himself. The commuters who have been listening are probably vaguely impressed also. Some of them will look into these new and remarkable tires; a few will buy them, as a result of this casually overheard conversation in a public conveyance. The sales of God-sent Tires may even turn out to be better than if these tires were advertised in the car cards and the newspapers which these same commuters have been reading; for word-of-mouth advertising, the unconscious salesmanship of the customers who have bought something, and like it, and tell their friends about it, is one of the most potent stimulants of trade. Most people remember the human voice longer than they do the printed word. Since the printed word frankly has an axe to grind, volunteer grinders are sometimes more effective. Think of your own life: of the number of books you read, the number of films you see, the number of things you buy because you heard someone else say that they were worth reading, seeing, buying.

The train jolts to a stop. "Well, here's where I get off," says the business man.

"Me too, Mr. Bradley," answers the chauffeur. They move down the aisle. Let us follow them and question them and find out if they realize what effect they may be having on the sale of God-sent Tires.

They get off, and we almost lose them in the crowd. Ah, here they are—must have left something behind, for they are climbing aboard the train again. But they're not getting on the right car. They're not even getting on it together; they enter at opposite doors and meet in the middle.

"Why, hello, John," says the business man, "I thought you'd be out driving the boss on a fine day like this."

The other commuters cannot fail to hear them.

"No, sir," answers the chauffeur. "I've been downtown ordering a new set of God-sent Tires for our Cadillac."

"God-sent, eh—is that a good tire? Mine are pretty well shot."

"Yes, sir. I figure it's the best tire on the market right now. Mileage? Say, the set we have on the Lincoln has gone twenty-two thousand miles and the tread is hardly worn."

"Now that's very interesting—what did you say the name of these tires was?"

And so on—line for line the conversation we heard in the other car. One by one of the commuters prick up their ears. They are interested, they all drive automobiles, they will all need new tires some day, and their sales resistance is gone because they are not aware that anyone is trying to sell them something.

If we follow John and Mr. Bradley we shall find them repeating this act, over and over again; we shall see them get out of one car and into the next as long as there are commuters left to listen to them. Just why are these two broadcasting their interest in God-sent Tires? Are they practical jokers? Or escaped lunatics? Or a vaudeville team out of work and rehearsing a new routine? Or recent members of some fraternal order going through an initiation stunt? Or sincere, but somewhat fanatical admirers of God-sent Tires, trying to make others hit the trail?

The answer in each case is, obviously, no. Mr. Bradley and chauffeur John are unemployed actors now serving as recruits in that small, secret, but growing battalion of professional word-of-mouth advertisers. If the struggle of advertisers versus consumers is, owing to increasing skill on one side and increasing immunity on the other, like the deadlock of trench warfare, these actors are an attempt to break the deadlock; they are the newest invention, they are invisible whippet tanks which sneak across no man's land under cover of their own ingenious smoke screen, place their bomblets of discreet propaganda deep in the unsuspecting enemy's territory, and as quietly depart.

If we observe John and Mr. Bradley now, with the sharp eyes of disillusionment, we shall notice things we did not notice when they seemed to be casual conversationalists: that their voices are a little louder and clearer than is quite necessary, that the name of the tire they are bringing to people's attention is very frequently repeated, and that their eyes have a way of wandering while they talk. This is not only because they know their lines by heart, and are not unnaturally a trifle bored by them, but because they must look about them and be sure not to do their act in the hearing of passengers who have heard it before. If they spot a familiar face they will shut up, and move away, and keep moving until they feel that their audience is again composed of strangers.

II

The "trained verbal propagandist" is something new in advertising. As yet—fortunately—he is not very common, but there may be a big future ahead of him. There are already a number of national advertising agencies, and some smaller and less reputable ones, which are experimenting on a large scale with verbal propaganda and believe in its value. The two men we have been watching are small cogs in a nationwide campaign for a tire—whose name is not of course "God-sent." While they talk and ride, and get out and ride and talk again, four other teams of verbal propagandists, dressed as they were and rehearsed in the same conversation, are working other trains, subways, and elevateds. A hundred times that same day homeward-bound citizens are attracted by loud clear voices, and look up from their papers to find a well-dressed chauffeur and a prosperous business man talking enthusiastically about a singularly cheap and reliable tire. Other products, in other cities, are probably even now being inserted into your innocent ears by the same method.

The theory behind this new method is highly plausible. Advertising which declares itself to be advertising—and almost all advertising sails under its true colors—is subjected by the public to a heavy discount. But the words of friends, the remarks even of casual strangers, are listened to without suspicion, and remembered. Therefore a good counterfeit of casual conversation can insinuate itself into places and produce results impossible to the frank and over-familiar salesmanship of the printed advertisement and the sponsored broadcast. The public, having listened, will pass the good news on in exactly the same way to its own friends. Word-of-mouth is probably the motive power of most buying anyhow. Here is a method of putting a few telling professional words into many amateur mouths.

The technic and economics are as simple as the theory. The advertising agency which employed Mr. Bradley and John and their eight colleagues undertook to cover Philadelphia with a barrage of God-sent tire talk for twenty-one days. Fifteen days would have been enough for a city of a million; a longer period would be necessary in New York. In any case the time may seem too short; but there are obvious hours and places where potential tire purchasers congregate, while a printed advertisement, not being movable upon two legs, must spray a much more indiscriminate area. For each pair of verbal propagandists the agency charges the God-sent Tire Company fifteen dollars a day. Add to this, carfare, hotel bills and incidentals. Add $17.50 for a supervisor to route the propagandists and check up on them, and report their travels, hours, and accomplishments. The total is not much more than two thousand dollars—less than the price of two full-page advertisements in one issue of one newspaper.

The working propagandists are paid about four dollars a day. They have to be imported from somewhere else, for they mustn't be recognized by their listeners. They have to be trained, for amateurs would be self-conscious, and a considerable degree of practice and skill is required in order to say something over and over again in public with complete naturalness. They must be dressed for the part or cast to fit its requirements. John and Mr. Bradley—though they earn less than thirty dollars a week apiece—are in character, and look like the men they pretend to be. If the agency contracts to spread *viva voce* propaganda for dresses, the operatives must be attractive and well-turned-out young women. If the client is a manufacturer of dentifrice, the pairs whose words spread the product upon the city's innocent toothbrushes must themselves have fine, white, flashing mouthfuls of teeth.

We have all seen, in subways and magazines, the pictures of those unbelievable young people with teeth like Dresden china. We don't altogether believe that our own battered, ochre chewing apparatus can become like that. But imagine that we find ourselves in the subway next to a handsome young woman talking to a young man. Her mouth flashes white, porcelain white with every syllable, as she says to him:

"You were a grouch last night, Joe; Mary says it was a toothache."

"Yes," answers Joe, "I had a terrible toothache."

"You know what, Joe, you should do what I did for a toothache—go down to the No-Pain-Easy-Pay Dentists downtown in the Jones Building and see if they don't fix you up so you never have another toothache like it happened to me. Yes, write it down—No-Pain-Easy-Pay, Jones Building."

We suspect of course that the propagandists don't talk quite as colloquially as this. They are given lines, and learn them, and speak them as they are written, and most advertising copy-writers don't write American dialogue like Ring Lardner or John O'Hara.

Do the verbal propagandists speak and act naturally enough for this new method to be successful? Apparently they do, for, besides tires and dental services, the propaganda agencies are known to have spread the good word for men's and women's clothes, furniture, radio programs, department stores, beverages, and vacation resorts.

Just how successful most of these campaigns were it is hard to say;

for secrecy, not unnaturally, veils this method as heavily as it does the work of international spying—which it somewhat resembles. Neither the agency nor the client boasts of the results in public; for though some of the dupes would laugh, most of them would be violently resentful.

We can, however, vouch for two instances. Both were large department stores, and department stores can "key" any given item so as to know pretty accurately the exact effect upon it of a particular medium of advertising. Instance number one: a department store, which was stuck with a great surplus of raincoats that simply would not move off the shelves, hired an agency to put squads of its talkers to work about the town. The talkers, talking raincoats all the time, rode up and down in elevators, haunted the street cars and the elevateds, mingled—still talking—with the crowds in moving picture houses. Seven thousand raincoats were sold within a week.

The second instance, while also a success story, has refinements and wheels within wheels which show how limitless is the horizon for engineers of verbal propaganda who are not too scrupulous. A manufacturer of women's gloves (let us call them Slicko gloves) found them hard to sell. The agency's talkers went to work—probably they were paid very little, for the job was a simple one. Every day for weeks some hundreds of women (sometime the same ones, but that wasn't noticed) went up to the glove counter of the town's chief department store and said, "Have you Slicko gloves? What? No Slicko gloves! Why don't you carry Slicko gloves? I want a pair of Slicko gloves!"—rather like an author trying to boom his own book.

The store's glove buyer was duly impressed by this popular demand and ordered some thousands of pairs of Slicko gloves.

If the manufacturer and the advertising agency had at this point rested on their oars, the department store would have begun to wonder why all the women who had been clamoring for Slicko gloves had suddenly gone out of town. It would be fatal if the gloves were not sold, if the sudden demand were as suddenly allowed to collapse. So the squads of glove-loving women, provided with nice new gloves by the manufacturer and a nice new line of talk by the advertising agency, began to march about the city in pairs, stretching out their gloved hands and saying, in elevators, street cars, film palaces: "These Slicko gloves are the best I've ever had! Lookit my Slicko gloves! I just love my Slicko gloves!" It worked; within a short time the gloves were sold.

The method may strike you as not quite ethical. The propagandists are in disguise. They are listened to and believed because they seem to be unbiased. That is their strength from the practical point of view; but there is another point of view. The agencies which deal in such propaganda do not think it wrong. One of their representatives puts the case for it fairly persuasively:

"I don't see how our methods," he says, "differ from those of any other publicizing or advertising organization. When a Fifth Avenue dressmaker wants to popularize his creations he hires models to mingle with the crowds in smart hotels, at the theater, at the races. They don't wear his label, they pass for society women. Over and over again in the magazines one can see the picture of a business executive endorsing some product. If the man in the picture isn't a business executive at all, but a photographer's model who looks the part, what of it? And those radio playlets in which some Park Avenue hostess (unnamed) is heard discussing the merits of a new face cream—does anyone object because she is really an actress trying to earn a living on the air? Our verbal propagandists are, like these people, simply trained talent impersonating imaginary characters for the legitimate purpose of increasing the sales of a legitimate product."

Let us remind you that this method is in its infancy, but growing. Probably very few of the kind words you hear in public about an article of merchandise are so paid for, but more and more reputable concerns are using it, or seriously considering its merits. These merits are obvious. Verbal propagandists are flexible, mobile shock troops. They can be thrown into any sector of the merchandising front upon very short notice. Their services are standardized and not expensive. They are secret, and as long as they remain secret, invulnerable; their campaigns, being surprise attacks under cover of darkness, do not instantly call forth the counter-attack of a competitor. Unlike all other advertising, they are uncensored, and can say things that would not be said in print.

And they can also perform tasks which no open advertising can perform at all: they can influence employees, and the public, in matters which have nothing to do with the buying and selling of goods.

III

Perhaps the first and certainly the best known of these propaganda agencies is the national organization of W. Howard Downey and Associates, with offices in New York, Chicago, Atlanta, and Toronto. It has helped to sell goods by the methods we describe, but it is chiefly remarkable for being the first such agency to substitute, in the breaking of strikes, subtle verbal propaganda for the traditional strong-arm methods of the Pinkertons and Pearl Bergoff.

The Downey strike method, which is now a routine recommendation of practically every other propaganda agency, is simple, painless, and neither gets people into hospitals nor itself into the news columns. Through the neighborhoods where the strikers live go small bands of trained propagandists, disguised as house-to-house canvassers and peddlers of women's silk stockings, brushes, and other household articles. When—as usually happens—the wife of a striker refuses to buy, the propagandist sympathizes with her:

"I can understand perfectly, madam, why you haven't any money to buy these bargains in fine hoisery. Your husband is on strike, isn't he? Well, of course it's none of my business, but I hate to see you folks deprived of the necessities of life just so these few strike organizers can ride around in big cars and draw down fat salaries. I was once a union man myself, but no more. See where it got me: selling stuff from door to door. Do you know what salary the labor organizer draws when your husband isn't on strike? Twenty-five dollars a week and no expenses. And when your husband *is* on strike? Why then that organizer draws one hundred dollars a week and plenty of expenses. Get it?"

The strikers' wives get it. When the strikers come home many of them find their wives on strike against the strike. We were told, by the representative of one of these propaganda agencies, about a recent long and bitter strike in Ohio. Three days after the house-to-house propaganda method was applied the strike was over.

Of course the use of words as invisible poison gas antedates the war, but the recent flowering and the subtle ramifications of commercial propaganda owe much to the methods that were so marvelously developed between 1914 and 1918. The propaganda agencies we are talking about do not deal in poison; they all emphatically deny part in the campaigns of whispered slander that sweep periodically across the country to the despair of many a manufacturer. Yet someone, possibly for a *quid pro quo*, is doing a great deal of dirty work. Rumor has wings; the dirtier the rumor the bigger the wings. No one knows exactly where or how commercial whispering campaigns start; in spite of offers of large rewards, no culprit and no real evidence have ever been found. They may be born in the imagination of salesmen, for salesmen are hard put to it, these days of bitter competition, to get ahead of one another. At any rate there are a great many more such epidemics of whispering than there used to be, and most of them were born in the last year or two, when our economic waters were lowest and more stagnant. The whispers, naturally, are always at the expense of the largest companies. It is an old axiom of salesmanship that the simplest way to get business is to take it away from the leaders.

Not long ago a large and country-wide chain of restaurants discovered, (a) that in New York it was losing Jewish patronage because of a wave of whispering that it discriminated against Jewish employees, (b) that in Boston it was being boycotted by Catholics who had heard that it hired only Protestants, and (c) that in upper New York State, Protestants were criticizing it for hiring only Catholics. Fortunately, the owner of the chain had a sense of humor. He made public these three contradictory rumors. Their sheer absurdity was placed before the patrons of each territory, and the whispering campaign was dissolved in laughter.

At the peak of the winter travel of 1934 there crept forth, simultaneously in New York, Boston, and Philadelphia, rumors to the effect that an American dollar was worth only sixty cents in Bermuda. So persistent were the rumors, that there might have been a serious slump in Bermuda-bound tourist traffic had not the Bermuda Development Board promptly put forth a series of advertisements stating the truth, which was that although Bermuda is a Crown colony, and, therefore, on a sterling basis, American and Canadian dollars are still accepted there at the pre-devaluation rate, and that Bermuda hotel bills have always been payable in dollars.

The case of a large tobacco company was not so fortunate. Over a year ago, almost simultaneously in a score of cities along the Atlantic Seaboard, there broke out a peculiarly villainous epidemic of whispering. There were two specific malicious falsehoods: that the executives of this company had contributed huge sums to the Nazi movement, and that several employees in one of its factories had been found to be victims of a vicious and contagious disease. To counteract the rumors, this company publicized a statement by the Mayor and Board of Health of the city in which the factory is located, vigorously denying and denouncing the report. In addition, the company offered a twenty-five thousand dollar reward for the arrest and conviction of those responsible for the rumor. It was never claimed.

Only a few whispering campaigns can be laughed away; only a few of them are punctured by plain, loud statements of the truth. Often such statements only make the prairie fire burn hotter. The sort of person who passes such rumors on will always put the wrong interpretation upon a denial, however detailed and frank. Besides, there is a perverse streak in mankind that makes people relish bad news and slander far more than good news or fair report. A compliment isn't worth bothering to pass on, but a scandal is always too good to be kept to oneself. Once such a whisper starts, it quickly gathers an irresistible momentum. A single careless or malevolent match can burn a thousand acres of timber.

There is also a large fraction of the American people which is always on the alert to sniff out, resent, magnify, and pass along any hint of prejudice against a race, color, or religion. It is as quick to find what it is looking for as a private detective. The group is a superb conductor of rumor, and once given a bit of slander by someone who has an axe to grind, or a neighbor's axe he wants dulled, will flash the lie all over the map in a very short time.

There is a chronic form of destructive rumor which, though milder than whispers about leprosy and religion, is almost ineradicable. It is spread by the makers and sellers of the less known brands of goods, and its victims are the better known brands. The retailer's margin of profit on the more obscure brands must be greater, because they lack advertising support and consumer acceptance. The manufacturer or wholesaler sometimes substitutes for this missing advertising unkind remarks about the better known brands. His slanders have their effect— the retailer finds the less known brands easier to unload, and the margin of profit on them greater when he does; he remembers the manufacturer's unkind remarks about the better known brands, and passes them on to his customers.

To offset this underhanded game, many of the better known brands have hired verbal propagandists. The propagandists (always in pairs, like Paris policemen) attend trade conventions, ferret out the damaging whispers, and try to counteract them. Or, representing themselves as customers, they go to a store suspected of slander, talk loudly and to as wide an audience as possible about their brand, the accepted brand, the advertised brand. They try to trip up the storekeeper, and if he repeats the rumor, attempt to squeeze from him where he heard it first, and how, and from whom.

Military men would call this counter-espionage. No one knows how many business spies and counter spies are busily at work; the public suspects practically nothing of all this. The public sees the honest open warfare of prices, quality, service, advertising. It does not suspect how many of the whispers it hears are well planned midnight raids on a great battlefront.

The impulse is not new, but the technic is. Individuals have always tried to build up their own business or take away the other fellow's by discreet remarks in the right place. But this hiring of mercenaries— trained, skilled, disguised, is a product of the fierce necessities and the ruthless logic of modern competition. It is to business rather like what atrocities and breaches of "civilized warfare" are to a world conflict. There was an armistice during NRA; now we may expect it to go on more bitterly and cunningly than before.

There are limits of course to the method so ably pursued by chauffeur John and Mr. Bradley. If too many manufacturers try to plant their own word-of-mouth good will, the public will eventually catch on. And the propaganda will become a nasty boomerang, for no one likes to be fooled in just this way. The trick may work beautifully a few times in a few scattered places, but let it once become general, and not only will the public be extremely cross, but peaceful private life will be poisoned. As people go about the city, they will be on the alert for chance remarks in which may be buried the barbed hook of salesmanship. Anyone who says an audible good word for something which may be bought for cash will be accused of talking for a living. Some of the most popular American topics of conversation, such as the merits of one's car versus one's neighbor's, the swapping of notes about radios, cigarettes, golf balls will be open to suspicion. Men who sit down on country club porches, in the smoking rooms of Pullmans, and say a few words, kind or unkind, about almost any well known article of commerce, will be asked whose payroll they are on, and how much they are getting. After a while nationally advertised brands might even dissappear from national conversation. For lack of their accustomed subjects of conversation, Americans might talk more than they did about God, Europe, politics—or, more likely the weather, which—thank heaven—is one commodity that no trained verbal propagandist will ever be able to make more popular or unpopular, more widely or less widely used, than it is already.

Questions for Study and Discussion

1. How do the two verbal advertisers described differ from the average commuter in their manner of conversation?

2. What comparison do the authors make between verbal advertising and international spying?

3. In what respects is verbal advertising superior to the written word?

4. What varieties of causes and products are promoted by verbal advertising?

5. Point out some effective propagandistic devices used by the authors in their discussion of the subject.

6. By the tone of the article do the authors reflect an attitude of approval, condemnation, or neutrality toward their subject? Explain.

Vocabulary Study

Define the following words and phrases as used in this selection: immune, potent, fanatical, ingenious, disillusionment, insinuate, *viva voce*, colloquially, ethical, Pinkertons, *quid pro quo*, malevolent, ferret out, mercenaries.

Writing Assignment

Write a composition discussing how honest advertising can benefit the public.

Forgotten Road to Success in Writing

J. D. Ratcliff

One of America's highest paid free-lance authors tells of opportunities often overlooked by people who want to write.

I can't understand why more beginners don't take the short road to publication—by writing articles for magazines and newspapers.

Last year over 250,000 articles were bought by general magazines alone. And that's only part* of a huge market that will pay well for pieces of almost any length on just about any subject that comes naturally to you. I've made a good living for 25 years writing articles, and I've enjoyed every minute of it.

A WONDERFUL LIFE

I've interviewed a dozen Nobel Prize-winners, including Sir Alexander Fleming who discovered penicillin. I've talked with heads of state, at least one king, and scores of leading industrialists. In the past year, I covered stories from Bangkok to Buffalo.

It's a wonderful life. No commuter trains to catch, no office routine. Whether I'm at home, or abroad on assignment, I write from 8 a.m. to noon every day—no more, no less. My afternoons are my own.

HOW TO PICK SUBJECTS THAT SELL

A big advantage of article writing is that you can break in with material right out of your own everyday experience. One of the first pieces I sold was about the adventures of a test pilot I knew. Another told the story of a friend of mine caught in a balloon that ran wild. Check the contents of any general magazine; chances are you'll find articles you might have written.

You can make good use of your special interests too. One of mine is science, and it's provided dozens of story ideas—from accounts of dra-

---

*11,000 newspapers and Sunday supplements also pay well for fresh material.

matic new heart operations, to a report on an astronomical observatory built out of salvaged junk. Your passion may be insurance or religion or football, raising roses or raising children. Whatever it is, you should be able to draw on it for articles that could inform and entertain thousands of readers.

Knowing *what* to write is about half the battle. The other half is knowing *how*. To produce saleable articles, you must master the tools and techniques used by all successful professional writers.

You might develop these skills on your own through sheer blood, sweat and rejection slips. But when I look back, I can't help thinking of all the time and agony I would have saved if I could have found a real "pro" to work with me.

Such help is now available to beginners everywhere through the Famous Writers School—founded by Rod Serling, Faith Baldwin, Bruce Catton, Bennett Cerf, Max Shulman, Mignon G. Eberhart, Bergen Evans, Red Smith, John Caples, Rudolf Flesch, Mark Wiseman and myself.

A NEW KIND OF WRITING SCHOOL

We poured all our secrets of success into a set of specially created textbooks and writing assignments. Then we worked out a method for bringing to each student, in his own home, the many hours of individual instruction a developing writer needs.

When you send an assignment to the School, one of our instructors—themselves all professional writers or editors—spends up to two hours analyzing your work. He blue-pencils corrections on your manuscript, much as an editor does with established authors. And he returns it with a long letter of specific recommendations on how to improve your writing.

Your course begins with the fundamentals upon which every writing career must be built. Then you get concentrated training in writing articles and other non-fiction. (If you prefer, you may specialize in Fiction, Advertising or Business Writing.)

STUDENTS BREAKING INTO PRINT

This training works well. Our students have sold their writing to more than 100 publications, including the *Reader's Digest, True, Redbook, The New York Times.*

Sharon Wagner, Mesa, Ariz., announces, "When I began your Course,

I was an unpublished writer. Since then, I've made 18 sales and now live on my writing income."

Stephan R. Novak, Wayne, N.J., writes, "I've just received a check from *Ellery Queen Mystery Magazine*. That's 11 stories sold in six months." Don Jones of Whittier, Calif., says, "Guided by your criticism, I rewrote my last assignment and sold it to *Nation's Business*."

"Your training has certainly paid off," reports Eileen Thompson Panowski, a Los Alamos, N.M., mother of four. "I've just sold my fourth book to the New York publisher, Abelard-Schuman." Doris Stebbins, S. Coventry, Conn., says, "Your Course made it possible for me to sell six articles to *Woman's Day* for $2,050."

Beyond the thrill of receiving that first check, our students find great intangible rewards in writing for publication. As my colleague Faith Baldwin puts it: "If one sentence you write opens a door for another human being...makes him see with your eyes and understand with your mind and heart, you'll gain a sense of fulfillment no other work can bring you."

Questions for Study and Discussion

1. What are the most persuasive ideas in the first four paragraphs? Explain.

2. Which sentence in the first paragraph of section 2 ("How to pick subjects that sell") has the strongest appeal to the interested reader? Explain.

3. Which paragraph in section 2 is the most educational? Explain

4. What is the effect of the word "secrets" in section 3 ("A new kind of writing school")?

5. Which paragraph in section 3 has the greatest appeal to the prospective student? Explain.

6. What major propaganda technique is used in section 4 ("Students breaking into print")?

7. Why does the author use four subheadings in this short article?

Vocabulary Study

Define the following words and phrases as used in this selection: Nobel prize-winner, "pro," intangible.

Profiles of Three States

CONNECTICUT OFFERS YOU "THE GOOD LIFE".

*Beautiful rolling countryside—a prosperous economy—fine
schools—great golf, swimming, living.*

People like Connecticut. They like to vacation in Connecticut; they like
to live in Connecticut, and frequently for the same reason.

The beautiful countryside that lures the vacationist back year after
year also provides rural or suburban settings for both the native and
the new resident. In compact Connecticut with its modern network of
efficient highways, it is possible to live in a rustic setting and yet be
within easy driving distance of office, shop or factory.

Beautiful old colonial homes looking out over quiet village greens
are only a few minutes' drive from advanced research centers; and
modern city apartments or a year-round house on lake or shore similarly
widen the choice of residence.

People like to live in Connecticut because of its prosperous economy.
It is a prosperity built on variety with the promise of job opportunities
for a variety of skills and talents. Both research physicists and skilled
technicians have helped to swell the migration that has helped to make
Connecticut the fastest growing state in New England and the twelfth
fastest in the entire nation.

People with families like to live in Connecticut. They respect the
state's topnotch public school system and some of them appreciate being
near the many private preparatory schools that have long been famous
throughout the nation. Some of them appreciate the state's system of
vocational-technical schools, and others the colleges and universities and
opportunities for graduate study. The keynote is still variety, training
for everyone.

They like Connecticut for its recreation facilities—its state parks and
forests never more than 25 miles away, its hiking trails, fishing streams
and rich green turf of its fairways.

For good living and for bringing up a family, Connecticut offers an unusual wealth of cultural opportunities. As one of the thirteen original colonies, it is rich in history. Its location between New York City and Boston makes accessible to its residents most of the advantages of both, but within its own boundaries it has unusually fine theaters and museums, libraries, concert orchestras and public events that reflect the presence of fine educational institutions.

A state of variety and a state of contrasts, Connecticut is the third most densely populated state in the country and 70 per cent of its land area is wooded. With its front steps on Broadway and a sideyard on Boston's Beacon Hill, it treasures the tradition of its colonial background and is completely attuned to the sophistication of tomorrow's fashion.

Of all the states in the country, Connecticut has the highest per capita representation in Who's Who. Connecticut is first in ratio of skilled workers to total workers, first in per capita value added by manufacture, first in percentage of people who own stock. Noted widely as a center of insurance and education, Connecticut has 81 per cent of the 480 industry types listed in the U.S. Census of Manufacturers.

At once rustic and urbane, cultural and mechanical, individual and diversified, Connecticut begins to represent one concept to the prospective vacationer and to the career hunter: Connecticut adds up to being the state where you can eat your cake and have it. There are always two cakes in Connecticut.

HAVE YOU EVER THOUGHT OF LIVING AND WORKING IN VERMONT?

Nearly everyone knows how beautiful Vermont is . what a perfect place to visit or vacation during every one of its four spectacular seasons.

But, what about Vermont as a place to live and work? How does it compare with where you are now?

Well, employment opportunities are at an all-time high here, especially for *professional, technical* and *skilled* people of practically all kinds, men as well as women.

Actually, Vermont is *booming* in its own quiet way, with numerous leaders in American technology locating or expanding here in recent years. Many long-established Vermont firms are also growing, as are dozens of new, active, smaller concerns.

Yet, *Vermont has no really big cities* with snarled transportation, strife, crime, bureaucratic waste, poor housing, air pollution and all the other seemingly hopeless problems of large metropolitan areas today.

We *do* have plenty of good stores, restaurants, hospitals, schools, colleges, churches, art exhibits, concerts and all the other cultural amenities and facilities of modern life within a few miles of almost anywhere in Vermont. We *do not* have so many people but what everyone can live within a few minutes of his work, and still have enough room for privacy.

Here, too, you'll have the time, energy and opportunity, with your family, to enjoy a wealth of outdoor activities the year 'round. You simply can't *get* more than a few minutes away from mountains and lakes in Vermont! Swimming, boating, fishing, hunting, horses, hiking, camping, gardening, golf, skiing—and so many others are all here. The air you breathe is fresh and clean.

Your children can grow up amid surroundings and with memories they will treasure all their lives. They will have deep roots in a land they can love, which is something fewer and fewer people have today in our ever more urban society.

If good career opportunities and the good way of life in Vermont sound like the kind of future you want for yourself and your family, the State of Vermont and these companies invite you to consider the job opportunities available right now.

NORTH CAROLINA'S BAFFLING MYSTERY

Stokes Penland chuckled quietly when that "city slicker" scientist came to North Carolina's high country and claimed those ghostly lights above Linville Gorge were reflections from automobiles. Old Stokes first heard about those lights 73 years ago.

LINVILLE GORGE—The legendary Brown Mountain Lights that dance in the sky between Hawksbill and Table Rock in the Blue Ridge Mountains have confounded scientists and geologists for more than a century.

They have also surprised many travelers who saw them from the highland route of the Blue Ridge Parkway. To be sure, those peculiar lights are astonishing.

But then, North Carolina is an astonishing state—from the scenic highlands to its historic coast. The modern parkway and winding byways that soar through the misty heights of the Blue Ridge and Great Smoky Mountains lead to a treasure-trove of things to do and see.

In the villages that snuggle against the towering slopes, "quaint" mountain craftsmen do fascinating things with their hands. And authentic folk singers do equally fascinating things with handmade musical instruments. And in places like Oconaluftee at Cherokee, real Indians live quietly and colorfully—and relive the past in the summer outdoor drama, "Unto These Hills."

Across the mountains at Boone, another outdoor drama, "Horn In The West," recreates the life of Daniel Boone.

A pleasant land, North Carolina's mountains. A rare piece of unspoiled nature for camping and hiking and fishing and looking—with just enough modern motels and hotels to keep near the comforts we've come to need.

But North Carolina is not all mountain country. To the east and to the south lie low rolling hills and flat plains, scenic farms, carpet-clean golf courses, restored Moravian towns, picturesque hunt country, sun-drenched beaches, shady rivers and sea-sized lakes.

On storied Roanoke Island, Paul Green's symphonic outdoor drama, "The Lost Colony," tells of the first tragic attempt to settle America. Nearby are the windswept Outer Banks, fisherman's and camper's paradise, that pulsate still with the spell cast by 18th century pirates and privateers.

Questions for Study and Discussion

1. Which one of the three profiles of states has the greatest appeal to you? Why?

2. Which one has the strongest emotional impact? Cite five sentences that contribute greatly to the emotional impact?

3. Which one has the greatest intellectual impact? Explain.

4. Point out three effective propaganda devices in each profile.

5. Point out the important educational values of each profile.

6. Why in these profiles are there no difficult words that require the use of the dictionary?

Writing Assignment

Write a composition praising the virtues of your native state or any state you greatly admire other than the three described in these profiles.

At Last! Instant Relaxation!

Now! A noted psychological researcher shows you how to PUT YOURSELF COMPLETELY AT EASE—*in seconds, with simple self suggestion*—EVEN IN THE MOST NERVE-WRACKING SITUATIONS YOU FACE EVERY DAY.

Yes! Situations that might otherwise tear you apart with tension, now become completely within your control when you use simple self-relaxing techniques like these:

For example—

Are you vulnerable to other people's insults? Does other people's rudeness, hostility, impatience cause you to be upset all day long?

Then by all means turn to page 145 of this revolutionary new book. Learn how easy it is to handle even the most antagonistic person—from rude sales help to waitresses to fellow workers to policemen. Prove to yourself that you can develop an invulnerable wall of self-confidence that quiets them down immediately . . . that puts you in command of the situation . . . that lets you walk away with a smile of self-satisfaction—and without the slightest rise in your blood pressure!

And this is just the beginning—

Do you have trouble falling asleep? Are your nights filled with shallow, dream-disturbed sleep that leaves you tired and dragged-out in the morning?

Then turn to page 139. You'll find four simple steps that will let you fall into a deep, refreshing sleep whenever you wish. Without drugs or tranquilizers—with nothing more than your mere desire to sleep.

You'll learn the secret of taking short "energy-naps" whenever you wish. That will rest you thoroughly in as little as ten minutes—give you a fresh charge of vitality upon awakening.

You'll even learn two "magic" words which, after you learn this amazingly simple system, will make you delightfully drowsy the moment you repeat them.

(The methods in this book are so effective that they have brought

deep, refreshing sleep to confirmed insomniacs. They will work for anyone. You can prove this yourself without risking a penny.)

And this is still just the beginning—

*Are you one of those people who frets and procrastinates about spend-
ing money for fear of making a mistake?*

Then read every word on page 169. You'll find an entire section
devoted to taking away the anxiety and worry usually connected with
buying a new home—purchasing an automobile—parting with any
amount of money.

And you'll also discover a special piece of wisdom that will allow
you to make up your mind in half the usual time—and cut your chances
of making an error almost to zero!

*Do parties and other social gatherings make you wish you'd never
received the invitation?*

You'd be surprised how many other people feel exactly the same way.
But there's absolutely no need to feel uncomfortable, awkward, ill-at-
ease at parties anymore. A simple technique described on page 229 will
show you the secret of relaxing from the very first moment you walk
in the door.

Yes, and you'll learn how to loosen up . . . express yourself freely . . .
make people like you at once . . . leave a lasting impression of warmth
and excitement—even if you knew no one in the room only one short
hour before!

Would you like to skyrocket your performance in sports—overnight?

Most people lose their smoothness and power because they "choke up"
with tension in the crucial moments—or when other people are watching them.

If you could eliminate this tension—if you could draw on all the
power and coordination that's really in your body—then you would have
a tremendous advantage over your competition before you even picked
up a club, a racket or a ball!

There are two entire sections in this book—starting on pages 228
and 239—that show you how to keep cool, calm, at top form . . . no
matter what the sport . . . no matter how high the tension mounts!

And the same exact techniques will be invaluable for you if you play
cards . . . invest in the stock market . . . or have to buck cut-throat competition in your job or business.

*And speaking of business, do you tie your stomach up in knots when
you have to make a crucial decision—sit in on a business discussion . . .
sell your boss or your co-workers on your ideas?*

Then don't miss page 194. It's the beginning of six startling pages that are alone worth the price of the book to you. It gives you a new technique for making right decisions—fast—without anxiety—and with all the facts at your fingertips for perhaps the first time in your life.

This one secret alone—of letting vital decisions *half-make themselves*—can build you a reputation for steel-nerved judgment that can alone be worth a fortune to you.

And then skip back to page 61, and discover how to automatically drain away anxieties the very moment *before* you begin to sell others your ideas. So you can be completely at ease, whether you have to address a crowd of one hundred, or convince a single man in the privacy of his office.

Plus, of course, a thrilling new concept of "psychological judo," that shows you how to win people over to your point of view no matter how antagonistic they've been to it before. Again—alone worth the low price of this book!

Yes—even if the thought of a trip to the doctor or dentist is torture to you. Even if the buzz of his drill sets your nerves tingling in anticipation of pain!

Then you need page 91. For here are six simple steps—self suggestion in its most valuable form—that actually save you hours of otherwise agonizing anticipation! We can promise you this: that they are so incredibly effective that you will actually be able to sit back in that man's chair and KNOW that the only thing you feel is relaxed!

An entirely different kind of book, to give you an entirely new power to relax!

But this is still just the beginning.

This book doesn't restrict itself to just the "big-tension" crises alone. It also shows you how to relax completely in the dozens of borderline-tension moments that pile up on top of you every day—that build up to exhaust you by the time you get home at night.

For example, here's how to relax completely while you're driving, even in the worst traffic jams. How to relax at meal-times—either in crowded restaurants or at home with the children—that turns meal-times from a torture to a pleasure.

You'll learn the one big mistake most people make about recreation—that leaves them more nervous and tired than ever—and how to cure it in seconds.

You'll learn how to double the enjoyment you get from your children—without having a cloud of mutual tensions ruin your relationships with them.

You'll learn how to use an hour in front of your TV set as a time—not to drain you of energy—but as a thrilling energy-restorer!

You'll find surprising secrets about complete relaxation while standing up. While sitting on a bus or train. While working at your desk. Any one of which could double the enjoyment and productivity you get out of every day!

And you prove every word of it, entirely at our risk. Here's how—

[The foregoing advertisement is intended to convince the reader of the incomparable merits of the book it describes. With permission of the advertiser the name of the book has been omitted.]

Questions for Study and Discussion

1. According to this advertisement, how many serious problems that often prevent the average man from being completely relaxed are satisfactorily solved by the advice given in this book?

2. What stylistic device is used to emphasize each of these problems?

3. What percentage of average readers of magazine advertisements would be likely not to be troubled by at least one of these problems?

4. Is it possible that the power of this advertisement is diminished somewhat by the claim that this book can satisfy too many needs of its readers? Explain.

5. What are the greatest merits of this advertisement?

6. What are its most damaging weaknesses?

Vocabulary Study

Define the following words and phrases as used in this selection: invulnerable, insomniacs, procrastinates, psychological judo.

Writing Assignment

Copy in context three sentence fragments from this selection, correct them in the most effective manner possible, and explain why you think the author (who certainly knows they are fragments) used them.

That's Why the Rich Get Richer

When You're Rich Enough To Buy A $145 Firmex Suit You Save Money On Suits. That's Why The Rich Get Richer.

It's economical to be rich. Yet, rich men don't have to think about economy. They don't buy Firmex suits because they last longer. They buy Firmex suits because they fit better. They hang more handsomely. They feel more comfortable. (But that's exactly why they last longer.) Our suits are cut of the very finest fabrics. Discoveries from Huddersfield, England, Edinburgh, Scotland or some special little mill in New England.

And they are cut by the most marvelously trained hands, which precision-measure each piece down to a sixteenth of an inch. So each part matches perfectly.

Then each Firmex suit is put together by hand. Because machine stitching is rigid, it's only good for the straight lines. So we give the body of our suit its curves and shapes with expert hand stitching.

We press and underpress as we sew, over thirty times, to mold the shape into the suit permanently. (Then no amount of cleaning and pressing can take it out.)

We go through a dozen processes on the lapels and collar alone to make sure they lie smoothly and snugly. When you slip into a Firmex jacket you can feel it weightlessly hugging your neck, rather than putting a weight on your shoulders. Your arms feel free to move. Your shoulders look naturally tailored.

See, rich men are more interested in how a Firmex suit feels, than how long it wears. But isn't it funny how money always goes to money?

[The foregoing advertisement was copied verbatim from a popular magazine except for the substitution of a pseudonym for the name of the product.]

Questions for Study and Discussion

1. Is this advertisement intended to be primarily for rich people? Explain.

2. What is the propagandistic significance of the last sentence in the first paragraph?

3. What is the most effective sentence in the fifth paragraph? Why?

4. What is the propagandistic intent of the last line?

5. What are the strengths of this advertisement?

6. What unfavorable criticism can you make of the advertisement?

7. Is the advertisement at all educational? Explain.

The Story of Whispering Love

Or how a certain time of day led to the creation of, perhaps,
the most tenderly beautiful perfume in the world.

The art of the perfumer, like the art of the musician, is elusive and mysterious.

But even the musician has certain laws of harmony and the eight notes of the scale to rely upon, while the perfumer is faced with an infinite range of fragrances, and only his intuition to guide him.

Common to all great art, however, is that moment, or event, which compels the artist to attempt to preserve it forever. (Who amongst us has led such a shallow existence that he was never moved to say "I wish I could paint that," or at least, "I wish I had a camera with me"?)

A moment such as this is the story of Whispering Love.

A man pauses to reflect on his walk home from work. The year is 1911. It is summer. There is nothing spectacular about the scene. No vivid sunset. No heavenly rays penetrating dark clouds.

To the contrary. The air is dark blue. The sky has lost the sun but not yet found the stars. And yet it is as if all the elements were conspiring to say something.

Something infinite. Something . . . tender. Something that simply cannot be translated into words.

The following morning a distinguished scientist returned to his laboratory and began work. For almost a year he struggled to capture that vibrant hush, the beguiling sweetness of closing flowers, the tender, infinite something that had overwhelmed him.

The result was Whispering Love, a finely balanced perfume composed with the passion of Musk and Rose de Bulgarie, and the naive loveliness of Iris and Heliotrope, subtly blended with fragrances from the far corners of the earth.

What happens when you apply Whispering Love to your pulse points, and its delicate scent starts to permeate the air around you? Ah . . .

That's another story.

[This advertisement was copied verbatim from a popular magazine except for the substitution of a pseudonym for the name of the product.]

Questions for Study and Discussion

1. What elements of style are responsible for the effectiveness of this unusual advertisement?

2. In what sense is the style appropriate to the product being advertised?

3. How does the first sentence set the tone of the entire composition?

4. What is the propagandistic effect of the first sentence?

5. Which paragraph has the greatest emotional impact on you? Why?

6. How does the implication in the last two sentences add additional strength to the entire advertisement?

Biographical Notes

STEPHEN E. AMBROSE is assistant professor of history at the Johns Hopkins University and associate editor of the ten volumes of the Dwight D. Eisenhower Papers to be published by the Johns Hopkins University Press. He is author of the definitive history of the U. S. Military Academy, *Duty, Honor, Country*, and is now completing a military biography of General Eisenhower.

ROBERT MCAFEE BROWN, born in Illinois and educated in U. S. and British colleges and universities, is both clergyman and educator. He has taught religion at several colleges and universities, including Stanford University. He has written seven books and has translated two others into English.

RUDOLPH FLESCH, a Viennese by birth and a lawyer by training, came to the United States to live in 1938. He earned the Ph.D. degree at Columbia University and now teaches business writing to executive and industrial groups. He is the author of seven well-known books, the most famous and controversial being *Why Johnny Can't Read*.

ADOLPH HITLER was leader of the Nazi party and master of Germany from 1933 to 1945. He was born in 1889 in Austria. He spent most of his time from 1906 to 1913 in Vienna where he tried to enter the Academy of Fine Arts, but he failed to qualify because he lacked a high school diploma and because his drawings were poor. He soon learned to distrust everyone; he despised the masses and hated the Jews. He was appointed chancellor of Germany January 30, 1933, and soon thereafter began a series of political moves that led to the beginning of World War II. He committed suicide in Berlin on April 30, 1945, as the allied armies closed in upon him and his trusted aides, but not before he had caused millions of deaths, wrecked Europe, and destroyed many of the cultural treasures of Western civilization.

BANESH HOFFMAN is professor of mathematics at Queens College, New York, and author of *The Strange Story of the Quantum*. After taking degrees at Oxford and Princeton he collaborated with Albert Einstein and Leopold Infeld on fundamental studies of relativity at the Institute for Advanced Study. He became involved in problems of testing when he published a criticism of the selection methods used by the Westinghouse Science Talent Search in 1943. He has written a book and several articles dealing with the problems of objective tests.

SIDNEY HOOK, professor of philosophy at New York University, is a frequent contributor to magazines and scholarly journals. He is also the author of several books in his field. He was educated at New York City Colleges and Columbia University, where he received the Ph.D. degree in 1927.

WILLIAM HUMMEL is professor of English at Kansas State University and a contributor to scholarly journals.

KEITH G. HUNTRESS was born in 1913 in Maine and was educated at Wesleyan University and at the University of Illinois, where he received the Ph.D. degree. He taught at Wesleyan at various times and has written five books as well as many scholarly articles. He is now professor of English at Iowa State University.

ROBERT M. HUTCHINS is president of The Fund for the Republic, U. S. A., a subsidiary of the Ford Foundation, and former president and chancellor of the University of Chicago. He is the author of eight books dealing with higher education in the United States. He was instrumental in establishing the Great Books Foundation in 1947, after having directed the growth and reformation of the University of Chicago for more than fifteen years.

NANCY G. LARRICK received the Ed.D. at New York University in 1955. She has taught a various colleges and universities and has published four books on the teaching of reading and writing, as well as four children's books. She is also a contributor to many educational journals.

WALTER LIPPMANN, a native of New York and a Harvard graduate, has been associate editor of *The New Republic* and editor of *New York World*. He is a syndicated columnist and a prolific writer.

ROBERT LITTELL, after studying at Harvard, became dramatic critic for two New York newspapers, and later senior editor of the *Reader's Digest*. He is author of *Read America First,* 1926; *Candles in the Storm,* 1934; and *Gather Ye Rosebuds,* 1934.

JOHN J. MCCARTHY, a former advertising executive, has long been an editor and free-lance writer.

JOSEPH R. MCCARTHY, who gained national attention as a U. S. Senator from Wisconsin, was born in 1909 and died in 1957. His practice of accusing persons in high public office of disloyalty and pro-Communist activity, in most instances unsupported by proof, was responsible for his notoriety and became known as McCarthyism. He was censured by his colleagues in the U. S. Senate for his unfair methods of "character assassination" of some of the nation's most distinguished statesmen.

EDWIN MARKHAM (originally Charles Edward Anson Markham) was born in Oregon City, Oregon, in 1852 and died in 1940. He attended the California State Normal School at San Jose and later graduated from the Christian College at Santa Rosa. He subsequently became a high school principal and finally headmaster at the Tompkins Observation School, Oakland, connected with the University of California. He abandoned school administration in 1899, after his poetry had won favor, and devoted his later years to writing and lecturing.

JOHN STUART MILL was an English philosopher and economist. He was born in London in 1806 and died in 1873. He was educated at home and is said to have begun the study of Greek at the age of three. Under his father's careful tutelage he became proficient in Greek and in calculus before his tenth year. His *System of Logic,* published in 1843, established him as one of the foremost thinkers of his time. Although radical in his philosophy, he was broadly humanitarian.

CLYDE RAYMOND MILLER, born and educated in Ohio, began writing as a reporter on local publications, then moved into the academic world as a lecturer. In 1937 he founded the Institute for Propaganda Analysis. For his contribution to the prevention of racial and religious prejudice, he received an award in 1945 from the National Conference of Christians and Jews. He is the author of many articles and books on education, prejudice, and propaganda.

JOHN MILTON was born in London in 1608 and died in 1674. He was first educated by a private tutor, then at St. Paul's School in London, and finally at Christ's College, Cambridge, where he took the degree of M.A. He traveled on the Continent and in 1639 returned to England where he became engaged in bitter controversies concerning the political policies of Charles I. His great poem "Paradise Lost," published in 1667, elevated him to a position in English literature second only to Shakespeare.

BENJAMIN QUARLES, professor of history at Morgan State College, Baltimore, is the author of many works on Negro history, the most recent of which is *The Negro in the Making of America* (1964). In addition, Dr. Quarles is a member of the editorial board of the *Journal of Negro History*, and is vice-president of the Association for the Study of Negro Life and History.

J. D. RATCLIFF was born in West Virginia and studied mining engineering before going to New York as a reporter in the mid-twenties. He is the author of four books and numerous articles which have appeared in such popular publications as the *Reader's Digest, McCall's, The Saturday Evening Post,* and *This Week.* He suggests that one of the reasons for the popularity of his magazine articles is that he rewrites each one six or seven times before submitting it for publication.

JONATHAN SWIFT was born in 1667 and died in 1745. He was dean of St. Patrick's Cathedral, Dublin, but was known primarily for his satirical writings, including the famous *Gulliver's Travels* (1726.) During the years of his greatest productivity there was an intense interest in politics as well as in manners and other social questions, and Swift became involved in the disputes that raged between the different factions of the British public.

EDWARD ANDREWS TENNEY, who earned the Ph.D. degree at Cornell University, has taught English at Michigan State, Oberlin, and Cornell. He is the author of several books and many articles in scholarly journals.

HENRY DAVID THOREAU was born at Concord, Massachusetts, on July 12, 1817, and died May 6, 1862. He was educated at Harvard and continued throughout his life to be a student of classical literature, which he found much time to enjoy and comment upon in the leisurely life that he chose for himself. He built a rough cabin near the shore of Walden Pond in an outlying section of Concord, where he lived alone for over two years. His most popular work is *Walden, or Life in the Woods.*

DANIEL WEBSTER, one of America's greatest orators, was born in New Hampshire in 1782 and died in 1852. In 1816 he settled in Boston, and during the greater portion of his life he was Senator from Massachusetts. He was widely recognized as the champion of the nationalistic view of the federal Constitution. He was the idol of New England until his Seventh of March Speech in 1850 when he advocated a compromise with the slave states in order "to save the Union."

Selected Bibliography

BOOKS

Childs, Harwood L. *Propaganda and Dictatorship*. Princeton: Princeton University Press, 1936.

Doob, Leonard W. *Public Opinion and Propaganda*. New York: Henry Holt, 1948.

Hunter, Edward. *Brain-Washing in Red China*. New York: Vanguard, 1951.

Lasswell, Harold D. *Propaganda Technique in the World War*. New York: Knopf, 1927.

Lerner, Max. *Ideas Are Weapons*. New York: Viking, 1939.

Lumley, Frederick E. *The Propaganda Menace*. New York: Century, 1933.

Packard, Vance O. *The Hidden Persuaders*. New York: McKay, 1957.

Qualter, Terrence H. *Propaganda and Psychological Warfare*. New York: Random House, 1962.

PERIODICALS

Bernays, Edward L. "Are We Victims of Propaganda?" *Forum*, LXXXI (March, 1929), pp. 142–149.

Burnshaw, Stanley. "Art and Propaganda: Reply," *Poetry*, XLIV (September, 1934), pp. 341–344.

Friedrick, Carl J. "Education and Propaganda," *Atlantic*, CLIX (June, 1937), pp. 693–701.

Gallup, George. "Why We Are Doing So Badly in the Ideological War," *Vital Speeches*, XVIII (June 1, 1952), pp. 501–504.

Huxley, Aldous L. "Notes on Propaganda," *Harper's*, CLXXIV (December, 1936), pp. 32–41.

McDonough, R. "Propaganda and the Writer," *Commonweal*, XX (May 11, 1934), pp. 35–37.

Monroe, Harriet. "Art and Propaganda," *Poetry*, XLIV (July, 1934), pp. 210–215.

Navasky, Victor S. "Advertising Is a Science, an Art, a Business?" *New York Times Magazine*, (November 20, 1966), p. 52+.

———."Professors and Propaganda," *The Nation*, CXXXI (July 30, 1930), p. 114.

———."Propaganda and Schools," *Elementary School Journal*, XXXI (May, 1931), pp. 642–644.

———."Propaganda That Is Good," *Saturday Review of Literature*, XIII (March 28, 1936), p. 8.

Selden, W. "Movies and Propaganda," *Forum*, CIII (April, 1940), pp. 209–213.

Thompson, William Hale. "Shall We Shatter the Nation's Idols in School Histories?" *Current History*, XXVII (February, 1928), pp. 619–640.

Tyson, L. "Education vs. Propaganda: Are They Incompatible?" *Vital Speeches*, IV (May 1, 1938), pp. 431–434.

Van Doren, Mark. "Literature and Propaganda," *Virginia Quarterly Review*, XIV (April, 1938), pp. 203–208.

Villard, Oswald G. "Propaganda in the Movies," *The Nation*, CXXXIX (December 12, 1934), p. 665.

Young, James W. "Do We Need a College of Propaganda?" *Saturday Review*, XLIV (February 11, 1961), p. 85.